DATE DUE

APR - 1 1997	
APR - 3 1998	
APR 16 1998	
JUN 1 5 1998	
MAR 1 9 2002	

BRODART   Cat. No. 23-221

DEBATING
DIVORCE

DEBATING DIVORCE

Moral Conflict in Ireland

MICHELE DILLON

THE UNIVERSITY PRESS OF KENTUCKY

Scholarly publisher for the Commonwealth,
serving Bellarmine College, Berea College,
Centre College of Kentucky, Eastern Kentucky
University, The Filson Club, Georgetown College,
Kentucky Historical Society, Kentucky State
University, Morehead State University,
Murray State University, Northern Kentucky
University, Transylvania University, University
of Kentucky, University of Louisville,
and Western Kentucky University.

Editorial and Sales Offices: Lexington, Kentucky 40508-4008

Library of Congress Cataloging-in-Publication Data

Dillon, Michele, 1960–
    Debating divorce : moral conflict in Ireland / Michele Dillon.
        p.   cm.
    Includes bibliographical references and index.
    ISBN (invalid) 0–08–131182–2 (alk. paper)
    1. Divorce—Ireland—Public opinion.   2. Divorce—Moral and
ethical aspects.   3. Divorce—Religious aspects—Catholic Church.
4. Public opinion—Ireland.   5. Divorce—Law and legislation—
Ireland.   6. Referendum—Ireland.   I. Title.
HQ878.D55   1993
306.89′09415—dc20   92–42597
                                                                CIP

For my parents,
Michael and Peg Dillon;
and for the next generation

Contents

As science does not, who is to answer the question:
"What shall we do, and how shall we arrange our
lives?"....Which of the warring gods should we serve?
Or should we serve perhaps an entirely different god,
and who is he?"

—Max Weber

Acknowledgments

This book started out as my Ph.D. Dissertation in sociology at the University of California, Berkeley. My most direct debt goes to my dissertation committee, Todd Gitlin, Kristin Luker, and Nancy Scheper-Hughes, each of whose own scholarship I greatly admire. I would like also to thank Ann Swidler for her comments, encouragement, and advice; Abigail Stewart and Conor Ward for comments on various chapters; and Peg Dillon and Geraldine Groarke for long-distance research assistance. My husband, Paul Wink, read this manuscript in its many forms; I value his intellectual and emotional companionship. I am fortunate also to have a caring and benevolent family and good friends.

Finally, I would like to express my gratitude to the people whom I interviewed as part of this study (see Appendix C); to Jack Jones, director, Market Research Bureau of Ireland, who very graciously responded to my requests for access to MRBI poll data; and to James Cantwell, Catholic Press and Information Office, Rhona O'Byrne, "Today Tonight," and Con Kelly, the Cork Examiner, for their cooperation.

CHAPTER ONE

Introduction

On April 23, 1986, the Irish prime minister, Garret FitzGerald, called a press conference at which he announced his government's intention to hold a referendum on divorce. The Irish electorate was being offered the opportunity to acknowledge formally the individual's legislative right to divorce, an established right in all other Western democratic societies.[1] The constitutional article prohibiting divorce legislation—"No law shall be enacted providing for the grant of a dissolution of marriage"—would be deleted and replaced with the following four-point amendment:

Where, and only where, such court established under this Constitution as may be prescribed by law is satisfied that: (i) the marriage has failed; (ii) the failure has continued for a period of, or periods amounting to at least five years; (iii) no possibility of reconciliation exists between the two parties to the marriage, and (iv) any other condition prescribed by law has been complied with, the court may in accordance with law grant a dissolution of the marriage provided that the court is satisfied that adequate and proper provision having regard to the circumstances will be made for any dependent spouse and for any child of, or any child who is dependent on, either spouse.

The form of divorce proposed was non-fault based and similar to that available in the United States, Great Britain, and other Western societies. In its other conditions, however, the Irish proposal was relatively restrictive. By American standards, the imposition of a five-year-failure clause appears excessively so, given that most states in the U.S. either prohibit judicial discretion to deny a divorce, or, in the case of a contested unilateral non-fault divorce, require a period of one year or less of separation. Viewed from a European perspective, the Irish five-year failure requirement appears less extraordinary. With the exception of Sweden and the Netherlands, which come closest to granting divorce on demand, other European societies take a much stricter view of marriage and its dissolution than does the United States.[2]

In announcing the divorce referendum, Garret FitzGerald also declared the government's intention of introducing new family law measures to accompany the amendment. This proposed legislation would set down guidelines regarding, among other points, age of marriage, a new family court system, and mediation, reconciliation, and separation procedures to be followed in the case of marital breakdown.

Following the announcement of the government's proposals, a national opinion poll found that over half of the electorate, 61 percent, expressed their intention to vote in favor of the amendment.[3] This level of support was consistent with previous surveys that sought to measure the public's attitude toward the removal of the divorce ban. Since 1971, when the question was first asked in opinion polls, the number in favor of removal of the ban has increased from a minority of 21 percent to a peak of 53 percent in 1983, with 77 percent expressing support for the introduction of divorce in certain circumstances.[4]

The government, therefore, in deciding to hold a referendum to establish whether the Irish people wanted to introduce divorce, had strong indicators that there was significant support, at least in principle, for divorce, and they had evidence of marital breakdown.[5] The initial poll published following the announcement of the government's proposals bore witness to pro-divorce sentiment. As the campaign progressed, however, subsequent polls indicated that the level of support for the introduction of divorce was dropping. And after nine weeks of a vigorous campaign during which pro-divorce and anti-divorce forces presented their respective cases to the public, the amendment was defeated, with two-thirds, 64 percent, of the electorate voting against it.[6]

The defeat of the divorce amendment can be seen on many levels and interpreted from many angles. It certainly presents as a curiosity. It seems anomalous that Ireland, a well-educated, urban, consumer society and a full member of the European Economic Community since 1973, differs so sharply from its fellow Europeans in its prohibition of divorce. Ireland's reaffirmation of the ban in the late 1980s presents as an oddity in much the same way, for example, that Switzerland's exclusion of the franchise to women in the 1970s presented.

Table 1. Irish pre-voting attitudes and intentions

	% in favor			% opposed		
	Nov. 1985	Apr. 1986	June 1986	Nov. 1985	Apr. 1986	June 1986
Gender						
Male	55	61	54	45	39	46
Female	50	62	36	50	38	64
Region						
Urban	62	69	47	35	29	53
Rural	40	52	42	60	48	58
Province						
Dublin	66	72	50	34	28	50
Leinster*	55	56	49	45	44	51
Munster	47	60	36	53	40	64
Connacht/Ulster	38	55	45	62	45	55
Social class						
Middle class	63	66	49	37	34	51
Working class	52	63	45	48	37	55
Large farmers	42	45	37	58	55	63
Small farmers	32	54	36	68	46	64
Total	52	61	45	48	39	55
(N)	(490)	(570)	(403)	(450)	(360)	(492)

Sources: Market Research Bureau of Ireland/*Irish Times*, Nov. 1985; April 1986; June 1986.

* Leinster excluding Dublin.

But anomalies are usually more than just that. Frequently they provide markers or keys to understanding the culture and the salient questions at issue in a society. The fact, therefore, that in Ireland a divorce amendment was introduced, and yet defeated, may provide insight into how a society grapples with issues of tradition and modernity. From this perspective, it says something about cultural tensions in Ireland, but it has also more general application to other societies dealing with related questions.

Another reading is to see the debate and the whole issue of divorce as one dealing with values and the way in which people try to reason about values. This is a complex question and has been the object of study and theorizing for a long time. It was Max Weber in particular who focused sociological thought on the place of values in social action,[7] and his discussion of the relationship between values and rationality continues to stimulate analytical debate among contemporary sociologists.[8] From this perspective, the Irish divorce debate gains universality by virtue of the fact that it dealt with perennial questions of human values: What shall we do and how shall we live? These are questions every society confronts. The issues raised by the Irish debate on divorce are in many ways no different from those debated currently in the United States and Europe concerning abortion and other moral issues such as AIDS prevention and genetic engineering. At the core of these questions is the issue of how we deal with values, morality, and religion in a modern, increasingly secular society that pushes for a stricter separation between state and church, but frequently at the price of anomie and alienation.[9]

The primary aim of this book is to understand the arguments articulated during the divorce debate, and through the discourse to shed light on why the amendment failed. In seeking understanding of how the Irish argued about the moral issue of divorce, I speak to the broader subject of Irish cultural values as well as to the question of values in general. In my research I apply a sociological perspective. I focus on the discourse of the divorce debate and analyze the arguments articulated to discover what they say about Ireland and about the values of the Irish, and to address the more universal question of how people reason about moral values in the Western world.

Just as the norms and rules regulating marriage and divorce in a given society are "major repositories of social values" and provide "symbolic expression of certain cultural ideals,"[10] how people argue about these fundamental questions equally signifies key cultural values and aspirations. Therefore, I treat the dialogue of

the debate as being significant in and of itself. How does Irish society argue for or against divorce in the late 1980s? I examine
the arguments put forward by the various players involved, the advocates and opponents of divorce, and the way in which the Catholic hierarchy and the mass media negotiated the questions raised
by the amendment as indicated by the nature of their respective discourses.

I begin chapter 2 by reviewing the salience of major themes in
Irish history and their impact on issues of marriage and divorce.
This chapter thus contextualizes the divorce referendum and the
complex questions it raised for the Irish. Chapter 3 introduces the
protagonists in the debate. I analyze the arguments put forward by
Garret FitzGerald in announcing the proposals and the arguments
articulated by him and other members of the government as the debate got underway. I also discuss the campaign arguments of the
Divorce Action Group. Founded in 1980 to lobby for the introduction of divorce, this group was the other primary pro-divorce player
in the debate. In particular, I address the questions: What are the
conditions necessary for introducing changes in values? How does
FitzGerald establish legitimation for his stance, and how does he
argue in favor of divorce? In other words, how do you introduce
revolutionary legislation in nonrevolutionary times, and how do
you argue for its acceptance?

Regarding the anti-divorce players, I analyze the arguments and
campaign themes of the one official anti-divorce group, the Anti-
Divorce Campaign (ADC), and the anti-divorce arguments expressed by individual members of Fianna Fail, the main political
party in Ireland, then in opposition. In discussing these arguments,
I take account of content, timing, sequence, and the fora in which
they were articulated. Just as advocates of divorce encountered
problems of legitimation, the same applies to the Anti-Divorce
Campaign. It was a different problem, however. In years past,
groups such as the ADC could appeal directly to religious teachings
in support of their cause, but now, in a changed society, one that
has become more modernized, this is not so easy. In chapter 3,
therefore, I probe the way in which the arguments invoked by the
ADC surmounted this dilemma.

The claim is often made that the right to initiate divorce proceedings is central to the independence and power of women in

society. It was not surprising, therefore, that both the pro- and anti-divorce groups singled out women as a focus to their respective arguments. In the Irish case, however, women overwhelmingly opposed the divorce proposals. In chapter 4, I explore the arguments that were directed toward women and articulated on their behalf, and relate these to the economic and social experience of women in Irish society. In doing so, I try to evaluate which arguments were likely to be more appealing to women. Here I argue that although similar themes to those invoked in the divorce campaign are typically used in debates in America on women's issues, the structural and cultural environments differentiate the appeal of comparable arguments.

In chapter 5, I consider the discourse of the Catholic church regarding the divorce proposal. It could be argued that the Church was key to the failure of the amendment. The argument that Ireland is a strongly Catholic society and that divorce is opposed by the Church, therefore the Irish people reject divorce, is understandably a tempting one. But things are not as simple as that. In looking at the disposition of the Church toward the divorce amendment, it is significant that the hierarchy itself did not officially participate in the campaign. Nevertheless, its pastoral document on marriage and divorce issued in 1985 and various statements by the hierarchy and by individual bishops during the debate provide evidence of a more complicated stance. Importantly, the Church's arguments embraced not just theological but sociological reasons.

In today's world, the mass media have become increasingly significant as they impose interpretive frames on a wide-ranging set of issues and events. In times of confusion or controversy, often it is to the media that the public looks for pointers in its search for clarity and understanding. The importance of the media in articulating cultural meanings is even more enhanced in Irish society. The homogeneity, smallness of scale, and paucity of elite groups in Ireland has enabled the media to secure for itself a position of legitimacy and credibility. Television, in particular, serves as a prime public forum for the articulation of competing arguments.

In this study, I treat newspapers and television separately since, as in most other societies, television is a significantly more regulated medium than print. Chapter 6 is an analysis of the arguments articulated in the editorial and regular feature columns of the three national daily newspapers. The editorial line in all of the newspapers, despite the sociodemographic and nuanced ideological differences in their respective readerships, was unequivocally supportive of the amendment. This unprecedented support for a cause, however, did not succeed in holding majority support among the public for divorce. This inevitably raises the question of the power of the print media to shape attitudes on fundamental questions. While this study is not an analysis of the causes of the defeat of the amendment and does not seek to examine why people voted as they did, nevertheless, I evaluate the editorial arguments themselves in terms of their potential as a forceful discourse.

In looking at the electronic media, I focus on television and RTE's (Radio Telefis Eireann, the Irish national broadcasting service) preeminent current affairs program, "Today Tonight." Accessible to all households that have a television set (98 percent), "Today Tonight" reaches a wide audience, and its popularity and legitimacy is consistently underscored by audience research studies.[11] As well as providing a representative picture of RTE's referendum campaign coverage, the focus on "Today Tonight" also shows how the electronic media dealt with statutory obligations toward objectivity, impartiality, and fairness during the campaign. The discussion in chapter 7, therefore, is based on a microanalysis of "Today Tonight" in which I give special emphasis to one of its campaign programs. My analysis focuses on the interpretive frames used by "Today Tonight," and I discuss how its representation of the issues raised by the debate highlights the dilemma confronted by broadcasters as they try to "balance" an unbalanced reality.

The concluding chapter summarizes the main points that emerge from the analysis of the divorce discourse in terms of a number of broad themes. Although the issues I discuss have special relevance in signifying Irish cultural values, they also apply to how people in general reason about morals and values. In particular, I address the multifaceted and concretistic nature of moral discourse, people's use of contradictory arguments in moral reasoning, the difficulty in trying to shift moral paradigms during nonrevolutionary times, and I comment on some cross-cultural themes and nuances in argumentation. The discussion also encompasses questions about issues of communicative style and about the limited power of the mass media in moral debates.

I argue that the various discourses articulated during the debate illustrate a tension in Irish society, but one not unique to it alone, between the forces of tradition and those of modernization. Commenting on some of the theoretical implications of uneven modernization, I try to understand the puzzle presented—at least with regard to the Western paradigm of modernization—by the non-alignment of cultural with economic change in Ireland.

Methodology

A study such as this inevitably raises methodological questions: how the evidence used was gathered and evaluated, and the biases of the author. As an Irish person studying an issue of great moral sensitivity in my own society I have to confront the question of the "objectivity" of my analysis. But then, of course, all knowledge of cultural reality is dependent on the perspective and the sociocultural location of the interpreter of that reality. As Max Weber phrased it: "All knowledge of cultural reality, as may be seen, is always knowledge from *particular points of view.* . . . cultural science . . . involves 'subjective' presuppositions insofar as it concerns itself only with those components of reality which have some relationship, however indirect, to events to which we attach cultural *significance.* . . . all evaluative ideas are 'subjective' " [emphasis in original].[12]

The advantage to my subjectivity is that in carrying out this study I did not have to face the problem an outsider encounters in studying the society of the "other."[13] Unlike so many who have done sociological and anthropological work on Ireland, I am deeply immersed in the culture. I was born and lived until my mid-twenties in the very center of Ireland, the townland of Killare, which is home to the Hill of Uisneach and Aill na Mireann. This was the legendary meeting place of the five provinces of ancient Ireland and the assembly where laws were made and military courts and markets conducted. And just as Killare marks the geographic center of Ireland, it is also in a sense on the center ideologically: it is neither the most traditional nor the most modern part of Ireland. But neither is it neutral. It represents some of the cultural jaggedness that I believe characterizes Irish society as a whole. This jaggedness was reflected in my own family's standing on the divorce amendment, with some in favor and some opposed to breaking the link between law and Catholic teaching.

But while it is disingenuous to pretend that as a researcher one can be neutral in studying realities, one has an epistemological obligation to try to attain a certain amount of detachment. One seeks to find a proper balance between cultural immersion and detachment. I was helped in this search by doing my graduate work abroad. As a doctoral student in Berkeley I was able to attain a certain amount of cultural distance from Irish society. I learned to ask of my native culture some of the more innocent but critical questions of the outsider. My hope for this study, then, is that my immersion within Irish society will add to the richness of my evaluation, while its honesty will be ensured by the distance I gained from it.

I approach the study of the arguments of the divorce debate as an investigator trying to probe and understand the various worldviews articulated and not as a partisan wishing to privilege my own worldview. I believe it is the duty of sociologists to document and try to explain the social world but not to evaluate or prescribe values or courses of social action. To assist in this objective, while I discuss the social and cultural significance of the various arguments articulated during the divorce debate, I try, to the best of my ability, not to evaluate the moral content of the arguments. I have also endeavored to be as comprehensive as possible in the research materials I use.

As this is a study of discourse, and not one of intentions or attitudes, my methodology relies primarily on an analysis of the texts of the various players in the divorce debate. My sources for chapter 3, the discussion of the pro- and anti-divorce discourses, are: organizational materials relating to all of the various players involved, including activist groups such as the Anti-Divorce Campaign and the Divorce Action Group, and the political parties; official transcripts of the parliamentary debate on the divorce amendment; transcripts I made of the party political broadcasts of the five parliamentary political parties in Ireland and of all of the eight "Today Tonight" television programs on the amendment; and official press statements of the various players. These sources, in addition to the press statements of the national women's organization, the Council for the Status of Women, were also drawn upon in the discussion of women and the amendment in chapter 4.

My discussion of the discourse of the Catholic church uses the hierarchy's definitive pastoral letter on marriage and divorce, *Love Is for Life;* all of the hierarchy's official statements regarding the divorce question preceding and during the campaign; official statements by the hierarchy and individual bishops with regard to other relevant issues, such as contraception and abortion; and supplementary Church documents and position papers. I also use a transcript I made of the sole "Today Tonight" interview with the hierarchy's spokesman, Bishop Joseph Cassidy, during the debate, and, in addition to its official statement, an excerpt from the hierarchy's (June 11) press conference transmitted on RTE's evening news.

The editorials and column pieces in the three national daily newspapers—the *Irish Independent,* the *Irish Press,* and the *Irish Times*—and the editorials in the *Cork Examiner* dating from April 24 until the end of June, constitute the materials used for the chapter on the print media. The transcripts I personally made of the eight "Today Tonight" programs directly relating to, and produced and transmitted during, the referendum campaign comprise the research material for chapter 7.

Finally, in an attempt to enhance my understanding of the debate, I interviewed several people who were involved directly or indirectly in the campaign, including, among others, William Binchy, the main spokesman for the Anti-Divorce Campaign; Jean Tansey, the chairperson of the Divorce Action Group; Bishop Brendan Comiskey of the Diocese of Ferns; and, from, "Today Tonight," presenters/anchors John Bowman, Brian Farrell, and Pat Kenny, and its then executive producer, Eugene Murray. (A list of the people interviewed as part of this study constitutes Appendix C.)

All research is like a journey. Some things are expected, and some things present themselves as a puzzle or as a happy surprise. The cultural journey we are about to embark on will take us, via the discourse of the divorce debate, to the core of modern Irish society and will alert us to important markers about broader questions of values.

CHAPTER TWO

Irish Cultural Themes

Why was a ban on divorce inserted into the Irish Constitution of 1937, fifteen years after independence from Britain? How is it possible for Ireland, a member of the European Economic Community since 1973, to remain the only European country along with Malta to continue prohibiting divorce? What specific forces precipitated the attempt to remove the ban on divorce in 1986? The answers to these questions span Irish history, culture, and society.

Historical and Cultural Themes in Pre-1922 Ireland

Ireland's is a rich, varied, and complex history extending from pre-Christian times and its Celtic culture of elaborate laws, customs, and rituals. Today, a sturdy reminder of this heritage is provided by Newgrange, the megalithic tomb in the Tara countryside. Also, for a small country, Ireland has given birth to a rich literary tradition, encompassing the writings of Swift, Goldsmith, Wilde, Joyce, Shaw, Beckett, O'Casey, Synge, and others such as O'Direain and O'Suilleabhain, lesser known because they wrote in Irish. The two main themes of Irish identity, nevertheless, are captured by the all-powerful images of the priest and the potato, representing, respectively, its Catholicism and its peripheralized agrarian economy.

Ireland's varied history notwithstanding, the focus here is confined to historical themes relevant to marriage and divorce. These coincide with the two major and interrelated strands of Irish history, Catholicism and over four centuries of colonial occupation. Since the arrival of the British missionary, Patrick, in the fifth century, Ireland has been distinguished for its Catholicism and its strong and vigorous monastic tradition. The monasteries were centers of religious and cultural learning, and Irish monks established many similar houses in Europe until the Golden Age of the Irish

Church ended in the ninth century as successive Viking conquests targeted Ireland's monasteries.

Acknowledging the importance of its missionary tradition, Ireland became known as the "Island of Saints and Scholars." An important cultural distinction, it created for the Irish a deep awareness that theirs was a special culture, a bastion of Catholic civilization in a European world of avarice and moral and cultural decline. With the Reformation, Ireland remained loyal to Catholicism whereas England became Protestant, thus further cementing the specialness of Irish values and deepening Irish-English tensions that had originated with the English Norman invasion of Ireland in 1169. Ireland's persistent struggle to maintain an independent identity in the light of consecutive foreign invasions was most severely challenged, however, by English colonization beginning in the sixteenth century.

The British colonization of Ireland occurred in the broader context of Counter-Reformation politics, whereby the British Tudor Crown sought to establish English Protestant settlers in Catholic Ireland. As part of Tudor plantation policy, Irish lands in the midland, southern, and northern regions of the country were confiscated and given to English settlers.[1] This policy caused active resentment among native Irish and previously settled Anglo-Irish families, even though many Catholics continued to own land and others managed to retain land tenancy. Violence against the new settlers was commonplace, as was exemplified by the 1641 Rising during which many English fled or were killed. To quell Irish opposition, Oliver Cromwell invaded Ireland in 1649, massacring thousands of Irish as he proceeded with his army through the country.

It was under Cromwell that the displacement of Ireland's wealth from Catholics to Protestants was consolidated. All of the Catholic landowners who had rebelled in 1641 were stripped of their land, while others who were innocent of rebellion since 1641 also forfeited their land and instead received an equivalent of one-third of their estate in Connacht, where land was poor. The land in the remaining three provinces, which was far superior to that in the west, was kept for non-Catholics, with Catholics working as laborers and tenants on the land. Demonstrating the sweep of English colonization, at the end of the seventeenth century, Catholics owned only 14 percent of Irish land.[2]

The final assault against Irish Catholic ownership was struck with the property restrictions under the penal laws operative from 1695 until 1829, which sought to ensure that Catholics "were kept in a position of social, economic and political inferiority."[3] As such the laws were concerned more with property than with religion,[4] even though they extended the religious repression that was so much a part of Cromwell's regime. The laws against property meant that no Catholic could purchase or inherit land previously owned by Protestants, hold land on a lease for more than thirty-one years, or hold land worth more than thirty shillings a year.[5]

As well as ensuring economic dispossession, the British Crown, again more from a purely political than religious motive, also sought to destroy the "popery" and Catholic faith of the Irish people. Toward this end, the penal laws prohibited the administering of the sacraments, terminated Catholic education, including the education and ordination of priests, and ordered the exiling of priests and bishops, with apostates encouraged with financial incentives.

The laws against religion, however, were ineffective in attenuating Irish Catholicism. The established Protestant church was mostly indifferent to the religious state of the people, and, at any rate, it "lacked the means to mount a serious campaign of evangelisation."[6] Despite the threats against it, the Catholic church managed to further organize its diocesan and parish system, which had initially been drawn into line with Rome in the twelfth century. The Catholic religious culture shaped during the penal era was based on the Tridentine pattern established in the early seventeenth century. As church historian Patrick Corish notes: "Religious life was rooted in the catechesis of the Counter-Reformation. . . . this stressed obedience to church authority, regular sacramental practice, centred on the Sunday Mass, and a regular round of prayers and devotions, especially to the Blessed Virgin."[7] Throughout the eighteenth century, Irish priests were trained in the seminaries of Continental Europe, and although there was some regional variation, Mass and devotions were regular features of Irish life, and Catholic booksellers and publishers flourished.[8]

The socialization of the Irish into the rigors of neo-Tridentine Catholic theology was underwritten, ironically, by the Protestant British state. In 1795, the British government came to the aid of the Irish Church, which was confronting a personnel shortage due to the closure of the Continental seminaries following Britain's war with France, and endowed the founding and establishment of Maynooth College, still the foremost Irish national seminary.[9] Here, Irish priests were trained under an allegedly French Jansenist influence—one that sacrificed humanist principles to strict disciplinary laws and precepts—in the moral and devotional austerity that became so much a part of late nineteenth-century European and Irish Catholicism.[10] One of the striking paradoxes of the British-Irish relationship was that by the nineteenth century the Irish Catholic church was well interlocked with the British state in the areas of education and social control—it took charge of children's education in 1750—enabling it, supported by the State, to act as a "civilising agent" on the undisciplined Irish.[11]

Even though the penal laws represent the most systematic British subjugation of the Irish, they were counterproductive insofar as they instead contributed to the consolidation of the Catholic church and Irish Catholic identity. Responding to their colonial domination, the economically dispossessed Irish appropriated Catholicism as a symbolic force against British Protestant oppression. Regarding Catholicism as signifying their unique status as a special "chosen people" in an exploitative Protestant world, it enabled the Irish to maintain a distinct identity from Britain and from the Anglo-Irish Protestant ascendancy. Catholicism and Irishness thus became intertwined as synonymous and gave the Irish people an inflated sense of social value grounded in a collective, rigorously Catholic identity.

Catholicism, therefore, acts as a central cohesive force for the Irish, providing them with a sense of community and unity, its well-defined values serving as a counterpoint against anomie and alienation. Cultural identification with Catholicism has also played a major role in the formation of a distinct Irish worldview. Dominant here is a tendency to obfuscate any distinction between the spheres of public and private life, in large part because of a widespread assumption that Catholic moral teaching should inform civil legislation. For Irish Catholics, the need to exercise personal conscience clearly recedes in importance when the civic culture is itself underpinned by the Catholic ethos. Thus Catholic teaching and public morality tend to be equated at the expense of an autonomous personal morality.

Related to this is a legalistic strand in Irish society. The catecethical tradition is one that outlines a clear set of duties and obligations that need to be executed,[12] with Irish moral theology tending toward "an overcategorisation of offences."[13] Extensively documented by empirical studies, many Irish Catholics exhibit a "dogmatic religious mentality."[14] They equate rigid observance of the law with morality, seeing this as the ultimate criterion in evaluating behavior, and ignore the relevance of personal values and moral principles as guides to behavior. As observed by moral theologian Raphael Gallagher: "We convince ourselves that we are morally good because we externally keep the law."[15]

Another distinction of Irish society and one that in part emanates from the Catholic tradition, is the absence of an established and well-accepted discourse of individual rights. Unlike the situation in the United States where it is commonplace for people to freely use a language that talks about their individual rights,[16] the use of a "rights" discourse in Irish society is uncommon. Although such a language is not totally absent—trade union leaders use a "workers' rights" discourse, for example—it is segmented and specific, and not readily available to the mainstream.[17]

Because of its communitarian emphasis, the Catholic view of individual worth is relational, dependent both on the person's benevolent disposition toward other members of the community and on acceptance of sacramental grace, which only the Church can confer. Thus, in Ireland, when an individual achieves success, it is not unusual to attribute this to the fact that "God is good," not that the successful person is good or deserved the reward in his or her own right.[18] This relational emphasis is well suited to a poor economy where preoccupation with economic viability preempts consideration of the post-materialist values represented by individual rights. Although the Irish endorse individual rights when asked such questions in surveys, for instance,[19] this more closely resembles affirmation of an abstract principle rather than the expression of a pervasive cultural ethic that values individual autonomy over obligations to family and society. In public moral debates such as divorce, therefore, where issues of individual freedom come into conflict with traditional notions of the social good, the Irish do not have ready access to a common language of individual rights that might be usefully appropriated in making a case for the introduction of divorce.

Economic Development

One outcome of colonialism, as we have seen, was its exacerbation of Catholic identity. But there are also other implications. Of particular significance was the moratorium that colonialism placed on Irish economic development through its stifling of economic growth.[20] British policies did not result in the obliteration of an Irish Catholic capitalist or bourgeois class but in the suppression of its capitalist spirit. Despite the plantations and the penal laws, a small minority of Catholic landowners and middle class survived. The repeal of various property laws beginning in the late eighteenth century—as of 1782 Catholics could buy land—facilitated the growth of Catholic economic wealth. Large landholding Catholics who were descendants of former proprietors secured ownership of land from Protestant landowners, while a substantial class of tenant farmers continued to exist.[21] In fact, the nineteenth-century Irish Catholic population was a remarkably stratified one, ranging from a minority of large landowners and merchants to large landholders, small tenant farmers, and laborers.[22] What is important in terms of Irish economic development, however, was the paucity and nature of the economic channels available to those Catholics who had excess capital.

The British occupation of Ireland occurred as Britain was entering the industrial age, and the economic policies that it pursued in Ireland were ones that suited its broader expansionist agenda. Most of Ireland was reserved primarily to function as Britain's farmyard, as a supplier of food for Britain's industrial classes, thus suppressing its own internal industrial development. The profits from Irish agricultural production were used by the British government to finance its own industrial growth as well as that of the Protestant, northern region of Ireland where, from the eighteenth century, industrialization was also pursued.[23] The results of this differentiation in colonial policy, industrialization in the North, and its virtual repression in the rest of the country, is crucial to appreciating the differentiated structure of nineteenth-, and subsequently, twentieth-century Ireland.

Colonialism accounts for the fact that as recently as the time of the Famine (1845–1849), when much of the Western world was fully industrialized, "almost half of the holdings in Ireland were below the minimum size even for manual agriculture."[24] The majority of Ireland's population was made up of tenant farmers renting from landlords, many without security of tenure. Part of the legacy of colonialism was to reinforce Irish agrarianism at a time when agriculture was being displaced elsewhere in the West with industrial and capitalist expansion. Whatever the chances of an entrepreneurial spirit emerging from the nineteenth-century Irish Catholic middle class, it was stifled by British maintenance of traditional, Irish peasant agriculture and its attendant economic values.

Moreover, the political and cultural implications of colonialism—the absence of an indigenous self-governing tradition, nonidentification with the colonizer, the attendant inferiority, insecurity, and instability of a colonized people, and the absence of a state-created environment conducive to entrepreneurial, industrialized culture—also militated against economic development. Reflecting the confluence of these factors, the expanding urban and rural middle class invested their excess capital not in industrial ventures but in the security and respectability of professional training, law, and medicine, for their children.[25]

The political-economic environment of nineteenth-century Ireland also accounts for the impact that the potato blights of the time had on Irish society. Had Irish laborers and tenant farmers outside of Ulster not been structurally dependent on the potato, both as a source of food and as a medium of capital exchange, the ravages of its failure would not have been as extensive as they were. Regarded as "a major dividing line in the history of modern Ireland,"[26] during the Famine "not far short of 1,000,000 people died either from disease or hunger,"[27] while millions of others emigrated. Continuing a pattern of mass emigration that had begun three decades earlier, over three million people left Ireland between 1845 and 1870.[28] In short, this period in history saw the Irish population decline by half, a major transformation for any society.

But especially significant about the Famine was the selectivity of its impact and the consequent social and cultural implications. It was the poorest classes in Ireland—the landless laborers and the cottiers (farmers with less than five acres of land)—whose numbers suffered the greatest decline, while the Catholic tenant-farmer class remained virtually intact.[29] After the Famine, land became scarcer as holdings were gradually consolidated, thus shifting the class balance in favor of the large tenant farmers.[30] Agrarian reform was a major political issue during the second part of the nineteenth century as the tenant farmers campaigned to establish a more secure, independent economic base. After decades of sporadic violence against the landlords and their representatives, they adopted more conventional tactics and joined the Tenant League, founded in 1850. Their demands were eventually resolved with the 1870 and 1881 Land Acts of Gladstone, which formally recognized the property rights of Irish farmers.[31]

It was not until the first years of the twentieth century, however, that legislation was enacted in Ireland that initiated the transfer of land from landlord to tenant and changed Ireland into a country of landowning small farmers. Encouraged by the Wyndham Land Act (1903), landlords sold entire estates to their tenants, who were advanced the money for the purchases by the state under very reasonable conditions. The success of this legislation was so immediate that by the time of Irish independence in 1922 "landlordism in rural Ireland had become a thing of the past."[32] Once the struggle for land ownership was over, the tenant farmers consolidated their influence as a highly conservative force in the shaping of the new Irish nation, an influence extending from the nineteenth century when they were the mainstay of the Catholic church, providing it with priests and money.[33]

The legacy of British domination in Ireland had important consequences for the issue of marriage and divorce. Small-scale agrarianism accentuated the importance of economic considerations in informing marital choices, while identification with Catholicism was maintained and publicly signified in post-independence Ireland through institutionalizing the sacramental definition of marriage.

Land and Marriage

For a people preoccupied with security of land tenure the question of marriage was harnessed to economic interests. In post-Famine Ireland, marriage was contemplated only if it maintained or enhanced the economic resources of the farmer. Such prospects were attenuated by a widening social class differential following the consolidation of farm holdings, which restricted the availability of suitable, that is, within-class, marriage partners.[34] Consequently, as demographers have well documented, the Irish exhibited high rates of postponed or late-age marriage and permanent celibacy.[35]

While various theories have been put forward to explain Ireland's distinctive demography,[36] Robert Kennedy's economic analysis seems the most convincing. He argues that the Irish, similar to their European counterparts, postponed or excluded marriage in order to maintain or improve their material and social ambitions. The meager economic resources of many people militated against their marrying because the acquisition of dependents would detract from their established standard of living.

At the same time, of course, despite its economic drawback, marriage was essential to the rural economy because it provided laborers to work the land and an "heir" to reproduce the viability of the family holding.[37] This tension was resolved by the institutionalized way in which inheritance operated—the stem-family system. Under this system, only one child (usually a son) in each generation could inherit the family holding, marry, and produce the next generation, and another (usually a daughter) could marry a locally inheriting heir. The rest of the siblings either emigrated or remained unmarried, because, had they married, they would have been unable to support a family at the same standard of living to which they were accustomed as members of a landholding family. Kennedy argues, therefore, that in spite of the Church's encouragement of marriage, many Irish people who might have married repressed their emotional and sexual needs in order to fulfill their economic objectives, or else they emigrated.[38]

The association of marriage and land was fortified by the prevalence of a dowry system in Irish courtship and marriage, a feature that remained in operation in some parts of the country until the

1940s.[39] Women brought to the marriage a dowry, either land or money, calculated on the basis of the value of the land of her future husband—to support herself and expected children, because with noninheriting siblings remaining on the farm, any extra demand on the existing resources would reduce the standard of living of the groom's family. The dowry thus enabled the inheriting son to marry, acquire further economic capital, produce an heir, and thus consolidate the family's generativity and economic security.[40] The availability of a dowry also increased the chances of marriage of the bride's inheriting brother, because, in turn, her marriage reduced the number of siblings dependent on her brother's resources, thus enabling him to marry, acquire more land or money from his wife's dowry, produce an heir, and consolidate his family's status. The dowry system, therefore, served as the linchpin in the relationship between land and marriage. As the Irish historian Joseph Lee has remarked, "Marriage might be a sacrament, but for the farmer the marriage contract was essentially, a commercial transaction."[41]

The importance of the dowry grew after the Famine because, among its other consequences, the Famine caused a deterioration in the independent economic status of women, who prior to then had an active economic role both in domestic industry (wool, linen, and cotton) and on the land.[42] The decline in women's marriage prospects attendant on their loss of economic resources was redressed by the availability of a dowry. Importantly, however, it also clasped women into a system of economic dependence on their fathers and husbands, and, along with the expanding moral disciplinary role of the post-Famine Catholic Church, cemented the notion that women's domain was that of the home.

Independent Ireland

Rather than being undermined by its framing as an economic question, the sacramental importance of marriage and women's dependency in relation to it became, after independence, a key marker of Irish identity. The achievement of political independence with Ireland's secession from the United Kingdom and the establishment of the Irish Free State in 1922 was not itself, of course, a total victory. The deep historical religious divisions, along which so much of

Irish cultural topography has its roots, continued. Differences in cultural identity were now officially institutionalized under the 1921 Anglo-Irish Treaty, which established two separate legal jurisdictions in Ireland: the twenty-six counties of the Irish Free State and the six counties of Northern Ireland, which remained part of the United Kingdom.

Reaction to the treaty and attendant questions of nationalism became the sole ideological axis driving Irish politics, the legacy of which is still evident today. Opposed by Sinn Fein, the precursor to Fianna Fail, and accepted by Cumann na nGaedheal, from which Fine Gael evolved, independence was followed by a bitterly fought Civil War (1922–1923), during which more than six hundred people died.[43] The treaty forces prevailed, and Cumann na nGaedheal under the leadership of W.T. Cosgrave became the first post-independence government. With the implicit support of the Church, which during the civil war excommunicated anti-treaty leaders, including Eamon de Valera, for their acts of violence against the new state, the Cosgrave government established democratic political stability. It remained in power for ten years until ceding to Eamon de Valera (now back in favor with Church authorities) and Fianna Fail, the party he founded, which has been a dominant force in Irish politics and society since then.

Despite the costs that the nationalist struggle had exacted, however, independence was not accompanied by the establishment of new institutions that would have allowed a complete break with Ireland's colonial past. None of the fervor that had successfully energized the fight for independence was converted into fashioning a new state that would embody the libertarian and republican principles officially proclaimed by the revolutionary leaders. Instead, the period following independence saw the continuation of the cultural themes that had distinguished the colonized Irish: Catholicism and agrarianism. And although church and state were separate institutions, they mutually affirmed a national identity grounded in Catholic teaching. This constituted part of the larger post-independence project of establishing a truly sovereign country that was independent not just politically but economically and culturally, an agenda that was interpreted by successive governments and endorsed by the electorate as one of economic and cultural protectionism.[44]

While the nations of the Western world were becoming more interconnected and interdependent, insular self-sufficiency became the dominant objective in Ireland. This led to agricultural policies that sought to increase the number of people working and living on the land. Tillage production was expanded and accompanied by guaranteed prices for crops, while grazing was discouraged and tariffs imposed on imported food products as well as on a large number of imported industrial products.[45] As Irish society became more "backward" relative to its modern, industrialized neighbors, the superiority of rural life and traditional values—de Valera's vision of "a countryside bright with comely maidens, athletic youths and romping children"[46]—became the cultural paradigm venerated by political and Church leaders.

The monolithic view was that Catholic values should be the definers of Irish identity, notwithstanding the existence of a substantial number of Protestants in the South.[47] Knowing, as he proclaimed, the hearts of the Irish people through looking into his own heart,[48] de Valera saw Ireland as essentially a "Catholic nation," a worldview that he eloquently explained: "Since the coming of St. Patrick fifteen hundred years ago, Ireland has been a Christian and a Catholic nation. All the ruthless attempts made through the centuries to force her from this allegiance have not shaken her faith. She remains a Catholic nation."[49]

Committed to upholding Ireland's uniqueness as a Catholic nation, de Valera's government enacted legislation supporting the principles of Catholic social teaching. It prohibited the sale and importation of artificial contraceptives, regulated dance halls, and taxed foreign newspapers. In keeping with the cultural consensus characteristic of the first decades of Irish independence, the previous government had already enacted legislation censoring books and films.[50]

Irish Catholic identity was most clearly demonstrated with the publication of the constitution in 1937. Reputed to have been single-handedly written by de Valera with advice provided by his close friend, John Charles McQuaid, who later became an influential archbishop of Dublin, de Valera explained: "Our people are a conservative people. For fifteen hundred years we have preserved the tradition and practised the rule of the Christian life. . . . If ever there was a time in which it was desirable for our people—whose spiritual history has been that of an uninterrupted spiritual crusade—to record a solemn declaration of their adherence to these fundamental principles, it is the time in which we live."[51]

The constitution thus represents "a synthesis of Catholic social principles."[52] It officially recognized the "special position" of the Catholic church in Ireland[53] and, in line with Catholic teaching, gives special recognition to the family "as indispensable to the welfare of the Nation and the State," affirming it as "the natural primary and fundamental unit group of society . . . antecedent and superior to all positive law." Consonant with the significance attached to the family, the constitution also pledges to "guard with special care the institution of Marriage . . . and to protect it against attack." Thus "no law shall be enacted providing for the grant of a dissolution of marriage"; in other words, no divorce.[54]

But while the boundaries between public and private morality were formally blurred by the constitution's privileging of Catholic morality, Catholicism and traditional values also account for the imposition of a strict separation of the domestic from the public sphere. The constitution defined women as the preservers of the structure and the values of marriage and the family. Expressing the official Irish view of women and underscoring the language of relational duties that informs perceptions of personal rights, the constitution states: "In particular, the State recognises that by her life within the home, woman gives to the State a support without which the common good cannot be achieved. The State shall, therefore, endeavour to ensure that mothers shall not be obliged by economic necessity to engage in labour to the neglect of their duties in the home."[55] The constitution thus formalized the Irish mother as "the organisational link between the Catholic Church and the individual," a relationship in place since the middle of the nineteenth century, which forged a powerful alliance between priests and women as family morality became the responsibility of mothers.[56]

Ignoring the active participation of women in its founding and the precedent of women in the public sphere set by Countess Markievicz, a minister in the first independent government,[57] the new state was committed to ensuring that women would execute their duties in the home. Accordingly, it enacted various legislative measures such as a ban prohibiting women from working in the public sector after marriage, which until repealed in the mid-1970s prohibited or obstructed the participation of women in the public sphere.[58] Reflecting these structural and cultural barriers, in 1961, a mere 5 percent of married women participated in the labor force, while many women in present-day Ireland continue to eschew the public for the domestic domain—currently, married women have a labor force participation rate of only 21 percent.

The constitutional prohibition of divorce in Ireland, therefore, is relatively recent in its origins. It came about as part of a broad attempt by the state to establish a society in which Catholic values would define national identity. Significantly, a divorce procedure that had been established by the British was still legally available in Ireland until 1937,[59] a situation that echoed the tradition of early Irish society when divorce was commonplace under brehon law.

But less than two decades after the establishment of the new Irish state, politicians had gained public approval for a constitution and enacted legislation that was in accordance with Catholic teaching. This influence extended from the immediate domain of marriage and sociosexual morality to inform also the formulation of education, health, and social policies,[60] resulting in a church/state consensus on public morality that continued virtually undisturbed until the late 1970s.

The one issue that threatened to crack the consensual relationship between political and Church leaders was an attempt in 1947 to introduce legislation that sought among other health changes to provide universal health care for mothers and their children.[61] First introduced by de Valera's Fianna Fail government, it was subsequently taken up by the coalition government that succeeded it in 1948. Known as the "Mother and Child" scheme, the Church formally communicated their total disapproval of the proposals to the government, emphasizing that they were "entirely and directly contrary to Catholic teaching on the rights of the family, [and] the rights of the Church in education."[62] The hierarchy further maintained that: "physical or health education is closely interwoven with important moral questions on which the Catholic Church has definite teaching. . . . The State has no competence to give instruction in such matters."[63]

Interestingly enough, the controversy only developed when the new minister responsible, Noel Browne, a young liberal maverick who was alone in those years in pushing for a greater autonomy between Catholic teaching and civil legislation, publicized the private correspondence between the bishops and the government on the matter. Once the dissension became known, the government, not wishing to engage in open confrontation with the hierarchy and reflecting many of the cabinet members' own ambivalence toward the scheme, withdrew it. The succeeding Fianna Fail government once again expressed commitment to the intent of the proposal, but when the act was finally passed into law in 1953, the bishops had received virtually all of the concessions they demanded.[64] The controversy clearly demonstrated that in the early decades of the newly independent Irish society, as Archbishop John Charles McQuaid stated: "The hierarchy cannot approve of any scheme which, by its general tendency, must foster undue control by the State in a sphere so delicate and so intimately concerned with morals."[65]

Ireland since the 1950s

While the opening years of the 1950s saw the forceful reaffirmation of Ireland's Catholic identity, the end of the decade would see the beginnings of a new orientation that would eventually challenge that hegemony. Strikingly high rates of unemployment and emigration became the hallmark of Irish society in the late 1940s and 1950s. It is estimated that between 1951 and 1961, 409,000 Irish people emigrated, an amount equivalent to about one-seventh of the total population in Ireland in 1961 (2.8 million).[66] With increasing evidence that an indigenous protectionist economic policy had failed to provide for the material needs of the Irish people, and extensive popular awareness throughout the country that those who emigrated were economically successful abroad, the Fianna Fail government, now under de Valera's successor, Sean Lemass, embarked in 1959 on a major overhaul of the economy. The results of the new orientation marked this period as the watershed in Ireland's modernization.[67]

Redirecting economic policy to focus on industrial development and its needed infrastructure, the government established economic growth as the dominant and uncontested project of Irish society.[68] The ensuing years recorded high and unprecedented growth in the national economy—between 1959 and 1963, for example, the annual growth rate was 4 percent per annum—accompanied by significant increases in the gross domestic product and personal disposable income.[69] The changes initiated by the government and fueled by Ireland's membership in the European Economic Community in 1973 transformed the Irish social structure and economy.[70] Agriculture was displaced by manufacturing industry and services as the main economic sectors.[71] Despite the quantitative decline in the numbers engaged in agriculture, however, the farming classes in general, and particularly the medium and large farmers who have benefitted disproportionately from Ireland's membership in the European Community, continue to exert a political influence their numbers belie.

Importantly, however, agriculture's lessening economic role became the engine for broader societal change. Attendant on this was the increasing urbanization of society, with one-third of the population currently residing in the greater Dublin metropolitan area; increased participation in education; the expansion of a white-collar middle class; increasing participation of women in the labor force; expanding consumerism; and, since television was introduced in 1962, extension of the reach of mass media.

As the social and economic structures underwent change, so too, but less forcefully, did the cultural environment, as manifested by a loosening of traditional values and attitudes. Since 1970 there has been, for example, a significant decline in fertility rates,[72] a steady increase in approval for divorce and contraception,[73] and slight evidence of a greater willingness to embrace the principle of church/state differentiation.[74]

The gains made by women in the political arena also reflect the interlocking changes. Since the early 1980s women have maintained a strong presence in national and European parliamentary politics, constituting an average of 8 percent of the seats in the national legislature, a rate surpassing that of many Western democracies including the United States and Great Britain.[75] Highlighted by the recent election of Mary Robinson as president of Ireland, the comparative political success of Irish women is in part because of Ireland's proportional representation electoral system, which, with its system of vote transfer, tends to favor "minority" candidates. It is also a testament to the strong interest that Irishwomen have in politics. Sixty-nine percent of women, similar to the figure observed for men (70 percent), express interest in current political and economic affairs,[76] and many women participate in political seminars and events organized by women's associations.[77]

Ideologically, Irishwomen present as a heterogeneous group holding a diversity of moral, social, and political attitudes ranging from conservative to liberal.[78] Their political orientation and level of confidence in political institutions displays a differentiated pattern similar to men's.[79] In terms of party affiliation, there is only slight evidence of a gender gap: more women than men support Fine Gael,[80] a difference that may owe more to that party's active efforts since the mid-1970s to recruit women members and candidates rather than to any ideological affinity with its progressive social platform.

But for all of women's political interest and activity, activist organizations that specifically represent women's interests and lobby on their behalf have not emerged as a strong force in Irish society. A promising Dublin-based women's movement, with women journalists in the forefront, formed in 1970 and received quite extensive national media attention, particularly for its lobbying efforts with regard to the liberalization of contraception. It quickly disbanded, however, because of the diversity in composition and ideology of its founding members,[81] which led to divisions over strategies and policies fueled by social class and nationalist conflicts. Subsequently, many of its original members were instrumental in establishing more focused organizations working on behalf of women's rights. The mushrooming of various women's groups encompassing a wide range of concerns led to the establishment of the Council for the Status of Women (CSW) in 1973, and it has coordinated action on certain issues, most notably in the area of economic participation. Lacking recognition as one of the nation's "social partners," however, it functions more as a national administrative body for women than as an activist lobby.[82]

In consequence, the extension of women's rights in Ireland owes more to Irish judicial review and equality directives from the European Commission than to the lobbying efforts of organized women.[83] The decriminalization of contraception was hastened by a 1974 Supreme Court case in which the justices ruled that its criminal status violated the right to marital privacy.[84] Following this, and after a number of failed attempts, Parliament eventually passed legislation in 1979—the Health (Family Planning) Act—which provided that both medical and nonmedical contraceptives could be purchased only for bona fide family planning purposes and only on the basis of a doctor's prescription.[85] This "Irish solution to an Irish problem"[86] remained intact until 1985, when Garret Fitz-Gerald's government extended the legal availability of nonmedical contraceptives without prescription to persons over eighteen years of age.[87]

The 1979 act also reaffirmed the nonlegal status of abortion, criminalized in Ireland since 1861.[88] Nonetheless, a right-to-life movement emerged in Ireland in 1980. Alarmed by the changes in Irish society, epitomized by the founding of a small "Woman's Right to Choose" group, and encouraged by Pope John Paul II's Irish visit in 1979 and the "Human Life Amendment Campaign" in the United States,[89] the Pro-Life Amendment Campaign (PLAC) successfully lobbied the political leaders to hold a referendum.[90] Pro-life lobbyists sought to copperfasten the criminalization of abortion by having a pro-life amendment inserted into the constitution that could then only be changed, not by Parliament or the Judiciary, but by public referendum.

After a vigorous and bitterly fought campaign, where an anti-amendment stance was equated, erroneously, with pro-abortion, two-thirds of the electorate endorsed the amendment.[91] Content not simply with a moral or symbolic victory,[92] since passage of the amendment, the pro-life movement has used it to successfully seek legal injunctions against the operation of nondirective pregnancy counseling clinics in Ireland, prohibiting them from disseminating information about abortion services in England.[93]

So, when Garret FitzGerald announced the divorce referendum in 1986, it was against the backdrop of a sociocultural environment that, despite its many modernizing changes, continues to affirm strong links between private and public morality. It was fitting, however, that FitzGerald should be the government leader who, in initiating divorce, attempted to forge a break between the public and private spheres of Irish life. Embodying the embryonic spirit of modern Ireland, just as de Valera had once forcefully represented its deeply embedded traditional values, for many years FitzGerald has publicly articulated an intellectual, pluralist vision of Ireland. Arguing that religious freedom is central to a modern heterogeneous society, FitzGerald, a devout Catholic himself, has argued for the displacement of the singular importance of Catholic teaching in informing public morality and for the removal of sectarian thinking from Irish laws and institutions.[94]

This is what FitzGerald proposed to effect with divorce, and this is what he needed to convince the Irish people of if they were to endorse the amendment. But just as economic questions have always played a pivotal role in Irish history and society, they would also impact on the divorce question. The divorce amendment occurred at a time when the longstanding cultural preoccupation with economic issues was revitalized by an economy in decline.

Notwithstanding its growth in the 1960s, Ireland's small, dependent economy is highly vulnerable to the state of the larger world market. Accentuated by the pressures of the global recession caused by the 1973 oil crisis, Ireland had to borrow heavily abroad in order to offset demands on its Exchequer, fueled, in part, by the rising expectations of the late 1960s and 1970s. The cumulative effects of an increase in the national debt caused a deterioration in labor market conditions, and since the early 1980s the problems of unemployment and emigration have once again become central concerns in Ireland.[95] In 1986, at the time of the referendum, the unemployment rate was 18 percent, with that of the youth labor market reaching 25 percent.

Irish preoccupation with economic problems is underscored in political election campaigns and opinion surveys in which economic issues are consistently ranked as top priorities. Although it is no surprise that people express interest in improving their economic status, Irish economic attitudes seem to demonstrate a more urgent acquisitive drive and concern with the immediate material situation.[96] Between 1982 and 1988, for instance, the Irish scored significantly lower than the European Community average on indices measuring satisfaction with both their household's financial situation and the general state of their country's economy.[97] Importantly, the gap between the Irish and the European score was at its greatest in 1986,[98] highlighting the extent to which the Irish were sensitive to economic difficulties at the time of the referendum.

The amendment, therefore, would bring together two key issues that over the centuries have been fundamental in shaping Irish national identity: Catholicism and economic status. Arguing about divorce, then, which is in and of itself both morally and economically charged, would penetrate directly the bedrock of Irish values. The difficulties that this debate presented for those engaged in it are the topics of this book.

CHAPTER THREE

Arguing about Divorce

The debate between the announcement of the divorce referendum and the final vote was a heated one. It involved the entire spectrum of Irish society from the chambers of Parliament to the local parishes. The pro- and anti-divorce arguments were featured prominently in the daily newspapers and were aired on radio and television. Spearheaded by the Fine Gael/Labour coalition government of Prime Minister Garret FitzGerald, the divorce proposals were supported by most, but not all, of the government ministers and Fine Gael parliamentarians[1] and were strongly supported by Labour under the leadership of Dick Spring, whose party had failed in previous attempts to win parliamentary approval for a divorce bill. The divorce proposals also received the support of the other minor parliamentary parties.

Also engaged in the pro-divorce campaign was an independent pro-divorce group, the Divorce Action Group (DAG). Founded in 1980 to lobby for the holding of a divorce referendum, the DAG is composed primarily of separated people. It has its headquarters in Dublin, the area from which it draws most of its support, and has branches around the country. The DAG was headed by Jean Tansey, a married woman, and, significantly, its executive committee comprises both men and women.[2]

The campaign against the government's divorce proposals was led, not, as one might expect, by the Catholic bishops or the opposition Fianna Fail party, but by a lay group, the Anti-Divorce Campaign (ADC), a group that was formally independent both of the Church and of party politics. Although the issue of divorce is central to the moral teaching of the Church and in the past the Church has condemned outright any legislation that sought to go against its teaching, the hierarchy confined its official participation to the issuing of episcopal statements discussing divorce. Similarly, the largest political party in Ireland, Fianna Fail (the party of de Valera, whose idea it was to have a constitutional ban on divorce), which continues to demonstrate a relatively conservative disposition on sociomoral issues, adopted an official line of neutrality.

Unlike the pro-divorce lobby, which was composed of a number of disparate groups, the one official opponent of divorce was the Anti-Divorce Campaign (ADC), thus making it a cohesive and unified player. The ADC did not represent a mass social movement against divorce but was an ad hoc group of Catholic lay people that formed only after the government announced the holding of the divorce referendum.

Despite the recency of the ADC's formation, its leaders were experienced canvassers on moral issues. Its main spokespersons and some of the members of its organizing committee were active in the successful pro-life amendment referendum campaign in 1983. Unlike the Divorce Action Group, which was led by a woman, the primary ADC figures were men.[3] The chairman of the ADC was Des Hanafin, a Fianna Fail Senator noted for his expertise as a fund raiser, his close ties to the Vatican, and his active role in the 1983 pro-life amendment campaign. The ADC's primary spokesman was not their chairman, but William Binchy, a barrister and author of a short book *Is Divorce the Answer?*, who was also a visible participant in the pro-life amendment campaign.[4] Two other members of the ADC's organizing committee who served as spokespersons were Joe McCarroll, a lecturer in ethics at the Dublin diocesan seminary, and Bernadette Bonar.[5]

The ADC was also able to draw on the active support of Family Solidarity, a social organization founded in the aftermath of the success of the right-to-life amendment as a lobby against what it perceives as increasing social and economic threats to traditional marriage and family life.[6] It is organized on a national parish basis, has the support of the Catholic clergy, and uses parish facilities for its meetings.

Importantly, the Anti-Divorce Campaign, through its affiliation with Family Solidarity, had access to an already established national parish network of active members and was able to use these local volunteers to canvass people in the various communities. This gave the ADC a significant organizational advantage over their opponents in the pro-divorce lobby, because both the pro-divorce

political parties and the Divorce Action Group have a more centralized regional structure, thus making them more distant from the
electorate in organizing campaign strategies for acceptance of the
amendment at the grassroots level.[7]

In addition to arguments expressed by the ADC and by Family
Solidarity, my analysis of the anti-divorce discourse also includes
arguments by Fianna Fail. Because, although Fianna Fail did not
officially participate as a party in the divorce campaign, not wishing, as it stated, to "politicise the debate,"[8] the majority of individual members who spoke publicly during the debate adopted a
clear anti-divorce stance. The party's leader, Charles Haughey, and
all of the shadow ministers expressed their opposition to divorce,
and its party political broadcast on the amendment was unequivocally anti-divorce.[9]

I propose to start my analysis of the divorce campaign right at
the beginning, with an analysis of Garret FitzGerald's opening
statement—a statement that, by what it said and what it failed to
say, provides a template for the understanding of the pro-divorce
strategies and arguments. FitzGerald announced the divorce referendum at a press conference held at Government Buildings. At this
time he outlined the details of the four-point constitutional amendment as well as the provisions of the accompanying legislation that
would be implemented if divorce was introduced. In elaborating on
the government's reasons for favoring the introduction of divorce,
FitzGerald stated:

The government is committed to seek and ensure the passage of the constitutional amendment through the House so that the people may be given
the opportunity to discuss their views on it. . . . Speaking for my own
party, Fine Gael, we will . . . be supporting it before the electorate, while
accepting that *individual members may on grounds of conscience not wish
to participate in this exercise because they hold a contrary view to the
amendment.* In thus providing the people with an opportunity to express
themselves on this subject, the parties in government are conscious that
diverse views may be held on whether the introduction of divorce on the
restrictive basis proposed is for the social good, or is necessary for the relief
of cases of marriage breakdown where spouses have entered into or propose to enter into other liaisons. *The parties believe that the balance of the
social good will be served by making this provision,* and while it is accepted that the divorce provision may have a negative effect on some

existing marriages, on the other hand, the number of people now involved in irregular unions and the number of children adversely affected by the situation is, in the considered view of the parties, more destabilising. The government is grateful to the churches for the manner in which they offered their views on the issues dealt with in the amendment and on the statement of the government's intentions with regard to marriage, separation and divorce. *The discussions with the churches were extremely constructive and the arrangements now proposed in relation to a number of these matters bear the mark of the views expressed by the churches. The government recognises, however, that some or all of the churches may have different views on some of the matters dealt with*, including the proposals for the provision of divorce, and that the churches will wish to put forward these views to their members [emphasis mine].[10]

The Private-Public Dichotomy

FitzGerald's remarks provide a complex text in which are embedded several arguments favoring the introduction of divorce. Importantly, in his opening address, FitzGerald both comments on his discussions with the churches[11] and remarks on the differences between him and the church authorities. Although he does not single out the Catholic church, it is the majority Catholic church to which he is primarily referring when he states that there may be different views held by some or all of the churches on divorce. Both the Catholic and Protestant churches oppose divorce on theological grounds, but it is only the Catholic church that opposes divorce as a civil response to marital breakdown.[12] FitzGerald's open reference to disagreement between the Church and him, and between him and members of his own party, on the question of divorce, constitutes a cornerstone of the pro-divorce campaign, and gives us insight into one of the most complex arguments raised in favor of divorce.

Given the strong association in Irish society between Catholic teaching and state law, in order to argue successfully for divorce, its proponents had to do two things. First, it was imperative that they establish their credentials, which, in part, meant convincing the electorate that they were good Catholics. Secondly, they had to succeed in forging a break between civil legislation and religious morality. FitzGerald had to demonstrate first the authenticity of his Catholicism and the attendant credibility of his government in holding a referendum with a view to introducing divorce. An attempt then had to be made at breaking the popularly endorsed relationship, embedded in tradition, between civil legislation and Catholic morality. The issue was: how to argue for divorce without undermining the well-respected traditional approach to marriage as a sacramental lifelong commitment and the attendant belief that state law should support this.

The Irish electorate had to be convinced of the public need for divorce, and, if they conceded this point, they then had to be convinced of the acceptability of having legislation in the civil sphere that was independent of and contrary to Catholic teaching. Accustomed to viewing marriage as a lifelong commitment and to thinking in terms of a direct relationship between (Catholic) religious morality and public morality, the Irish people, with the introduction of divorce, were being asked to overturn these two bedrock values in their culture and have them displaced with counter value positions. For them to vote in favor of divorce would thus demand a fundamental change in worldview.

It is understandable then why, in his opening statement introducing the divorce referendum, FitzGerald emphasized his consultations with the churches. It seems clear that the reference to his consultations with church authorities has to be construed as an attempt at legitimation of his newly proposed legislation. It enabled FitzGerald to show respect for all denominational perspectives, but particularly, given its dominance, the Catholic ethos, and to underscore his deference to the Catholic hierarchy. It also served to emphasize that FitzGerald's decision to hold a referendum was not an impulsive one but was the result of careful deliberation, including deliberation on the Catholic church's position on divorce. It indicated his concern to take full account of the needs and wishes of the Irish people and his personal desire not to introduce a form of divorce that would be totally at odds with Irish cultural values.

Accordingly, while his evaluation of the problem of marital breakdown in Ireland convinced him that divorce was needed, his consultations with the churches had helped him to construct divorce proposals that were relatively restrictive. Consulting with the Catholic church resulted in a reaffirmation of the Church's opposition to divorce, but, FitzGerald was saying, it also provided the opportunity for him to hear more fully the bishops' concerns about marriage and marital breakdown in Ireland. Having given serious consideration to these concerns, the government was in a position to take account of the fears and reservations expressed. The subsequent divorce proposals and accompanying pro-marriage legislation he had introduced were, in part, a product of these concerns. In a fairly direct way, therefore, FitzGerald was attempting to gain personal legitimacy by referring to his talks with the church representatives and to his incorporation of some of the ideas that they put forward, a legitimacy he needed if his government's divorce proposals were to be acceptable to the Irish people.

It is significant in this regard that other senior members of the cabinet also stressed the consultations with the churches. Opening the Parliamentary debate on the amendment, the minister for justice, Alan Dukes, stated:

In deciding on the form of the constitutional amendment that should be presented and in forming its further proposals, the Government have taken fully into account the views expressed by the various persons and groups who have contributed to the debate, including the views expressed by the various Churches in their meetings with the Taoiseach [prime minister] and myself. The Government have carefully weighed the various arguments on each side, both from the point of view of the individuals directly involved and of society as a whole. In the Government's considered view, the balance of the social good lies with the introduction of divorce in limited circumstances.[13]

Similarly, Dick Spring, the deputy leader of the government [Tanaiste] and leader of the Labour party, maintained: "It's very difficult to establish perfection in any solution. But I believe that after careful consideration and after consultations with the church authorities, I believe that the government has brought forward a very balanced amendment to the constitution to cope with very serious problems in Irish life."[14]

More important, however, FitzGerald's reference to consultations with the churches reflects one of the main thrusts in the strategy to break the link between Catholic and civil morality. By referring to the consultations with the Church, acknowledging disagreements, and yet proceeding forward, FitzGerald, with one swift blow, challenged the Irish conflation of the public and the private spheres of life.

In proposing divorce, as with liberalizing contraception legislation one year previously, FitzGerald in his opening remarks challenged the absence of autonomy between the personal and the public. He introduced a proposal that not only went against Catholic dogma but that was contrary also to the commonsense view that public legislation should bolster personal Catholic belief. By stating that the Catholic bishops and some individual legislators, his own party colleagues, took a view contrary to his on the divorce question, FitzGerald with his own actions demonstrated that this posture was acceptable. While politically it may have ultimately undermined the credibility of his agenda, nonetheless, the greater point that seemed central to FitzGerald's argument was the fact that a modern society is characterized by a multitude of individual value positions. Moreover, the subtext of his argument says that this diversity of values and beliefs is not problematic for the maintenance of social order, precisely because there is a formal autonomy between privately held values and public law.

Just as he was willing to accept the autonomy of personal conscience and to respect the wishes of parliamentary members of his own party to act contrary to the collective agenda of Fine Gael, it was implicit in FitzGerald's remarks that he was asking the Irish people to adopt the same attitude to those whose personal conscience allows them to avail of divorce. Allowing divorce to be publicly available, he was suggesting, would enable those who wish to avail of it to do so and would still allow those people who object to divorce to maintain their personal commitment to lifelong marriage. The introduction of divorce, FitzGerald was saying, while formally making divorce publicly available, was not imposing a new private morality, because the two spheres were distinct. Private morality could be maintained independently of the changed civil law, because personal morality and public morality, while they are related, are not one and the same thing.

The distinction between personal belief and civil legislation and the argument that the introduction of divorce was not an attempt to undermine religious teaching or the family were also stressed by other members of the government. Peter Barry, the minister for foreign affairs, for example, argued that "the forthcoming referendum. . . . is about freedom for the people of this country to follow their conscience in matters of private faith and morality. . . . We respect the incalculable contribution of the Christian Churches to our national way of life and we want to preserve our Christian identity. We cannot do this by denying people their conscience."[15] Alan Dukes, minister for justice, contended: "In promoting legislation to permit divorce the Government are not opposed to marriage. The Government are fully committed to the protection of marriage."[16]

In sum, FitzGerald's challenge to the Irish tendency to equate private and public morality was a bold move that served the dual purpose of preserving his own legitimation and supporting the cause of divorce. At the same time, however, articulating such an argument was a difficult undertaking in a society where the two concepts have been historically conflated. Yet, in many ways, this is what FitzGerald and the pro-divorce forces had to confront if the divorce proposals were to have a chance of success. To argue for the introduction of divorce was a difficult and complex undertaking precisely because it challenged such fundamental Irish attitudes. It was not simply a question of overcoming a specific religious tenet. Rather, because of the sociocultural influence of the Catholic church, the privileging of its teaching in civil legislation, and the pervasiveness of the association of Catholic and public morality, the proposal to introduce divorce challenged the basic cultural identity and worldview of the Irish.

The Social Good

We saw that FitzGerald, in his opening remarks to the divorce debate, attempted to justify his legislation by arguing for a separation of private and public morality. At the same time, he invoked also the notion of the social good in support of his cause. This invocation of the social good, just as did his reference to the private/public distinction, attempted to break the link between Catholic morality and civil legislation. While the notion of the social good is one well known to the Irish, FitzGerald injected it with new meaning and stripped it of its traditional Catholic-based connotation.

FitzGerald argued that divorce would serve "the balance of the social good" in view of the significance of marital breakdown in Irish society.[17] While he acknowledged that divorce would have some negative effects on existing marriages, he contended that these would be outweighed by the stabilizing effect divorce would have by, for example, enabling the instability caused to society by the pervasiveness of new illegal unions of separated people and the children involved in these irregular situations to be redressed.

Throughout the debate, FitzGerald stressed the significance of the problem of marital breakdown, stating, for example: "We face the situation where there is a very large number of marriage breakdowns. Many more than there used to be. There is a huge volume of human misery. . . . These problems are on such a scale, and so many of them have in fact entered into other unions and have children in many cases, that it is not a problem that we can ignore and sweep under the carpet."[18] The project of the achievement of the balance of the social good, FitzGerald argued, would be aided by the fact that the government's divorce proposals were a restrictive response to the problem of marital breakdown, requiring as they did, the fulfillment of specific criteria before a divorce decree could be granted.

FitzGerald maintained that the absence of divorce would lead ultimately to the undermining of marriage as an institution, as increasing numbers of people, experiencing marital breakdown and unable to divorce and remarry, would opt to cohabit without the social and legal sanction of marriage. Significantly, throughout the campaign, he elaborated on the importance of marriage as a societal institution and its role in contributing to the common good of society. Attendant on this, he argued that the introduction of divorce should be viewed as supporting, not undermining, the common good, as well as reflecting social values of diversity, tolerance, and compassion. Thus FitzGerald stated: "On the merits of [the divorce proposals] there are not merely deeply divided opinions; there are deeply divided approaches to the whole matter. . . . The first of these approaches involves the application of the criterion of the common good. I believe that this is in fact the most important criterion that we should apply to the issue because of the social nature of marriage itself. I have always held this view."[19] The minister of state at the Department of Justice, Nuala Fennell, similarly argued that: "The divorce referendum Bill . . . strikes a balance between the interests of society generally and the need to deal humanely and fairly with people whose marriages have broken down. . . . the reality of life is that many marriages break down. . . .

we must face up to it and deal with the consequences. The non-existence of divorce in our society is itself a destabilising factor at this stage in that many people whose marriages have broken down openly live in a relationship outside of marriage."[20]

Since the Irish electorate is well familiar with the notion of the social good, the invocation of it by FitzGerald and other proponents of divorce seemed at first like a promising strategy. The appeal is made to a culturally accepted concept that can then be used to support the controversial and nontraditional issue of divorce. However, the concept of the social good as used by FitzGerald was far removed from the meaning attached to it by the Catholic church. According to the perspective articulated by the Catholic hierarchy, the social good is achieved by the implementation of the Church's moral and social teachings. The Catholic good is the social good; a definition that has never formally been challenged in Irish society. As far as the Irish people were concerned, the social good traditionally was maintained by explicitly prohibiting divorce. Therefore, the attempt by FitzGerald to use the notion of the social good in the service of divorce has to be seen as yet another attempt by him to, creatively, break the link between the public sphere and religious morality.

In arguing that the introduction of divorce was necessary as a way to serve the social good, FitzGerald was challenging directly the understanding of the social good already prevalent and deeply rooted in Irish society. He was challenging the Irish people to move from a situation where the constitutional prohibition on divorce was popularly thought to serve the common (Catholic) good to one where, in his opinion, the introduction of divorce would serve the common good, but in a way that would be independent of Catholic teaching. It was not sufficient, he was arguing, to equate the social good with that which supported only the ethos of the Catholic majority. Rather, the social good must include honesty in recognizing social problems and tolerance of opposing views and minority interests. As Dick Spring, the leader of the Labour Party, phrased it, "the test of the social morale and fabric of a society is how it caters for its minorities."[21]

The complexity of the notion of the social good as it applies to the introduction of divorce was intensified by the fact that divorce can be and has traditionally been perceived as primarily serving the needs of the individual: the individual's right to be liberated from an unsatisfactory marriage and the freedom to establish a new legally sanctioned union. This focus on the individual and the importance of individual rights, however, does not fit so easily with Irish cultural values. The tension in FitzGerald's pro-divorce position was thus heightened by the fact that in introducing divorce he was explicitly emphasizing the needs of individuals and stressing the need to give those in broken marriages the option of divorce and remarriage, even though this went against the ethos of Irish society. Notwithstanding that the government divorce proposals were contrary to the teaching of the Catholic church, were contrary to the commonsense notion of the social good, and were proposals that demanded a new vision of the individual—to see the individual as an autonomous person rather than primarily as a member of a larger community with family and societal obligations—throughout the campaign, FitzGerald boldly maintained that divorce would, on balance, serve the social good.

Indissoluble Monogamy

During a television interview following the press conference at which he announced the divorce proposals, FitzGerald stated: "On the specific issue of provision for divorce, the Catholic church has a theological position and also a sociological view which it will, I'm sure, want to put forward. We as a government don't have a theological view. We may have it individually, and indeed *we have our own attachment to indissoluble monogamy as individuals.* But we do have to take a sociological view and that view is perhaps somewhat different to that of the Catholic church" [emphasis mine].[22]

This statement in many ways summarizes the thrust of the arguments of the pro-divorce campaign and points yet again to their difficulties. In a somewhat convoluted and intellectualized manner, what FitzGerald acknowledged in the interview was that he as a good Catholic did not want a divorce for himself—he believes in indissoluble monogamy—but that in introducing the legislation he is arguing for the freedom of a hypothetical Irish person who should be able to partake of this option.

These remarks were problematic because if, as Catholics, FitzGerald and his colleagues in government believed in indissoluble monogamy, then it was also likely that their fellow citizens and coreligionists felt likewise. FitzGerald had already acknowledged that the Catholic church opposed divorce and stated his acceptance that members of his own parliamentary party may "on grounds of conscience" not wish to participate in the pro-divorce campaign. At the same time, he was prepared to ask the Irish electorate to detach themselves from their personal beliefs and circumstances, conceptualize an abstract Irish citizen in a hypothetical broken marriage who hypothetically wanted to divorce and remarry, and thus vote in favor of the proposals even though they did not want a divorce for themselves and indeed were opposed to it on moral grounds.

Confronting the electorate with a hypothetical situation may not be the best political strategy, and invocation of the distinction between theological and sociological perspectives may be of little use in a society where the former subsumes the latter. Yet, if the divorce amendment was to pass and if FitzGerald's vision of a pluralistic Irish society was to materialize, then this is what the Irish people had to do. They needed to be sensitive to these distinctions and willing to make the break with the traditional relationship between Catholic morality and state law. In articulating these remarks, therefore, FitzGerald was reiterating the social project at issue if divorce was to be permitted.

FitzGerald's use of the phrase "indissoluble monogamy" in this context is also significant because it demonstrates, from the outset of the debate, some of the tensions that surrounded the pro-divorce arguments. Clearly terms like "indissoluble" and "monogamy" are not words used in everyday discourse. While the Irish believe in marriage as a lifelong commitment, they do not consciously think of it as being one specific form of matrimony, indissoluble monogamy.

FitzGerald's use of the term "indissoluble monogamy" does show the inevitable tendency toward intellectualization and abstraction that was forced upon him and the pro-divorce advocates. In Ireland the most popular and authoritative forms of argumentation tend to be grounded in religion and/or economics. In presenting reasons for the introduction of divorce, however, neither of these could really be used by the pro-divorce lobby. Clearly, religious arguments in support of divorce could not be articulated because the introduction of divorce goes against both Catholic teaching regarding divorce per se and the traditional expectation of the relationship between Catholic morality and civil legislation. Neither could an economic discourse that would have articulated the material and practical effects of divorce be initiated, because this would run the risk of being regarded as the imposition of a secular framework on what, for many people, is fundamentally a sacramental issue.

Unable to resort fully and effectively to either of these authoritative discourses, therefore, FitzGerald and the pro-divorce lobby were drawn to the use of abstract intellectual concepts—as was the case with their call for a separation between the public and the private and the way in which they used the concept of the social good. This more intellectualized approach characterized their arguments throughout the campaign. FitzGerald maintained this perspective even in the chambers of Parliament. Reiterating his initial argument, he stated: "Even though it has been repeatedly repudiated by the authorities of the Roman Catholic Church . . . [the attitude exists] that the theology and law of that Church should be the foundation of, or even constitute the content of, the civil law of our State. While personally committed to the indissoluble character of sacramental marriage in the Church of which I am a member, I reject that approach, in common with the authorities of my Church and the vast majority of the Irish people."[23]

The use of the term "indissoluble monogamy," therefore, can be seen as crystalizing the legitimation difficulties and tensions involved in being an advocate of divorce. The tension in the question posed by the divorce referendum ran thus: if you are a good Catholic you cannot be pro-divorce; but if you are pro-divorce, can you be a good Catholic? The answer is probably yes, but it is a complex answer and one that is not necessarily well suited to political discourse.

Pro-divorce Economic Arguments

Even though the pro-divorce lobby did not use economic points as the linchpin of their case, they did make recourse to an economic discourse. However, economic arguments were used by them hesitatingly and frequently in a secondary, reactive, defensively justifying mode. In his opening statement on divorce, the same context in which he dealt with the social good and the public/private distinction, FitzGerald referred to the possible negative economic effects of divorce, but he linked the issue of divorce and economics in a somewhat weak and negative manner. FitzGerald stated: "The legislation will include provisions to enable the Family Court . . . to make various financial orders with a view to ensuring that the interests of spouses and dependent children are adequately protected and appropriately provided for. These orders will relate to maintenance, lump sum payments, and property owned by the spouses, including the family home. . . . A dependent spouse will not be prejudiced in any determination of property rights by virtue of the fact that he or she gave up employment to attend to duties in the home. And provisional support for families in distress will be reviewed with a view to ensuring that as far as possible support will be made that will allow [families] to stay together."[24]

Rather than putting forward a positive claim that divorce may be beneficial insofar as it would give dependent spouses a more equitable share in the couple's joint resources than the current legal situation allows, FitzGerald stated that divorce would not harm people: with divorce, he said, dependents' interests would be "adequately protected," "appropriately provided for," and "not prejudiced." From the perspective of economic security these are rather tentative arguments for favoring divorce.

Subsequently, in rejecting a journalist's claim that the proposals being introduced would provide "divorce for the rich but not for the poor," FitzGerald acknowledged that financial problems always exist in any case of separation, but stated, without elaboration, that the government's divorce conditions required that adequate economic arrangements would have to be made before a divorce could be granted.[25] Later, in response to the economic criticisms expressed by opponents of divorce, FitzGerald found it necessary to, in his words, "clarify" some points that had arisen. These related to the alleged negative economic effects of divorce on women and children. He stated: "The children of the first marriage remain the children of a family founded on marriage, with full rights under the Succession Act. . . . the dependent spouse has her or his interests protected better than at present. . . . No dissolution of a marriage with a right of remarriage will be constitutionally possible unless adequate and proper provision is made for a dependent spouse and dependent children."[26]

Continuing this defence of their proposals, other government spokespersons emphasized throughout the debate that negative economic consequences would not accompany the introduction of divorce. The minister for justice, Alan Dukes, stressed that: "The provision in the proposed amendment . . . clearly states that a divorce cannot be granted unless a court is satisfied that adequate and proper provision having regard to the circumstances, will be made for any dependent spouse and any dependent child of, or any child who is dependent on either spouse. . . . the constitutional and the succession rights of the first family are unaffected."[27] It was also emphasized that the status of social welfare entitlements would not change with the introduction of divorce. Dick Spring argued: "All spouses can be absolutely assured that they will *not be disadvantaged* in terms of their social welfare entitlements as a result of their legal status being changed from married, separated, or deserted to divorce."[28] The minister for social welfare, Gemma Hussey, similarly stated that "the social welfare code is sufficiently flexible to cater for a wide range of families in different circumstances."[29] Responding to claims that "family farms" would be lost, the minister for agriculture, Austin Deasy, reassured farmers that divorce "poses *no threat* for the family farm."[30] The minister for justice, Alan Dukes, also gave assurances that: "A court, before granting a divorce will have to be satisfied that the provision made for the [farmer's] wife takes into account the fact that she will be losing inheritance rights."[31]

Similar to the government, the DAG did not initiate economic arguments in support of their case, but, as the campaign progressed, they too responded to arguments made by those opposed to divorce that women and children would suffer economically in a divorce situation. The DAG emphasized that women already suffer— "deserted women, battered women, women whose husbands receive foreign divorces"—and that divorce could only help to improve their economic deprivation.[32] Counter-arguing that the wife and family from the first marriage would not lose their inheritance and succession rights if divorce was introduced, the DAG emphasized that the divorce amendment would economically favor women in particular. Jean Tansey maintained: "In fact, what the legislation does is it brings forward women's rights with regard to succession. The time of marital breakdown, that is the time when women need to have financial and property arrangements sorted out, not in ten or twenty years or when somebody dies."[33]

When divorce clearly has a range of economic consequences for those involved, it is significant that FitzGerald and other advocates of divorce did not initiate economic arguments nor demarcate the economic dimension as a central consideration regarding the amendment. This can be understood in terms of the problem of legitimation that I have already highlighted. Advocates of divorce did not have the legitimacy to initiate an economic discourse because this would have been perceived as trivializing marriage.

To initiate the argument that divorce would redress some of the economic problems currently confronted by deserted or separated people would have been a valid contention, but an inappropriate one. The imposition of a secular frame on what is, after all, a sacrament would have ensured that FitzGerald's proposals would be viewed as anti-Catholic, a label that proponents of divorce needed to avoid if their case was to be heard. The use of economic arguments in support of divorce was constricted, therefore, by the legitimation dilemma confronting those arguing in its favor. They were free to invoke economic reasons only in response to the economic arguments of anti-divorce campaigners. In campaigning for the introduction of divorce, FitzGerald and others already were going against the traditions and values of the Irish regarding marriage. To have then initiated arguments for divorce grounded in the context of its practical and economic consequences would have been to exacerbate the radical nature of their proposals and to delegitimate further their agenda.

Arguments against Divorce

After FitzGerald's announcement of the government divorce proposals, the anti-divorce position was stated by William Binchy on "Today Tonight" immediately following its transmission of the government press conference. It was a brief interview. Nonetheless, from the outset, Binchy took the initiative, was on the offensive, set the tone for the debate, and defined the issues. He stressed the legal and consequent economic implications of divorce, which he argued would follow if the government's proposals were accepted. I quote below the full exchange between William Binchy and the interviewer, John Bowman.

BOWMAN: You are campaigning against divorce. What is your response to the fact that your campaign against it has now failed since the government is proposing it?

BINCHY: Well I think it is interesting to note the type of divorce system that the Taoiseach [prime minister] has proposed here. The divorce system that is now going to be put before the country is in fact the type of modern divorce laws which exists, really one could say, throughout Europe, North America or the world.

BOWMAN: How can you say that? In a lot of those jurisdictions one has what is known as quickie, no-fault divorces. The provisions here are very strict.

BINCHY: Well, in fact, this is divorce based on demand, delayed demand. It is not hard divorce but easy divorce. It transforms marriage from a lifelong commitment into a commitment that either spouse provided they are willing to stay long enough apart can get a divorce. Once one does this in one's society, once one transforms marriage into a revocable commitment, then necessarily all the social support that we know, the maintenance entitlements, the succession entitlements, the Family Home Protection Act, as we know from other countries, once divorce has been introduced . . . we know that all these processes happen. They happen because marriage is no longer for life, and it would make no sense attaching to marriage the type of entitlements that are based on marriage being for life.

BOWMAN: But some of the entitlements which you claim would be ended are in fact those points which are covered in the supplementary document . . . and the people would have to be referred to again if there was to be any slippery slope, which is what you seem to be describing.

BINCHY: That's right, but I think you misunderstand me there. The type of divorce system that is now on offer means that the type of maintenance entitlements that exist under our existing law that were introduced ten years ago, the type of succession entitlements that exist under our existing law, would be modified because marriage is no longer for life and it makes no sense attaching to non-lifelong marriage the type of support and scaffolding, legal scaffolding, that we have in our country at the moment.[34]

It is evident from this exchange that William Binchy's opening remarks, just as did those of FitzGerald, contain outlines of several arguments to be elaborated and fleshed out by the ADC during the campaign. Binchy argues that the government proposal was for a "modern," easy divorce, that it would change the nature of marriage from a lifelong to a revocable commitment, and that, as a result of the changed status of marriage, the legal and consequent economic protection currently offered marriage would no longer hold. Binchy's remarks are striking in that they contain the seeds of two very different types of arguments. The first set, and the one to be emphasized by the ADC throughout the campaign, is very this-worldly, down-to-earth, and practical. Here fit Binchy's arguments concerning the unrestrictiveness of the proposals and the eradication of the constitutional and legal economic benefits attendant on marriage. The second set of reasons, however, the one deemphasized during the campaign, has clearly an other-worldly, moral cum spiritual tone; here belongs the issue of lifelong commitment.

Easy Divorce

A prominent theme in the arguments of the anti-divorce campaign was an emphasis on the unrestrictiveness of the proposals. On the night after the amendment was announced, Binchy elaborated that the proposals were not as restrictive as the government was claiming because the word "failure" and not "separation" was contained in the proposed amendment. He stated, "if one examines the proposal that is going to go to the people there is no mention whatsoever of separation . . . all that is necessary is that the marriage should have failed. . . . the type of divorce that is proposed is divorce that doesn't even require one week of separation between the spouses."[35]

Binchy contended that because failure entailed a subjective judgment on the part of an individual spouse or judge, it was a more vague and flexible criterion than if the constitution itself contained a provision requiring an objective separation period of five years before a divorce could be granted. "Failure," Binchy argued, "could mean anything." Thus he stated: "If anybody who is married thinks about the notion of failure of a marriage, what do they say it means? I'm not sure what it means. I suggest that perhaps you're not sure. I suggest that the viewers . . . will not be sure. It could mean, for example, a case where a woman got married and the husband was an obnoxious guy, I'd be thinking . . . that would be failure. It could mean . . . an unhappy relationship with my husband or wife as the case may be; it just simply hasn't fulfilled me. That's a form of failure. . . . Failure could mean any form of failure."[36]

Because "failure" would have such subjective meanings, Binchy and other ADC spokespersons argued that "failure" as a criterion for divorce would mean that if one spouse defined the marriage as a failure from his or her perspective, then a court would have to grant a divorce, even against the wishes of the other spouse. The form of divorce that the government was proposing, therefore, Binchy reiterated, was "an easy divorce law." Thus, "under this wording . . . any married person can literally walk out on the other, claim that his or her marriage has failed. . . . What judge can say 'No, I think your marriage has not failed'? It's only the person himself who could be the judge of that."[37]

Joe McCarroll similarly stressed that the amendment was so permissive that if it was endorsed, "all of the marriages that are over five years will be able to be dissolved immediately."[38] Another anti-divorce activist, Bernadette Bonar, argued that the type of divorce being proposed was "the most liberal form of divorce we could possibly have. It took England nearly one-hundred years to arrive at that type of divorce."[39]

The ADC emphasized that, if the amendment was accepted, the Irish would have a situation whereby people could be "divorced against their will"; that, as one campaign slogan stated, "you could be forced to divorce"; as long as one partner wanted the marriage dissolved, then that would be sufficient for a divorce to be granted. The ADC continuously stressed that the form of divorce being proposed was so liberal that: "DIVORCE COULD BE OBTAINED BY ONE SPOUSE AGAINST THE WISHES OF THE OTHER. . . . WHILE IT TAKES A COMMITMENT FROM TWO TO GET MARRIED, LEGALLY, IT NEEDS ONLY ONE TO BREAK THE MARRIAGE" [emphasis in original].[40] Joe McCarroll reiterated this position, arguing that divorce would "introduce the idea of a throw-away spouse . . . if a problem comes up you just throw away the spouse and throw away the children."[41] Further highlighting the unrestrictiveness of the proposals, the ADC contended: "If this Amendment is passed, it will be easier to dismiss a spouse than an employee. In an age of unemployment, employees are better protected and more secure than your wives and your husbands will be if this amendment is carried."[42]

Like the ADC, spokespersons from the Fianna Fail party also argued that the proposals were unrestrictive. They too expressed concern that the notion of "failure" of a marriage was weak, vague, and ambiguous. Their primary anti-divorce spokesman, Michael Woods, argued, for example, that: "If one spouse considers that the marriage has failed, will anybody be able to say in those circumstances that it has not?. . . . The word "failure" is subjective. . . . I do not think there is finality in the word. . . . I regard the word "failure" as a weak word and one that sets a low threshold."[43] Another Fianna Fail member, Padraig Flynn, who represents a constituency in the west of Ireland, similarly maintained: "I understand that failure, breakdown, or whatever word is used is nothing more than a formula of words to allow 'no fault' divorce to be introduced into this country. The ordinary person in the street sees it like that—as easy divorce in certain circumstances. . . . This will not be restrictive legislation. . . . [it] will make for easy divorce being made available in this jurisdiction."[44]

Related to their emphasis on the unrestrictiveness of the proposals, both ADC and Fianna Fail spokespersons claimed that the introduction of divorce would lead to the development of a divorce culture. The ADC stated: "We believe that divorce introduces a climate of opinion that militates against the success of each and every marriage. The acceptance of divorce in a society introduces the concept of defeatism into every marriage."[45] Importantly, the ADC emphasized that this was not simply their viewpoint, but was based on "facts,"[46] facts from the divorce experience of other countries. In support of their position they argued that: "International statistics and the international experience of divorce shows that . . . if divorce is available . . . the numbers of people resorting to divorce will be high and will increase[47]. . . . In England alone, divorce has resulted in an increase from 75,000 applications . . . to 175,000 applications . . . from 1970 to 1985."[48] Echoing this ADC approach, a Fianna Fail parliamentarian similarly stated that: "Experience in countries where divorce is available. . . . underlines the fact that divorce breeds divorce and in some countries has led to what is tantamount to a breakdown of marriage as an institution."[49]

In the context of this argument, Fianna Fail speakers challenged Garret FitzGerald's contention that divorce would serve the social good. Taking a dichotomously opposed perspective to FitzGerald, Michael Woods equated the introduction of divorce with evil, graphically portraying it as a "constitutional Frankenstein." He argued: "If this proposed amendment is put into the Constitution and divorce becomes common, as it has in other countries, legal reasons will be sought for terminating the financial shackles of previous marriages. This trend has clearly emerged already in Britain and the USA. In this context the government's proposed amendment could in future be used as a sledgehammer to crush the rights of the first family. . . . Could it be that the Government have unwittingly created a 'constitutional Frankenstein' which may sleep for a time but then rise and stalk the land?"[50] Charles Haughey, the leader of Fianna Fail, similarly argued that the consequences of introducing divorce "would represent a major change in Irish society" and dismissed FitzGerald's argument as "just not credible."[51]

Economic Effects

Throughout the divorce campaign, its opponents also highlighted the economic consequences of changing the legal and constitutional status of marriage. In fact, the consequences of the erosion of legally sanctioned economic support for marriage served as the primary theme of the anti-divorce discourse. In elucidating their opposition to divorce, the ADC concentrated on what Binchy defined as the "legal pitfalls"[52] in the proposals, weaknesses they posited, that would have particularly serious economic implications for the dependents from the divorced person's first marriage.

Elaborating on one of the initial statements made by Binchy, the ADC argued: "Once we decide that the marriage is no longer for life, then all the legal supports for marriage as a lifetime commitment are eroded. The protection given to wives, husbands and children by the Succession Act, the Family Home Protection Act and the Family Law (Maintenance of Spouses and Children) Act, would be weakened significantly by divorce."[53] Throughout the debate, the ADC further contended that "the law would shift its support to the second family to the disadvantage of the first family. The second family of a divorce would become the primary focus of the

constitutional protection. . . . THE DIVORCED FAMILY WOULD LOSE
ALL THE CONSTITUTIONAL RIGHTS AND PROTECTION WHICH ARE
POSSESSED UNDER OUR LAW BY A FAMILY BASED ON MARRIAGE"
[emphasis in original].[54] As William Binchy phrased it, the proposed amendment would lead to a "legal schizophrenia" that
would force people to redirect all their resources into a second
marriage.[55]

The ADC argued that the introduction of divorce could only have
negative economic effects on all the parties involved. They suggested that in the case of a couple owning property, the family
home or business or farm would have to be sold in order for an
economically equitable divorce settlement to be made. Given the
economic circumstances of many people, they maintained, the pro-
ceeds from such a sale would not be sufficient to continue support
of the family from the first marriage and to support a second marriage. Accordingly, the ADC emphasized that the consequences
would be devastating for all concerned. Binchy presented a vivid
depiction of the likely scenario: "The implications of this prema-
ture liquidation of the man's assets, assuming that he is the person
with the property . . . is going to be equally alarming for him [as
for his wife]. He is going to have to produce, if the settlement is to
be any way other than grossly inadequate, he is going to have to
produce a significant proportion of his assets there and then. Now
most people who have a house . . . a farm or a business already
have some degree of mortgaging or charging on those properties.
The reality of that means that if the husband has to produce one-
third of his value at the time of the divorce, that means the sale of
the house certainly . . . in many cases . . . farms or businesses . . .
the sale of part or all of the property."[56]

Quite apart from the implications of this type of situation, the
ADC argued that the salary of a divorced man would not be sufficient for him to fulfill his financial obligations to two wives and
families. As they emphasized, because a second marriage added to
the number of dependents, the first family would have to share an
unenlarged economic pie with a greater number of people, thus re-
ducing their individual share. The ADC was unequivocal about this.
Joe McCarroll stated: "Divorce doesn't multiply a man's income
by two. If a man can just about scrape by on one income and then
he sets up a second relationship, I think the society is unwise to

transfer the stamp of social approval to that as if it were something responsible, when in fact, the money isn't there."[57] And as Binchy reiterated: "If one has the right to remarry that means the right to establish a second family, and the reality of life is that unfortunately if a man enters into a second family, his salary doesn't increase, doesn't double. It is just one salary and in these circumstances the one salary has to cover two families."[58] In particular, the ADC constructed the negative economic effects of divorce as having a detrimental impact on women. "Wives," they argued, "tend to suffer a massive drop in living standards."[59] As dependent spouses, married women would be most vulnerable to divorce because they would lose all their rights—the right to the family home, the right to their husband's land or property, the right to their husband's pension, the right to social welfare benefits. In sum, Binchy argued that divorce "deprives the first wife of her [economic] rights as wife." He stated: "The right to remarry . . . says that it is reasonable that the second wife . . . should have a whole range of rights. The only way that the second wife can have a whole range of rights is at the expense of the first wife."[60]

The constitutional amendment that was proposed included a criterion stating that a divorce could not be granted unless "adequate and proper provision having regard to the circumstances" was made for dependent spouses and children. The ADC contended, nonetheless, that this clause would favor the primary or sole earner of the couple, most usually the man, and they delineated what this would mean in practice. Thus William Binchy argued: "Practical implication one, the succession rights of the first wife are removed. Practical implication two, the succession rights of the children of the first family are reduced. Practical implication three, a person can be divorced against their wishes. Practical implication four . . . a working spouse, a working wife will receive no protection under the amendment the way it is drafted. . . . a final practical implication. . . . [The amendment] does not consider the position which might arise, say two or three years after the divorce where a divorced wife is injured in a traffic accident or sick."[61]

In support of their argument that divorce causes economic hardship for women and children, the ADC again invoked statistics from other countries. They stated, for example, that "in the United States . . . sixty to eighty per cent of fathers ignore court orders and currently owe some four billion dollars to their former families[62]. . . . the reality in the world where divorce has been introduced, and this is a matter of fact, in every country where divorce has been introduced, women and children have suffered from the introduction of divorce . . . married women have suffered . . . and women with young children have been particular casualties[63]. . . . No matter what country in which you examine the issue and study it you find that it is women and children who are suffering."[64]

Because of the harsh economic realities that women and children would experience with divorce, it was the ADC's claim, in part as a response to a pro-divorce slogan "Put Compassion in the Constitution," that compassion was due, not solely to individuals whose marriages had broken down, but to the "unilaterally repudiated" first spouse (wife) and children. The "balance of compassion," the ADC contended, "demands an unequivocal NO to divorce."[65]

The ADC argued that the overall impact of divorce would be to "bulldoze people into poverty,"[66] thus leading to the establishment of a new category of social welfare dependents. Supporting these "victims of divorce," the ADC maintained, would cost the taxpayers at least an additional one million pounds per week. The ADC stated: "The implications for the State have not been costed but there are suggestions that it would amount to a need to generate extra taxation of more than a million pounds a week to aid the victims of divorce."[67]

The post-divorce scenario that was elucidated by Fianna Fail opponents of divorce was also clearly one of negative economic consequences.[68] In the opening statement by Fianna Fail to the Parliamentary debate on divorce, their justice spokesman, Michael Woods, depicted what he regarded as the devastating economic effects of divorce on the first family. He specifically pointed out that the dependent wife and children would be economically disadvantaged; they would become "constitutional orphans."[69] Continuing to focus on the dependent situation of women, and simultaneously paying attention to the specific consequences of divorce for farmers, Woods highlighted the negative post-divorce situation of farm wives and children: "The effects of the proposed amendment on succession would have very serious implications for the farming community. For example, if a farmer gets divorced the wife who may have contributed substantially to the development of the farm as a farming enterprise will . . . be deprived of her home on the farm and her way of life. If the farmer dies intestate, she will have no share in the inheritance. Her children may also be excluded from inheriting even though one or more of them may have been working the farm with the father before his death."[70] The economic costs of divorce, Woods argued, would fall not just on those in the divorced situation, but, significantly, on the taxpayer. He emphasized that the "main effect" of the government introducing divorce would be that every citizen regardless of their attitude to divorce would have to contribute to the State's underwriting of it.[71]

Economic Interests and the Irish

The two opposing sets of arguments articulated during the divorce debate, those by both pro- and anti-divorce forces, reflected cogent, thoughtful ways of approaching the question at issue. The anti-divorce arguments, however, strike as clearly more potent than those expressed in favor of divorce. They were strong, graphic arguments, vividly depicting likely post-divorce scenarios of negative eventualities. The emphasis by the ADC on tangible, this-worldly, economic arguments resulted in a forceful message, possibly a decisive one in the debate.

The dissimilarity in the content and tone of the pro- and anti-divorce arguments was underscored by the contrast in the opening arguments of Garret FitzGerald and William Binchy. FitzGerald's arguments were relatively abstract with no attention paid to the practical implications of introducing divorce. He talked instead about the social good, indissoluble monogamy, the right of individuals to object to divorce on grounds of conscience, and the difference between his and the Catholic church's assessment of the sociological impact of divorce. His remarks addressed social-philosophical points rather than pragmatic considerations. Distinguished from FitzGerald's, Binchy's approach focused directly on the immediate practical implications of introducing divorce. His naming of the removal of specific legal and economic entitlements that divorce would entail was concrete and spoke directly to people's basic concerns with issues of economic security.

The ADC discourse was important not only because of its concreteness but also because it appealed to the long-standing keenness of the Irish for a language of economics. Economic-related arguments hold a strong attraction for the Irish because, as outlined in chapter 2, they appeal to historical preoccupations with economic security and, in the case of the divorce amendment, addressed immediate concerns renewed by the depressed state of the Irish economy at the time of the referendum. By recourse to practical, economically grounded arguments as a way of articulating their opposition to the amendment, the anti-divorce lobby empathically connected with the Irish people and their sensitivity to economic issues.

The anti-divorce contention that divorce begets negative economic effects clearly echoes post-famine Ireland's association of marriage with economic costs. Modern divorce, its opponents contended, has adverse consequences for an individual's standard of living. The opponents of divorce were arguing that if the promise of marriage is to provide economic security and perhaps even to enhance people's standard of living—particularly given the fact that for many women it is through marriage that they maintain the social status of their parents or achieve upward mobility—and, through succession and inheritance rights, to ensure the continuing security of the family, divorce, with certainty, yields the opposite effects.

The Irish had succeeded in establishing ownership of their land and property, and the anti-divorce narrative predicted that this would be put in jeopardy. By voting in favor of divorce the Irish would become confronted once again with economic dispossession. Implicit in the anti-divorce arguments was the warning that this time, however, the material dispossession would be of their own making.

The power of the anti-divorce economic discourse was also grounded in a second important source, one more immediate, embedded as it was in the environment of current economic crisis highlighted by the high unemployment rate. This further enhanced the direct appeal by opponents of divorce to the economic preoccupations of the Irish, clearly highlighted by campaign posters that read: "Jobs we want, not divorce. Vote no!" Significantly, the anti-divorce groups depicted not only the economic costs that would be incurred by divorced families, but they also elucidated the economic consequences that divorce would bring for people in general as taxpayers. The argument posited by anti-divorce activists that acceptance of the amendment would lead to an increase in personal and societal economic costs was key, therefore, to concentrating people's attention on the negative implications of divorce.

Marriage as a Lifelong Institution

In the preceding discussion I have argued for the effectiveness of the ADC's economic discourse as well as contended that the pro-divorce lobby could not forcefully use economic arguments because this would be seen as trivializing the issue of divorce. But the following question comes to mind: should not this argument apply equally to the ADC? The answer is contained in the second string of arguments articulated by the ADC. These were moral cum religious objections that spoke of the changed definition of marriage that would ensue with the legal recognition of divorce. Although deemphasized, these provided the ADC with legitimacy and freed them to stress the economic and practical implications of introducing divorce.

The ADC argued that, by introducing divorce, the understanding of marriage as a lifelong institution would no longer apply. They stressed that the legal acceptance of divorce entailed a redefinition of marriage. Divorce, as Binchy argued in his initial remarks, "transforms marriage from a lifelong commitment into a revocable contract that either spouse provided they are willing to stay long enough apart can get a divorce. . . . once one transforms marriage into a revocable commitment . . . marriage is no longer for life."[72]

Underlying the ADC's opposition to the removal of the legal status of lifelong marriage was their adherence to the concept of a natural right to lifelong marriage. Joe McCarroll argued that the introduction of divorce "violates and abolishes two natural rights of married people." He stated: "We have a natural right to marry and marriage is lifelong. We have a natural right to a whole marriage and not to a slice of a marriage. And secondly, we have a natural right to legal protection for marriage."[73]

So although the ADC emphasized the negative economic consequences of divorce and stressed the unrestrictiveness of the specific proposals, paralleling this, they also expressed their objection to the principle of divorce. Stating: "WE OBJECT TO DIVORCE ITSELF" [emphasis in original],[74] the ADC underscored its opposition to the particular amendment at issue and to divorce in general. Accordingly, it would seem that the ADC would have opposed any divorce proposals, regardless of how restrictive they might have been. Joe McCarroll further demonstrated the ADC's position in an exchange with "Today Tonight" interviewer, Pat Kenny.

> KENNY: Let's get it quite clear. You're against any divorce, not just this bill as it is drawn up. You're picking holes in this bill but your basic point is no divorce no matter how tight, how restrictive, how conservative it might be?
> McCARROLL: Yes, I believe that divorce is unjust.[75]

Therefore, while the ADC stressed the unrestrictiveness of the government divorce proposals, it is evident that even if there was a separation requirement of five years or longer written into the constitution, it would still be opposed by the ADC. For them any provision for divorce is in itself too permissive because it violates both the right to lifelong marriage and the right to legal protection for lifelong marriage. Concomitant with the ADC's opposition to the principle of divorce was commitment to the principle of lifelong marriage. For the ADC, the two principles were mutually exclusive: "Divorce by definition is the destruction of marriage."[76] Reinforcing this position, Family Solidarity argued: "When divorce is available, the State no longer recognises or supports marriage based on lifelong commitment. Divorce undermines the institution of marriage. . . . Divorce violates the right to lifelong marriage. . . . WE HAVE A RIGHT TO LIFELONG MARRIAGE . . . Divorce destroys marriage as a lifelong commitment" [emphasis in original].[77]

Opponents of divorce, therefore, expressed their resistance to any legislative or social action that would not provide the family based on *lifelong marriage* with protection and support. In arguing against the introduction of divorce, they were simultaneously campaigning to maintain the state's protection of marriage as a lifelong commitment. As William Binchy argued: "There are certain gaps in the present law, but one thing that can be said . . . is that marriage as a lifelong commitment is protected by it."[78]

We thus see that although the ADC argued their case against divorce primarily on practical and economic grounds, it also had a moral objection to the principle of divorce. In this regard, the ADC demonstrated a theological position clearly similar to that of the Catholic church, which defines marriage as an indissoluble lifelong commitment.[79] In line with McCarroll's argument that people had a natural right to state protection for lifelong marriage, many others who campaigned against divorce carried placards that read "God says no to divorce," implying that the Church's teaching on marriage should thus be enshrined in state legislation. What the ADC omitted to point out, however, was the fact that the Catholic church does not demand that their theological position on marriage be enshrined in state legislation simply because of its theological status.

Here again, Fianna Fail's position also accorded with that of the ADC. While Fianna Fail speakers raised objections to the specific form and procedural details of the government divorce proposals, it was evident that their opposition was more deeply rooted. There was a strand to the Fianna Fail anti-divorce discourse that suggested that they too were opposed to the principle of divorce. To introduce divorce, they maintained, would be, essentially, to abolish marriage. Sean Treacy, for example, stated: "For me and the vast majority of the people I represent, marriage is a sacrament. It is indissoluble. We accept as our credo that what God hath brought together no man has the right to pull asunder. . . . Divorce . . . is alien to the Christian way of life. . . . Marriage as a lifelong union becomes legally obsolete. . . . Divorce destroys the concept of marriage as a sacrament. It makes a mockery of marriage as a permanent institution."[80] Padraig Flynn similarly argued: "The Christian ethic cannot lightly be set aside. . . . Introducing divorce would give respectability to actions totally at variance with Christian ethics. Those who facilitate actions that offend that ethic must share in the consequences for society afterwards."[81]

In objecting to the principle of divorce therefore, its opponents expressed a view of marriage that was coincidental with the theological position of the Catholic church. Once again, just as with the economic arguments, this set of arguments was very powerful, since it now appealed to the other sphere of Irish life, the Church and the tradition of Irish Catholicism. In Ireland, being opposed to divorce is itself significant because it reaffirms commitment to Catholic teaching about lifelong marriage and the attendant historical and cultural expectation of state support for lifelong marriage. Specifically invoking the concept of lifelong marriage and arguing against divorce on the grounds that it violates this, opponents of divorce underscored further their empathy and concurrence with the Irish religious tradition.

Issues of Emphasis and Tension among ADC Arguments

The ADC, therefore, put forward two powerful sets of arguments, one speaking to economic concerns and the second speaking to the religious values of the Irish. These were forceful arguments. Jointly they spoke to both this-worldly and other-worldly values. Interestingly enough, however, as I have documented, the ADC appeared to emphasize the this-worldly economic arguments and de-emphasize the other-worldly religious strand in their opposition to divorce. This difference in emphasis was well illustrated by William Binchy, who maintained that the position of the ADC bore no relation to religion.

Toward the end of the campaign, when challenged by "Today Tonight" interviewer John Bowman that the ADC's opposition to divorce "coincided with that of the Catholic hierarchy," Binchy responded that in objecting to divorce he was not taking a theological, but a sociological, position. Binchy insisted that the reason he opposed divorce was because of the "clear injustices which it would cause to the first family," and he argued that his objection had "nothing to do with religion."[82] As he stated on "Today Tonight," he saw the religious as the sphere of the Church, while he and the ADC were concerned with addressing the legal, economic, and sociological implications of introducing divorce. Binchy and the ADC thus sought to maintain differentiation between their practical economic objections to divorce and the theological arguments of the Church.

For Binchy to try to adhere to the distinction between economic/ secular and religious arguments was understandable since pastoral guidance is the prerogative of the Church. But, as documented above, contrary to Binchy's claims, this distinction was not consistently adhered to by him or by other members of the ADC. One good reason for not complying with this distinction is that the religious arguments provided a powerful justification and backing for the secular discourse of economics. It could be argued that only by skillfully blending the two traditions could the ADC avoid the problems of legitimation that proved continuous for the pro-divorce forces.

Although, as we can tell, it was important for the ADC to weave into their discourse strands from both the secular and religious traditions, nevertheless, it was also important for them to try to keep separate the two lines of argumentation. According to Binchy, the ostensible reason for this was a simple division of labor between the Church and the ADC. However, another reason relates to the fact that moral cum religious and economic lines of reasoning make for strange bedfellows. After all, the economic argument draws on a this-worldly discourse of rationality, empirical facts, and evidence. Objections to divorce grounded in this tradition are by necessity contingent and subject to revision in view of the available and future data. Therefore, Binchy, the sociologist, economist, and lawyer, would seem to have to accept the need for divorce if the empirical evidence argued in its favor.

But moral objections to divorce are of a very different kind to those grounded in sociology and economics. The other-worldly arguments of religion and morality are neither contingent nor grounded in empiricism, nor are they subject to change. One clearly does not reconsider a moral objection to divorce as a result of a conclusive empirical study stating that on the average people are happier with the option of divorce than without it. Although I do not claim that the decision to keep the this-worldly and other-worldly arguments was a deliberate strategy of the ADC, nevertheless, it is quite understandable that things just had to happen this way. Drawing on these two traditions clearly strengthened the ADC's hand, but at a price: one of contradiction if not incompatibility.

In the final chapter, I argue that the fact that the ADC reverted to both secular and religious arguments in its campaign against divorce and the fact that this strategy was never challenged is of significance well beyond the narrow issue of how people debate matters of values and morality. I will show how it provides an important insight into the transitional status of contemporary Irish society and, at the same time, sheds light on the relationship between traditionality and modernity in general.

Marginal Themes

The discourse of the divorce campaign is significant in terms of its focus and emphasis. The range of arguments articulated facilitate a mapping out of the values and cultural tensions that characterize and distinguish Irish society. But the questions that gained only marginal attention during the course of the debate are also of significance. Two issues in particular stand out: the notion of divorce as a civil right and the amendment's relevance to Northern Ireland. At first glance, these two important questions strike as the sorts of substantive concerns that might have provided legitimation for the pro-divorce forces. Their marginalization, however, was well-grounded in the cultural realities of Irish society.

Divorce as a Civil Right

Importantly, as the proposer of divorce Garret FitzGerald adamantly maintained that the divorce provision should be seen in its social context, serving the social good as opposed to being regarded as an individual civil right. Like his counterparts on the anti-divorce side, FitzGerald rejected the "liberal position that there is an individual right to divorce."[83] Instead he, as did William Binchy from the anti-divorce campaign, emphasized his view that divorce was a social question, stating: "I don't believe there is a civil right to divorce. I believe it is a social issue,"[84] a view that was also stressed by his parliamentary party colleague, John Kelly, himself a professor of constitutional law.[85]

The DAG's main contention throughout the debate was that divorce was a necessary response to the increasing problem of marital breakdown, and they argued that, as such, it should not be seen simply as an individual civil right. Nevertheless, in appealing to broad societal values of honesty, compassion, and tolerance, they argued that a 'yes' vote was "a vote for an Irish society which cares about social and personal suffering . . . It is a vote for the recognition of individual rights, for tolerance, for social maturity."[86] Similarly, Jean Tansey alluded indirectly to her belief in the right to divorce, stating: "A [yes vote] is a vote for the recognition of individual rights. . . . What people object to at the end of the day is the right of people to remarry."[87]

Tansey claimed, however, that those who want to legally re-marry want to do so not because of their ideological belief in the libertarian rights of individuals but out of respect for the serious-ness with which Irish people regard the legal and social framework within which the institution of marriage operates.[88] In this regard, the DAG distanced themselves from the perception that advocates of divorce are permissive and from the media-created image that di-vorce undermines social control. It was significant, for example, that the DAG opened their campaign by stating that they did not want a form of "quickie divorce or a California type divorce."[89] Rather, they commended the government for introducing a "re-sponsible procedure" and continued throughout the debate to em-phasize the restrictiveness of the proposals.

The notion of divorce as a civil right was also mentioned by pro-divorce politicians. Dick Spring, the leader of the Labour party, for example, stated that in the situation of the divorce proposals being accepted: "I believe we as a State will no longer be seen as prohib-itive, as a State which denies its people that which other democra-cies have regarded as a legitimate civil right."[90] Some members of the Fine Gael party also endorsed the notion of divorce as a civil right.[91] Significantly, however, this stance was more commonly ex-pressed by minor voices in the debate. The Irish Congress of Trade Unions (ICTU) argued that "divorce is a human and a civil right . . . recognised in virtually all the countries of the world."[92] Arguing that its prohibition is discriminatory and sectarian, and broadening the implications of the divorce referendum to other socioeconomic issues, an ICTU spokesperson claimed that those who oppose di-vorce are also "opposed to workers' rights and the right of trade unions to defend and improve the economic conditions of workers. They are not just opposed to divorce. They are opposed to social progress and the emergence of a secular Irish State."[94]

The Irish Council for Civil Liberties (ICCL) also argued that di-vorce was a civil right. Failure to endorse the amendment, they stated, would "endorse a society where caring and compassion have no meaning." In a statement, the ICCL argued that "divorce is a civil right. . . . If this amendment fails, our constitutional democ-racy will become the clubhouse of a moral majority, where the prej-udices of the day are labelled constitutional laws."[94] Similarly, the Workers' Party, a parliamentary socialist party, stressed that: "In a

Democratic Republic civil divorce is a civil right for those whose marriages have failed. It is undemocratic and intolerant to deny such people that right. . . . YOUR VOTE IS VITAL FOR A SOCIETY WHICH GUARDS THE RIGHTS OF MINORITIES AS WELL AS MAJORITIES" [emphasis in original].[95]

Such arguments, nonetheless, did not constitute the main thrust of the pro-divorce case. The notion that people had a civil right to divorce was not a key argument systematically articulated by those directly involved in either the government's or the DAG's pro-divorce campaign. As I discussed in chapter 2, a language of individual rights is not commonly used in Irish society. Consequently, it was not readily available to proponents of divorce. The concept surfaced during the debate, but, significantly, compared to Fitz-Gerald, the government, and the Divorce Action Group, it was other more marginal groups and political parties who framed the introduction of divorce in terms of an individual civil right.

It is understandable that these organizations freely used the argument of a right to divorce, despite its marginality, since issues of public legitimation were not their concern during the campaign. Their more peripheral status made it less imperative that they maintain credibility with the Irish people. Moreover, the groups who explicitly stated that divorce is a civil right are accustomed to speaking a specific language of rights—among others, the rights of workers to fair wages, the right to strike, the right to justice. It was relatively easy for them, therefore, to incorporate the "right to divorce" within the discourse of rights they customarily articulate.

Northern Ireland

If divorce was introduced into the Republic of Ireland it would make the situation there more comparable with that of Northern Ireland, where no-fault divorce is legal.[96] In light of the Republic's constitutional aspiration to a united Ireland, one might expect that the issue of Northern Ireland would be an important consideration during the divorce debate. It could be argued that the passing of the amendment in the South would send a signal to Protestants, and indeed, to Catholics, in Northern Ireland that people in the South were willing to make practical changes that could be seen as facilitating unification, even though in and of itself, divorce would not be a catalyst for change.

At the press conference announcing the referendum, however, FitzGerald stated, in response to a reporter's question, that "the situation in Northern Ireland is essentially subsidiary" to the problem caused by the scale of marital breakdown in the Republic.[97] Subsequently, during the Parliamentary debate on divorce, he strongly reiterated this assertion but noted that the passing of the amendment would have incidental relevance to the relationship between North and South:

I believe that this debate has also an importance that extends outside the boundaries of this State. . . . This debate, and the subsequent wider public discussion, together with the eventual decision taken by the people of this State, will, of course, be watched particularly closely by people of both traditions in Northern Ireland, many of whom will, I believe, be influenced to a degree in their attitude towards this State and towards each other by the manner in which we act in this matter. That will not be a primary consideration when this matter will be put to the test. But it should not be ignored either. And to the extent that electors conclude that this proposal should be adopted on its own merits to meet the social needs of this State, to that extent they will also be helping incidentally the relationship between North and South, and between the communities in Northern Ireland. At a time when the situation in Northern Ireland is so delicately balanced this is not something we can reasonably ignore.[98]

Another member of the government, the Labour minister for health, Barry Desmond, also suggested that the broader issue of Northern Ireland was relevant to the success of the divorce amendment. He argued: "Few are naive enough to believe that the introduction of divorce in the Republic would persuade the Unionists to look with more favour on their Catholic neighbours. However, in the proposed referendum we cannot ignore the implications of a decision to maintain the constitutional prohibition on divorce for our aspiration to bring peace and stability to this island. A 'no' vote will reaffirm the traditional view of southern society that one moral principle of one Church, the indissolubility of marriage, is more important than the moral principle of fundamental respect for the rights of others, A 'yes' vote will, on the other hand, be a vote in favour of a new Ireland with which all traditions might identify."[99]

At the launching of the Fine Gael party's pro-divorce campaign, however, its director, the foreign minister, Peter Barry, argued that the outcome of the referendum would have no impact on the Northern Ireland question. Barry stated that in the event of the referendum being defeated, he doubted "that the people of Northern Ireland would see the outcome as proof that the Republic is a Catholic State for a Catholic people."[100] Putting the relevance of the Northern Ireland dimension to the divorce amendment more bluntly, the Fine Gael parliamentarian, John Kelly, contended: "I do not see that this matter has anything to do with the North of Ireland. . . . The argument that we have to change the law here to bring ourselves into line with the North or to disarm criticism from non-Catholics or those who think this is some kind of spiritual dictatorship run by the hierarchy, is wrong."[101] Independent Senator Catherine McGuinness, who is herself a Northern Protestant, strongly emphasized that, to the contrary, the defeat of the amendment would be "a blow in the face to all moderate Protestants who are trying to make the Anglo-Irish agreement work . . . It will reinforce the view that this is a society where home rule is Rome rule."[102]

With this one exception, therefore, the Northern Ireland angle, while not ignored by the pro-divorce forces, was underplayed by them. Its relevance to the amendment was more forcefully dismissed by opponents of divorce. William Binchy argued that unification was a completely separate issue,[103] while members of Fianna Fail argued that "granting divorce here will not make one whit of difference to a united Ireland."[104]

The issue of Northern Ireland is one of well-grounded historical relevance to Irish and Anglo-Irish politics and continues to dominate political discussions in Ireland. Some may find it puzzling, therefore, that it was so marginalized during the divorce debate. One way in which its omission can be explained is that, as a sociopolitical issue, the "problem" of Northern Ireland essentially spotlights questions of minority rights.

Talking about Northern Ireland focuses attention on the problem of minority Catholic rights in the North and the problem of minority Protestant rights in a possible future united Ireland. In the context of the divorce debate, it can be used to indirectly remind people that there is also a minority in the Republic of Ireland, a minority who would like to divorce and remarry. After all, this was what the referendum was about: the concession of the legal right to divorce and remarriage to those who wish to avail of it. Remarks by the foreign minister, Peter Barry, in defending his dismissal of the Northern Ireland dimension, highlighted this. He argued: "Because Northern Ireland was not referred to in my script, that does not mean it is not important. In any republic concern for the rights of a minority is extremely important. I believe myself that we have a Republic and that I am living in a Republic. I would hope that the government and every government would ensure that the rights of minorities are upheld."[105]

But, in Ireland, just as arguments invoking individual rights do not find ready acceptance, the same difficulties confront those arguing the case of minorities. There is a preference for causes that are seen as more broadly benefitting the family, the community, or the larger society. Given this cultural context, many people perceive divorce, for instance, in negative terms, as essentially granting to an individual and to a minority, rights that take precedence over broader societal ideals. As far as many of the Irish people are concerned, while they would genuinely like to help people whose marriages are broken down, and in the case of the Northern Ireland problem, they would like to see the conflict there brought to a peaceful resolution, at the same time, they sincerely believe that they should not vote in favor of a proposal that, in their eyes, would undermine a greater good—with respect to the divorce amendment, lifelong marriage. Consequently, in arguing for divorce, it was in FitzGerald's and the government's interest to deemphasize rather than to emphasize the relevance of Northern Ireland, while for the anti-divorce forces, its introduction as a topic would have clouded unnecessarily their already sharply focused anti-divorce arguments.

There is also another reason, one which might easily elude non-Irish readers, why the government did not emphasize the importance of the amendment to North/South relations. It can be explained by a lack of real commitment in the South to Northern Ireland. Contrary to what many non-Irish people, particularly Irish-Americans, may think, for the most part, the majority of people in the Republic do not regard the unification of Northern Ireland as a major priority.[106] The Irish Republican Army (IRA) receives little support for its political agenda from people living in the South, and it is likely that this minority support would be even further attenuated if there was a greater awareness that related to the IRA's agenda is the objective of a united, socialist Ireland.[107]

The Irish have more immediate concerns with the economic and social issues in their own jurisdiction and those that impact on their everyday lives. Certainly, there is no shortage of nationalist rhetoric by politicians and others, and aspirations toward a united Ireland are frequently articulated. But an aspiration toward a united Ireland is a long distance from commitment to the real costs it would entail. It is not certain that a majority of people living in the South would be prepared to make adjustments—economic, political, social, or cultural—as a way of accommodating, or assimilating with, those in the North.[108]

Given the distance that people in the South have from the Northern Ireland question, therefore, it would only have further delegitimated the pro-divorce case of FitzGerald and the government. Indeed, it would have been counterproductive. The Irish would have asked, "Why should we be more concerned about the political impact that introducing divorce would have on our relations with Northern Ireland than with the consequences of divorce on our own society?" As the astute parliamentarian, John Kelly, declared, "We will run our affairs to please ourselves."[109]

To recapitulate, those making the case for the introduction of divorce into Irish society had to accomplish two things. They had to establish a break between the equation of state law and Catholic morality and, at the same time, to maintain their own credibility by not undermining the traditional approach to marriage as a lifelong sacrament. Advocates of divorce had to establish credibility with an electorate for a stance that was contrary to bedrock Irish religious and cultural values. The challenge was to establish authority for a position that was so at odds with the dominant societal ethos. They had to argue for the acceptance of secular legislation without appearing to be challenging the prerogative of the Church to define both private and public morality.

Precluded from relying on economic or religious arguments, the pro-divorce lobby used a broad, intellectualized discourse. The tension in Irish society between tradition and modernity meant that while they were trying to appeal to modern values such as the distinction between private and public morality, at the same time, they had to be careful not to offend the majority, who regard marriage as a sacramental lifelong commitment. Their task was to try to preserve a balance as they negotiated questions of their own credibility and legitimation, their presentation as authentic Catholics, and their arguments in support of the introduction of secular legislation.

Discussion of the anti-divorce discourse revealed that two types of concerns preoccupied opponents of divorce: economic, and moral or religious. Throughout the debate, the ADC and members of Fianna Fail who opposed divorce publicly emphasized its this-worldly practical economic effects. At the same time, however, they gained credibility from their other-worldly reason, their moral objection to the principle of divorce. Jointly, their use of economic and moral arguments was powerful because these two sets of arguments appealed to the primary cultural concerns of the Irish: economics and religion. A basic inconsistency, however, character-ized the ADC's discourse because it drew on two different tradi-tions—evidence and doctrine—which, when juxtaposed, are incompatible, but which, significantly, went unchallenged during the debate.

CHAPTER FOUR

Women and the Divorce Campaign

Can anything further be added to our understanding of the debate by looking at the arguments from the perspective of women? We might well expect that the inclusion of women and arguments relating to them would give a different slant to the debate. After all, there is a long tradition of seeing divorce as of special interest to women and central to the cause of women's equality. Since the early part of the nineteenth century, demands for divorce law reform were prevalent among feminists in Western Europe, who saw divorce as one way of giving legal protection to women's uncertain status relative to the de facto independence of men.[1] Traditional legal marriage and divorce based on adultery of the wife reinforced the patriarchal family structure of Western society and thus subordinated women to the authority of their husbands. Based on the common-law doctrine of coverture, whereby women assumed the legal identity of their husbands, "the wife became . . . a legal nonperson, living under her husband's arm, protection and cover."[2]

As with other questions concerning women's equality, reforms in the area of domestic relations were slow. In England, where the Christian conception of indissoluble marriage prevailed, it was only after 1857 that the modern notion of divorce as the dissolution of a valid marriage and the right to remarry became legal.[3] But, despite changes in the law, the basic understanding of marriage as a permanent union continued and was supported by restrictive divorce laws. Reflecting its English common-law roots, this was also the case in the United States.[4] Before the twentieth century, therefore, it was common for Western families to stay together, and "public divorce or even private separation was a rarity."[5]

By the turn of the century, however, most American states had enacted divorce laws grounded in the traditional principles of fault, one party's guilt, post-divorce continuation of gender-based marital responsibilities, and financial compensation.[6] This was the type of divorce that prevailed until the 1960s when it was displaced in subsequent years throughout America and Western Europe by non-fault based divorce. With Ireland an exception, "between 1969 and 1985, divorce law in nearly every Western country was altered."[7]

Encompassed in much of the new divorce legislation was the objective of ensuring greater gender equality through giving each spouse an equal share in the marital property and economic resources, the interpretation of which brought forth some unanticipated negative consequences for women. Simply dividing the couple's joint economic resources at the time of the divorce did not compensate those women who had been inactive in the paid labor force because of mothering and/or housework activities and who, therefore, subsequently encountered a reduction in their future earning power as a result of lost work experience and seniority. Failure to acknowledge the cumulative economic impact of wives' noneconomic contribution to their husbands' current and future earning power, in addition to the fact that gender wage differentials favor men, meant that, relative to their husbands, many post-divorce women suffered a decline in income.[8] In short, establishing the principle of legal equality in divorce settlements could not override the unequal social and economic status of women in society. As Lenore Weitzman observed, those responsible for proposing the new laws "were so deeply convinced of the fairness of the new law that they did not foresee how de jure equality might not result in equity in a society lacking de facto equality."[9]

What was reflected in the reforms was the institutional dominance of a male worldview. It was a predominantly male legal profession working with a predominantly male legislature that formulated and endorsed the new laws, and this may well explain the erroneous gender equity assumption.[10] Absent in the formulation of the divorce reforms were women's voices. Organized feminist groups were not active participants in efforts to reform the American law,[11] while similarly elsewhere, in Italy, for example, the initial attempt to introduce divorce legislation was not framed as a women's issue.[12]

But these earlier divorce reforms were set in place prior to the public impact of the second wave of feminism—the resurgence of

women's liberation movements in the late sixties—which partially
explains the dearth of women's perspectives in the new thinking on
divorce. Irish divorce, in contrast, was proposed in the late 1980s
following twenty years of vigorous feminist organization and activity in the West, including the formation in Ireland of various
women's organizations and the establishment of a national administrative body for women, the Council for the Status of Women. We
would thus expect the active participation of women and women's
groups in the debate. Moreover, because the Irish divorce proposals
also sought to effect gender equality and were presented as being
pro-women—it was envisaged that divorce settlements would compensate wives for their non-economic contribution and also allow
women redress against deserting husbands who default on economic obligations—we would expect women to argue vigorously
in favor of divorce.[13]

This was not the case, however, even though, as I discussed in
chapter 2, Irish women are actively involved in politics. More sur-
prisingly, a significantly greater number of women than men opposed the amendment. At the end of the campaign, 64 percent of
women compared to 46 percent of men expressed their intention of
voting against divorce.[14] This was so despite majority support
among women for divorce at the outset of the debate and in previous opinion polls, where equal numbers of men and women favored divorce; in one poll, for instance, 67 percent of men and 64
percent of women agreed that divorce should be permitted in certain circumstances.[15] Therefore, while support for divorce as a
whole decreased from 61 percent at the outset of the campaign to
36 percent on referendum day, something also happened during the
course of the debate to affect a gender difference in attitudes toward divorce.

It was not that women were disinterested or indifferent to the
proposed change. To the contrary, many women participated in the
campaign, but they did not articulate a distinct women's agenda
regarding marriage and divorce. The participation of organized
women was limited to the Council for the Status of Women (CSW).
Established in 1973 and underwritten since 1980 by an annual government grant, the CSW represents over seventy women's organizations, encompassing all shades of political opinion and including
professional, trade union, farming, health, educational, feminist,

social activist, and religious groups. Its main role is to provide a central information resource for women and women's organizations and to lobby on agreed policies regarding all aspects of Irish life. The CSW is expressly committed to considering any legislative proposals of concern to women and to representing women's views on matters of public concern.[16]

Regarding the amendment, the CSW welcomed the referendum and the government's divorce proposals, stating: "The Council is convinced that divorce legislation on the lines outlined by the Government will be of immense *advantage* to those women for whom it will be a merciful release from the prison of a long dead marriage. The Council therefore, urges everyone to vote in favour of this referendum" [emphasis in original].[17] It also emphatically rejected the argument that the divorce proposals would cause women and children to suffer: "Divorce is a response to a situation not a cause. . . . To suggest that women or children will *begin* to suffer if divorce is introduced demonstrates ignorance and thoughtlessness about the situation which already exists. It is unacceptable that people in an unhappy marriage should be obliged to stay together through financial pressures even if they wish to part" [emphasis in original].[18] A public meeting held by the CSW two days prior to referendum day addressed the impact of the divorce proposals on social welfare and legal entitlements and countered, in particular, the anti-divorce argument that deserted or separated women would lose their social welfare benefits with divorce.[19] The CSW took issue also with the "degrading image of women being portrayed by the anti-divorce lobby," arguing:

To suggest that this amendment will impoverish women is untrue. Impoverishment of women exists because our society relegates women to a subordinate role and, in marriage, to a dependent status in which society continues to ignore the lack of legal and economic equality which all women should have by right. . . . Listening to recent statements made by the anti-divorce lobby, one would be forgiven for thinking that all women in Ireland are extraordinarily passive creatures, unable to sustain marriages if divorce legislation exists, and who are married to men likely to abandon them at a moment's notice.[20]

Importantly, however, as the sole national representative body of the various women's organizations in Ireland, the CSW did not engage in an *activist* role during the debate. Although it expressed its endorsement of the amendment, it did not actively campaign in its favor. It did not, for instance, organize a nationwide canvassing campaign or lobby women through advertising or the mass media to endorse the proposals. In short, it adopted a very low profile during the debate.

The stance adopted by the CSW during the debate, despite its supportive endorsement of the amendment, underscored its function as an administrative organization for women's groups rather than an active national women's lobby.[21] Because of the social and ideological diversity of its affiliate membership, it appears that the CSW does not have the de facto legitimacy to speak on behalf of all women or to organize a national grassroots campaign in support of a particular demand (in this case, either pro- or anti-divorce) when a controversial question affecting women and society at large is at stake. Consequently, although the divorce referendum represented the first occasion in the history of the state when an issue with major implications for women was open to resolution by public vote, the CSW did not canvass on the issue nor actively articulate the implications of divorce for women.

With the CSW's disengagement from active participation in the debate and their recalcitrance to articulate publicly a cohesive position addressing women's interests and divorce, the same protagonists who argued the case in general, activists and politicians, were the ones who most specifically focused on women and divorce. Let us look first at the anti-divorce arguments.

The Anti-Divorce Campaign

As was the case in the ADC's overall campaign, the main emphasis was placed on issues of economics, with the impoverishment of women one of the central motifs of the anti-divorce discourse. From the outset of the campaign, the ADC's William Binchy argued that divorce would negatively affect married women by depriving them of their existing marital economic rights—the right to succession, maintenance, and the family home.[22] With posters stating, "This amendment will impoverish women: Vote NO!" the ADC accentuated this theme throughout the debate.[23]

The ADC argued that dependents from the first marriage would have no claim on the economic resources of the husband/father. Accordingly they would suffer a sharp decline in their standard of living and in many instances become dependent on the state for basic social welfare payments. In short, the ADC argued that divorce was not a viable option for dealing with marital breakdown because it would propel women and children into poverty, a claim they supported by drawing on evidence from other countries, for example: "in Britain 60% of women who get a divorce go straight on to social welfare. . . . 88% of low income parents are women. 63% of that 88% of low income parents are divorced women."[24]

Do Women Want Divorce?

Opponents of divorce did not deny that marital breakdown was a problem in Irish society. What they took issue with was both the alleged extent of the problem and the wisdom of dealing with it by introducing divorce.[25] The ADC contended that many deserted and separated women themselves did not want to divorce and remarry, nor did they favor the introduction of divorce into society.[26] It was necessary for women in other jurisdictions to initiate divorce proceedings, they argued, precisely because unlike the state provision of welfare benefits for deserted women in Ireland, in countries where divorce is available, filing for divorce is the only possible way in which women whose marriages have broken down can get financial support. Thus Bernadette Bonar argued: "At the point where a woman seeks divorce her husband has already gone off and left her to set up home with somebody else. And this is the only legal channel open to her to try and get maintenance [and] the family home. . . . But don't forget that the men just don't pay maintenance to their wives. 60% of them in England go straight onto social welfare. And in America, 85% of men, even after a court order, refuse to pay maintenance to their wives."[27] Also of importance, Bonar argued, was the divorced woman's loss of social status: "Divorce . . . will take all status from the [deserted] woman. As it is she feels she has a husband even though he is not living with her. His position is going to be made legal and respectable and she will be left with no hope of any sort."[28]

The threat of the hopelessness of being a divorced woman, of becoming a "non-person," was further reinforced by the ADC's slogan, "You could be forced to divorce: Vote NO!" Specifically targeted at women, it emphasized that divorce would allow the further exploitation of their already vulnerable status as dependents of their husbands. Reiterating the anti-divorce position, law professor Mary McAleese argued that divorce would mean state approval of "a man who leaves his wife and children so that he can be happier with another woman."[29]

Gender Discrimination

While the ADC emphasized the traditional view of women as dependent solely on marriage for social and personal as well as economic status, importantly, they linked this to the structurally unequal position of women in Irish society and highlighted the problems caused for women as a result of sexual inequality. It was precisely because of gender discrimination, the ADC argued, that women needed to be protected from the consequences of divorce. Rather than allowing themselves to be depicted as being against the rights of women, the ADC conveyed a strong message that it was pro-woman to be anti-divorce.

The ADC argued that because of the sexual discrimination in society, the state's legal support for marriage as a lifelong commitment was the best way in which to compensate women for the discrimination they confronted. William Binchy argued: "There are inequalities in society and there is sex discrimination. Divorce, in a society where there is such sex discrimination and sex inequality in terms of opportunity, would yield a massive increase in needless hardship for precisely the categories that you or I would wish to protect. The woman who is older, who has sacrificed her career by rearing a family within the home, the woman who is younger who has children. These two categories, studies throughout the world have shown again and again, are the categories that have been hit hardest by the introduction of divorce based on failure of a marriage."[30] From the perspective of the ADC, therefore, the current unequal position of married women as dependent wives would be undermined further by divorce because it would remove the legal protection and social status offered married women.

Fianna Fail parliamentarians echoed the ADC stress on the negative economic effects of divorce on women.[31] Their education spokesperson, Mary O'Rourke, acknowledged the suffering of many women in broken marriages and women's changing expectations regarding marriage and work. Arguing, however, that the divorce question was ultimately about balancing the traumatic effects of marital breakdown against the stability of marriage in society as a whole, she contended that the divorce proposals were not "for the betterment of society,"[32] a position reiterated in the Senate by her Fianna Fail colleague, Tras Honan.[33]

The range of arguments put forward regarding the negative consequences of divorce on women was best summarized by Alice Glenn of Fine Gael, whose active opposition to divorce highlighted the legitimation difficulties that Prime Minister Garret FitzGerald's divorce agenda confronted. At the time of the referendum, Glenn represented a predominantly working-class Dublin electoral constituency and was noted for her conservatism and outspokenness on social issues. From the outset of the debate she expressed strong opposition to divorce, in particular to its negative consequences for women.[34] Contributing one of the most graphic arguments against divorce, Glenn contended that: *"any woman voting for divorce is like a turkey voting for Christmas"* [emphasis mine].[35] This was because, as Glenn elaborated:

No account is taken of the woman who is discarded. The woman will be the victim of this legislation, the cast aside spouse women are denied succession rights but the position as regards family home protection is self evident. If a husband leaves his wife and children, what family home are we talking about? Reason would suggest that the family home is that of the second liaison. The Constitution is to protect the family but *a woman cast aside is not a family. She becomes a non-person.* She loses all protection under the Constitution. The wife and children are diminished but the opposite happens to the male. He will have formed an alliance with somebody in the workforce who is bringing in plenty of money. That is all he is interested in [emphasis mine].[36]

While a crude metaphor, the meaning of Glenn's remarks was clear and underscored the image of women as victims in need of protection, the theme that pervaded the anti-divorce discourse as a whole.

It was, apparently, as evinced by the decline in support for divorce among women, an effective image. Why was this anti-divorce message so persuasive? What is it about the substance of the arguments that might explain the shift in women's attitudes to divorce?

Appeal to Women's Traditional Role

The women-related themes of the anti-divorce discourse ensured their appeal to a broadly based constituency. The arguments contained themes that spoke to the values embodied by the traditional notion of lifelong marriage, and they were also relevant to a large segment because the economic thrust of the discourse focused on women's objective status as "dependents." Relating to the actual situation of the majority of Irish women, opponents of divorce framed women's identity as being inextricably linked to marriage; thus, a woman's status was dependent on her role as wife and homemaker and was not related to engagement in the public sphere. Within this framework, they argued that divorce would mean the loss not just of economic but of social and personal status. Divorced women would become "non-persons." Positioning themselves on the side of women who are full-time housewives/mothers, opponents of divorce stressed the inequities and injustices that divorce would mean for such women by its undermining of lifelong marriage and how, consequently, their vulnerability would be further exploited. As Family Solidarity argued: "The family occupies a central position in society so the State has a right and duty to watch over it and give it special care and protection. As our society developed, marriage laws were introduced, out of compassion and in the interest of justice, *to help the weaker and more vulnerable members of the family, the women and children especially*" [emphasis mine].[37]

Out of expressed concern for dependent wives and their role in preserving the family, those arguing against divorce contended that the State should continue to protect legally marriage as a lifelong institution. In their view, when women depend on marriage for economic, social, and personal status, marriage as a lifelong, irrevocable commitment is the only guarantee they have that their personhood will be legitimated. In sum, anti-divorce advocates opposed divorce because: "*Divorce takes all status away from the*

*woman. . . . Women will be the victims of [divorce] . . . woman
will be the cast aside spouse. . . . The woman cast aside becomes a
non-person"* [emphasis mine].[38]

Women's victimization, therefore, was a central theme in the
anti-divorce discourse. The pervasiveness of this motif extends well
beyond being just an Irish phenomenon, however. It is an image
that is also found in political debates in America. Documenting its
use among American anti-abortion activists, Faye Ginsburg notes
that the frame of women as victim fits into a long historical pattern
in which the biological, social, and cultural bases of gender differences were seen by women as the only way in which to activate support or maintain state protection for women's structurally
vulnerable position.[39] As she explains: "The themes expressed by
right-to-life activists in the contemporary abortion controversy—
the dangers of male lust, and the protection of the weak against the
depredations of self-interest unleashed—are similar to concerns
voiced by women activists in America over the past two centuries.
They have been most prominent in female-led moral reform movements. . . . These movements emerged with the material and cultural separation of wage and domestic labor that came to be
identified as male and female arenas of activity."[40] Importantly,
Ginsburg further observes that the current use of the theme of female nurturance in opposition to male self-interest is applied not
just against males, as it was historically, but also against those
women who appear to have eschewed their dependent and nurturing roles in the pursuit of non-domestic interests.[41]

The debate over the Equal Rights Amendment (ERA) has also
been construed as a conflict over women's role. Those campaigning
against the ERA claimed that its passing would mean that women
would be treated on an equal basis to men, thus delegitimating
their need for special protection. "What was at stake in the battle
over the ERA was the *legitimacy* of women's claim on men's
incomes,"[42] an inevitable source of tension once some women
work in the labor force and some remain full-time housewives.[43]

Presenting women as victims, therefore, is to argue for the traditional definition of woman's role as an economically dependent,
full-time mother and homemaker. It is a paternalistic argument
that maintains that woman's "natural" nurturing role needs to be
protected from those who undermine it: economically independent

women engaged in the public sphere; men who default on their responsibilities toward women; and "male" laws, which exploit women's vulnerability.[44]

William Binchy's attempt then to use the status of women to argue against divorce, was, despite the qualifications to his argument, sexist. It was not sexist because it raised the possibility of
gender differences but because no serious attempt was ever made to
distinguish which of these differences were due to temporal, cultural, and historical circumstances. Equally, there was no attempt
made to come up with remedies that would alleviate the "vulner-
abilities" of women and thus set the stage for the implementation
of a non-fault based divorce. Rather, sexual inequality, his dis-
avowal to the contrary, was represented as natural, inevitable, and
a just reason for insistence on "legal lifelong marriage and women's
dependent status within it."

The forceful authority of Binchy's argument emanated, ultimately, not from his acknowledgment of sexism in Irish society
but from its direct compatibility with the sexism in Irish society.
Although the theme of women's victimization has universal appeal
because of the historical subjugation of women, such an argument
would appear to have greater salience in Ireland, where the disem-
powerment of women and their economic dependence is far greater
than in the United States. In Ireland, the vast majority of married
women are dependent economically on their husbands. Only a
small number, 21 percent, are engaged in the labor force, compared to 56 percent of married women in the United States and 42
percent in the European Community as a whole.[45] Notwithstanding their image in literature and film, which, rightly, presents Irish
women as strong characters, the centers of initiative and industry,
undaunted by cruel fate, it is no accident that they tend to be portrayed as holding forth only in the domestic domain.[46] Reflecting
deeply embedded cultural attitudes regarding the role of women
and the remnants of structural barriers against their economic participation, the life chances of the majority of Irish women revolve
around marriage and domesticity, an arrangement that is the expressed preference of a majority of Irish married men.[47]

Thus while the economic emphasis in the anti-divorce discourse
in general was powerful because of the cultural sensitivity of the
Irish to economics, its importance was further accentuated when

the focus shifted to women. Stressing the negative economic consequences of divorce for women—its exploitation and victimization of their de facto economic dependence—was fully grounded in the immediate economically dependent situation of women, for many of whom legal lifelong marriage is a necessary "protection" against their currently unequal status. The ADC arguments appealed to this reality, exploited it, and reinforced it, without ever attempting to remedy it in an active fashion other than preserving the status quo.

Another reason why the ADC arguments were powerful is because they reinforced the disposition advocated by the Church. The consonance between the ADC's arguments and the Church's teaching on the indissolubility of lifelong marriage was likely to carry greater force with women. Women's socialization, as argued by Nancy Chodorow and Carol Gilligan, predisposes women to greater emphasis on other-orientation and communal investment.[48] This is reinforced in Irish society by women's historical role as the moral guardians of the family and its stability. Irish women are thus accustomed to subsuming their personal interests to those of family considerations. Moreover, Irishwomen's greater participation in Church activities and their greater confidence in the Church's teaching would enhance their predisposition toward the ADC's emphasis on lifelong marriage.[49] Here again, therefore, we see how women's socialization and cultural experiences would have made them more impressed by the anti-divorce message.

For Irishwomen to vote in favor of divorce, would demand their going against powerful forces: the traditional social and economic structures within which lifelong marriage and women's status are embedded, the moral authority of the Church, and other-oriented socialization patterns that find further support in Irish society because of the underemphasis on individual rights. Given the forces that divorce was challenging then, what kinds of arguments did its advocates articulate in making divorce seem like an attractive option for women and advantageous to their situation?

The Divorce Action Group

The main argument of the Divorce Action Group was that women want divorce, and DAG activists repeatedly expressed confidence that women in particular would endorse the amendment.[50] DAG invoked legitimacy for its case by arguing that the proposals were supported by the various groups who have campaigned on behalf of women's rights in Ireland. Thus Jean Tansey argued: "All of the women's organizations who have fought for women over the years . . . are behind this divorce legislation. And I think it is possibly because women know that within a marriage they are more vulnerable, emotionally and financially . . . and they recognise the need to have a right to a recognition that a marriage has failed and that they want to have another chance."[51] Taking issue with the passive, dependent image of women presented by opponents of divorce, Jean Tansey accused them of portraying "the image of women as spineless creatures who are in marriage only because there is a marriage certificate there, and once divorce is permitted, that women would be rejected."[52]

As evidence that women favored divorce, its advocates argued that in other countries it was primarily women who initiated divorce proceedings, thus indicating their desire to be freed from the binds of an unhappy marital relationship.[53] As Tansey explained, women favored divorce because its introduction could not possibly make deserted or separated women worse off economically than they were presently. Divorce, according to the DAG, would accelerate and make more equitable the process whereby property and material resources are divided. Consequently, as DAG maintained: "It is women who are saying to us that they want to have divorce. It is women who are deserted by men and left penniless. . . . This amendment is pro-women."[54]

The Political Parties

In keeping with the pattern of their general stance, the politicians supporting divorce all argued that divorce would benefit women. Like the DAG, pro-divorce politicians maintained that because currently many deserted wives live in poor economic circumstances and many separated women voluntarily surrender their succession rights, the proposed divorce legislation would strengthen their economic status.[55] It was Garret FitzGerald who most forcefully argued that divorce would enhance the rights of women. In a final statement to the electorate on the eve of polling day, he specifically assured women that divorce would protect their interests, and he appealed to them to vote in favor of the amendment. FitzGerald passionately implored:

Can we say "no" to our people whose marriages have failed? I say we must be more generous. I ask this particularly of the women of Ireland. Over the course of the campaign many of you have been led to believe that a "yes" vote would be a vote against the interests of women. I guarantee you this is not the case. The opposite is true. If it were not, I would never have been associated with this proposal. A "yes" vote will, in fact, lead to the strengthening of the position of wives—giving them property rights that they do not now have in the family home. . . . A "yes" vote will give those women and children who are presently trapped in unhappy situations a choice. I believe they deserve this choice.[56]

In view of the feminist tradition of framing divorce as central to women's equality and in light of the low profile of the Council for the Status of Women in calling for divorce, it seems reasonable to expect some spokeswomen to emerge as representatives of women's interests and divorce. What was the role of women politicians during the debate? And did any women elites, academics or journalists, for instance, argue for divorce on women's behalf?

Women Parliamentarians

Women members of the government and other pro-divorce political parties, as well as nonparty independent senators, all argued vigorously in favor of divorce. Nuala Fennell, the minister of state for women's affairs and a long-time campaigner for women's rights, declared that the divorce proposals would "for the first time . . . provide a charter of rights for women in the event of marital breakdown."[57] Opening the Senate debate on divorce, she argued that one of the central aims of the divorce proposals was to ensure that "the interests of dependent spouses and children were as fully protected as possible." Fennell emphasized that the proposed legislation empowered the courts, in determining property rights and maintenance payments, to recognize the relevant circumstances of the divorcing couple and in particular, to take account of the dependent wife's contribution to the family,[58] while the minister for social welfare, Gemma Hussey, reaffirmed that women would not lose their social welfare benefits with divorce.[59]

Fennell, Hussey, and others reiterated the argument of their male colleagues that the existing domestic relations legislation was inadequate in protecting the rights of married women, thus enabling divorce to enhance women's economic position. This position was most forcefully articulated by Fine Gael back-bencher, Monica Barnes, an active feminist and a representative from Ireland's most liberal electoral constituency, Dun Laoghaire, the borough south of Dublin city. Barnes drew attention to the limitations of the existing benefits that anti-divorce advocates were arguing protected married women. She argued:

Women . . . consider that the Family Home Protection Act is one of the most important protections they have been given. People have bleated here about the family home of the first wife of a marriage and her children. They probably do not even realise that that Act protects a woman only to the extent that without written consent by her the home cannot be sold. . . . if she is not in joint ownership of the home, no matter how many years she has given to the home and the family, legally she is not entitled to a penny from the price of that house. Neither, legally is she entitled to any part of the contents of the family home unless she can prove that financially and independently she paid for such property.[60]

Barnes highlighted the especially vulnerable economic circumstances of women whose marriages have broken down and who have formed new nonlegal relationships. These were the women, she contended, who needed to be given greater legal protection; protection, she maintained, that would come only if the form of divorce being proposed by the government was accepted. Thus she argued: "Take the case of a deserted wife who forms a new liaison and has a second family. As it stands at present she has no right to support from her new partner. She cannot claim maintenance nor succeed to his estate when he dies. The Succession Act does not enter into it. She has no rights under the Family Home Protection Act. She cannot obtain a Barring Order in the event of violence to her or her children. If deserted she is not entitled to deserted wife's benefit or allowance. If he dies she is not entitled to a widow's pension."[61]

The issue of constitutional protection for women and families was also a major part of Senator Mary Robinson's lengthy contribution to the parliamentary debate. Arguing that there was an urgent need for greater legislative protection and support for women involved in marital breakdown, she, too, elaborated on the shortcomings that deserted and separated women encounter in the present legislative situation.[62] A similar stance was taken by renowned family lawyer Senator Catherine McGuinness, who gave special emphasis to women's loss of succession and other rights in separation and nullity cases.[63]

Emphasizing the changing expectations and role of women in Irish society, pro-divorce women politicians attacked the "scaremongering" and "anti-women" claims of the anti-divorce lobby.[64] Presenting themselves as the defenders of women's emotional and material interests, they took issue with the dependent and passive image of women depicted by anti-divorce campaigners. In this regard, they were sharply critical of Glenn's "turkey" metaphor and denounced it as insulting to Irish women. The criticisms expressed by Mary Harney of the Progressive Democrats typified the range of reactions. She stated:

I reject this and feel insulted that women are treated like this in this House [Parliament] and in this country on matters of this kind. It is degrading; it is offensive; it is insulting to Irish women and I hope that throughout this debate people will refrain from discussing women in this way and from implying that this legislation will make women and children suffer more than they have suffered over recent years as a result of the kind of legislation we have. . . . Women are generally supposed to be the moral guardians of all that is right and proper and, if something goes wrong, it has to be the fault of a woman.[65]

Women Academics

Academics in Ireland for the most part do not actively engage in public debates on social or political questions. The context dependency of knowledge notwithstanding, a fairly strict distinction is maintained between personal beliefs and analytic discourse. And while some professors have a relatively high public profile, their contributions tend to represent detached analysis rather than dialogic exchange. During the divorce debate, as with previous issues, a number of academics publicly expressed support for the amendment.[66] Women were not at the forefront in this, however, even though there is a vibrant women's studies community in Irish academia. Two women law professors who were active in the campaign, Senator Mary Robinson and Mary McAleese, were active independent of their academic position and were already identified partisans on divorce, expressing pro- and anti-divorce arguments respectively.[67]

As I noted above, Mary McAleese, basically echoing the arguments of the Anti-Divorce Campaign, warned women of the threat posed by divorce to their economic status. Arguing for divorce, Mary Robinson grounded her position in a discussion of Irish constitutional law and its recognition of the inalienable and imprescriptible rights of the family.[68] Emphasizing that family rights come into being on marriage but are not dependent on the subsistence of the marriage to continue, Robinson argued that divorce would not terminate the family rights of spouses and children. She acknowledged the concerns expressed regarding dependent wives' loss of legal protection with divorce but maintained that proposed changes in legislation and in the social welfare code should "ensure that there will be no economic loss."[69]

Women Columnists

The comments of the women columnists in the national press, Mary Holland and Nuala O'Faolain of the *Irish Times* and Nell McCafferty of the *Irish Press,* all well-known Irish feminists and advocates of women's rights, were distinctive for the paucity of remarks specifically discussing divorce and women. Out of four articles written on the amendment by Mary Holland, for example, only one referred to women's situation. What the columnists said, nevertheless, spoke directly to the issue of women's inequality in Irish society.

Nell McCafferty took a humorous approach to the divorce question. Teasing as to what would be the story resolution of "Dallas," the soap opera, and the outcome of the Irish divorce referendum, McCafferty drew out the moral message of "Dallas" and its relevance to the divorce debate: "If Dallas preaches anything, it preaches this—children come first, their mothers will be financially taken care of, and their fathers will never desert their posts, come

separation, nullity or divorce, even though America has no constitutional provision regarding the rights of women as mothers" [un-
like the Irish constitution].

Continuing to point at Irish hypocrisy in relation to official
proclamations regarding the sanctity of motherhood, McCafferty
challenged anti-divorce campaigners "who go on about the constitutional rights of mothers being under threat" to show how the
state, in line with its constitutional commitment to protect wom-
en's economic situation, would be successfully forced to pay mothers for their work in the home.[70] In a later article, McCafferty
called the Church's preference for nullity rather than divorce an old
"feminist solution to an Irish problem"—in practice, the abolition
of marriage and private property and collective responsibility for
child-rearing.[71] So, although clearly tongue-in-cheek, Nell McCafferty forcefully communicated her disregard for the inconsistencies
in the anti-divorce platform.

The message from the *Irish Times'* columnists was more ambivalent. Commenting on the apparent success of anti-divorce campaign slogans such as "This amendment will impoverish women"
and "You could be divorced against your will," Mary Holland argued that these "were aimed at women with children who are wor-
ried not just about property but about their place in the community
generally." Without elaboration, she commented: "It tells us something desperately sad about the situation of women in Ireland today that such slogans should have had a major impact on the
debate." Holland warned that the reality and implications of marital breakdown would have to be eventually confronted and that
the divorce issue, "unlike abortion, cannot be pushed out of sight
on the Liverpool boat" [one means by which Irishwomen travel to
England in order to have an abortion].[72]

The status of women in Ireland was explicated more bluntly by
Nuala O'Faolain, Holland's colleague at the *Times*. Themes evident in O'Faolain's remarks during the divorce debate were the
overemphasis in Irish society on the sanctity of motherhood and
the family and the obeisance of Irish women to the Church.[73]
Grounding her argument in a forceful and compassionate critique
of the economically and socially impoverished circumstances which
many married women experience, O'Faolain denounced the inher-
ent anti-woman bias of marriage and argued that divorce would be

no better: "The great majority of women subsisting on the Deserted Wives Allowance, or cowering behind barring orders . . .
have little to gain and much to lose by entering into the kind of
transactions the proposed divorce legislation would entail. . . . In
any case, divorce is about remarriage. It was marriage that did
them in the first place—marriage as a social imprimatur for having
the children. It is rearing the children that makes them powerless.
They always got less out of marriage than the blokes."

Explaining why women might be acting in their own self-interest
by opposing divorce, O'Faolain stated: "Women, particularly, are
facing the demise both of the unchallenged status of wifehood and
of the implicit security of an indissoluble marriage. They have to
have security somehow, for the years in which they bear and rear
the race. Using a man's income was never the best way of doing
this, but there aren't many other likely alternatives." O'Faolain's was
the only voice in the debate that noted that women's lives are fundamentally different to men's because of women's "nurturing responsibilities," a difference, she suggested, that makes "their view
of their purpose different from men's, even in ideal marriages."[74]

But this sensitivity to the institutionalization of gender difference was not used by O'Faolain or by others, including the Council
for the Status of Women, to demarcate systematically women's interests with regard to the divorce proposals at issue. Although
women politicians and the DAG under Jean Tansey's leadership
argued adamantly that divorce would favor women, they did not
engage women in forceful, consciousness-raising discourse on divorce. Nor did women academics or journalists—despite the strong
feminist credentials that can be found among both groups—advocate a women's agenda on divorce.

Women, in short, did not present themselves as a cohesive bloc
during the divorce campaign.[75] In a debate dominated by male
voices—both the pro- and anti-divorce platforms were led by men,
Garret FitzGerald and William Binchy, respectively—there was no
attempt either by the CSW or pro-divorce activists and politicians to
organize women as a distinct constituency or to coordinate a unified women's voice that would have challenged the status quo. Organized women as an independent lobby were absent similarly
from the earlier abortion and contraception debates and from national economic debates where the interests of farmers, industrial

employers, and trade unionists predominate. Unlike the concerns of other interest groups in Ireland, women's interests as women seem to get mediated, or indeed marginalized, by larger issues such as with divorce, the greater value of the family, or with abortion, the greater value of prenatal life. The peripheralization of women's voices was well illustrated during the 1983 pro-life amendment debate, where, from their public contributions to the debate, groups of lawyers and medical doctors, and even the farming organizations, appeared to have a greater stake in the outcome of the referendum than did women.

The pro-divorce case was clearly hindered by the absence of an independent activist women's group that would have moderated the debate and raised consciousness regarding the benefits that would accrue to women with divorce. While the message of women's equality articulated by pro-divorce advocates might ultimately be an appealing one, it was not forceful enough to provide a counterpoint to the sexist, anti-divorce arguments of Binchy and others. For a link to be forged between divorce and women's equality, especially in light of the formidable social, economic, and moral structures that maintain women's traditional status in Irish society, it is not enough for a pro-divorce message to be verbalized by a few women. Some channel through which to target women's consciousness as women appears necessary.

This would entail the constitution of a clearly identified women's organization that has the authority—unlike the csw because of the ideological diversity of its broad based affiliate membership—to articulate publicly a cohesive women's rights discourse and, as part of this, to pursue actively and systematically a pro-divorce agenda. Such a group cannot just express support for divorce; they must canvass and use campaign strategies that show consistency with their expressed belief in the value of divorce for women. A group that would have the organizational capability to do this effectively cannot be expected to emerge spontaneously once a divorce referendum is announced. Unlike the sprouting of the Anti-Divorce Campaign, there is little affinity between Irish values and an ad hoc organization that would emerge to challenge the inevitability of women's dependent role.

Given the absence both of an activist women's organization and a distinct women's agenda in the debate, coupled with the cultural and socioeconomic experiences of Irishwomen, perhaps it is not so surprising that women did not vote for divorce, which, if implemented, threatened, as its opponents contended, to delegitimate women's status in the home and exploit further their dependent "vulnerability".

CHAPTER FIVE

The Catholic Church and the Referendum

It is both easy and tempting to try to explain the failure of the divorce referendum by pointing to the Catholic church's opposition to divorce. After all, Ireland is among the most Catholic of Western countries, with a well-developed parish system where 87 percent of its predominantly Catholic population attend Mass weekly and participate regularly in other Church rituals and activities.[1] Anyone who has read James Joyce's *Portrait of the Artist as a Young Man* will have no doubt as to the fervor and the vividly this-worldly style of Irish Catholicism.[2] Yet, to attribute the demise too hurriedly to the Church would be both simplistic and an injustice to the genuine moral and practical dilemma with which the referendum confronted the Irish bishops.

Clearly, the issue of divorce is central to the teaching of the Church and fits squarely and legitimately in its pastoral jurisdiction. As we noted in chapter 2, during the Mother and Child controversy the Church did not hesitate to take a direct and forceful role in sociomoral debates. This was particularly true of the 1940s and 1950s, when the Church explicated the incompetence of the state to legislate public morality. Yet the role of the Church in relation to the state in Ireland, as elsewhere, became much more complex as a result of the great watershed event in the history of the Church, the Second Vatican Council (1962–1965).[3]

Under the visionary guidance first of Pope John XXIII, who died in 1963 shortly after it was convened, and then his successor, Pope Paul VI, Vatican II enabled the Church to conduct a "fundamental reappraisal of its doctrine, liturgy and relationship to the world."[4] Cardinals, bishops, theologians, and invited lay people deliberated in Rome concerning moral and doctrinal issues, often in open dialogic disagreement, a dissent made public by the journalists who managed to circumvent the limits imposed on the press by the Council. Sweeping in the breadth of its changes, the impact of Vatican II is most popularly associated with transformations in Church ritual, specifically concretized by the move from the Latin to the vernacular (native language) Mass, relaxations in Church rules regarding penitence, and in visibly significant changes in the dress and lifestyle of nuns and priests.

Regarding issues of church-state relations, the Council officially endorsed the autonomy and independence of each sphere and rejected the notion that the Church was entitled to give Catholics specific guidance in their activities as citizens.[5] It also addressed the issue of tolerance for diverse worldviews and beliefs and noted the importance of personal conscience and its role in informing views on sociomoral questions such as divorce.[6] Of particular relevance to Irish society, given the dominance of the Catholic church and the formal constitutional recognition accorded it, the Council pointed out that even if the circumstances of one country caused one religious denomination to receive special civil recognition, the rights of other religious communities and citizens to religious freedom should be acknowledged and made effective.[7]

Responding to changing times, evinced both by the new spirit of openness within the larger Church and the increasing modernization of Irish society, the Irish hierarchy adopted a different form of self-presentation and discourse. The first evidence of a shifting and more liberal position in the stance of the Irish Church on matters of church and state can be seen in the early 1970s debate over contraception.[8] In 1973, for the first time, the bishops publicly acknowledged the distinction between secular law and Catholic morality. Stating that it did not wish to intervene in the process of government, the hierarchy argued that, even though the two spheres may not always coincide, it was the duty of governments to govern and of bishops to preach. In accordance with Vatican II, the hierarchy pronounced that civil legislation and Catholic teaching could be independent of each other.

The Irish Episcopal Conference declared: "The question at issue is not whether artificial contraception is morally right or wrong. The clear teaching of the Catholic Church is that it is morally wrong. No change in State law can make the use of contraceptives morally right, since what is wrong in itself remains wrong, regardless of what State law says. . . . It does not follow, of course, that the State is bound to prohibit the importation and sale of contraceptives. There are many things which the Catholic Church holds to be morally wrong and no one has ever suggested, least of all the Church herself, that they should be prohibited by the State."[9] This position was clearly less dictatorial than their attitude two years earlier when the bishops stated: "Civil law on these matters [contraception, abortion] should respect the wishes of the people who elected the legislators, and the bishops confidently hope that the legislators themselves will respect this important principle."[10] A few years later, in 1978, once again in a debate over contraception legislation, the hierarchy repeated its declaration on the distinction between law and Catholic morality and argued further that: "Those who insist on seeing the issue purely in terms of the State enforcing or not enforcing, Catholic moral teaching . . . are missing the point."[11]

But despite the collective statements of the hierarchy affirming the autonomy of church and state, the occasion of the "pro-life" referendum in 1983 found the hierarchy adopting a much more tenuous position. Both the firmness of the hierarchy's commitment to assuming a noninterventionist stance when moral legislation was at issue, and the consensus among the bishops regarding nonintervention came into question. The hierarchy's position during that debate directly deviated from the stance of previous statements affirming the autonomy of law and morality.

Although the bishops stated that they recognized "the right of each person to vote according to conscience," at the same time, they called for a "yes" vote, which they argued would "constitute a 'witness before Europe and before the whole world to the dignity and sacredness of all human life from conception to death.' "[12] Notwithstanding the hierarchy's collective clear-cut endorsement of the pro-life amendment, the then archbishop of Dublin, Dermot Ryan, dissented and went one step further than his co-bishops. In a separate personal statement he strongly advocated that people vote "yes" and omitted any reference to freedom of individual conscience.[13] Three days later, however, on the Sunday before polling day, the hierarchy's spokesman, Bishop Joseph Cassidy of Clonfert diocese, clarified that the bishops were "advising [Catholics] strongly to vote 'yes,' " but also pointed out that "if they

have a conscientious conviction that they cannot vote 'yes,' then
we acknowledge, fully acknowledge, their freedom in conscience
to do that."[14]

The most forceful articulation of the hierarchy's noninterventionist stance was seen in 1984 on the occasion of official talks
concerning the future of Northern Ireland at the New Ireland
Forum,[15] where the bishops' delegation declared: "The Catholic
Church in Ireland totally rejects the concept of a confessional State.
We have not sought and we do not seek a Catholic State for a Catholic people. We believe that the alliance of Church and State is
harmful for the Church and harmful for the State. . . . We have repeatedly declared that we in no way seek to have the moral teaching of the Catholic Church become the criterion of constitutional
change or to have the principles of Catholic faith enshrined in civil
law."[16] Keeping to this line of church/state differentiation, when
legislation was enacted in 1985 extending the provisions of the contraception law, the joint statement of the Conference of Bishops
stressed that artificial contraception was in itself morally wrong.
Significantly, the hierarchy did not go so far as to declare that it
was thus morally wrong for legislators to enact such legislation.
Once again, however, a number of bishops, including Archbishop
Kevin McNamara of Dublin, departed from the collegial stance es-
pousing autonomy between civil law and Catholic morality and argued instead that legislators should not make a false distinction
between private and public morality but should dutifully respect
Catholic teaching.[17]

The hierarchy's continuing affirmation of the autonomy of
church and state represents a new departure for the Church. However, the ambivalence of the bishops in adhering to a noninterventionist stance, fueled, perhaps, by the conservatism of Pope John
Paul II,[18] demonstrates the inevitable tension in the Church as to its
role in contemporary moral debates. Given that both the pro-life
and contraception debates saw the Catholic hierarchy vacillating
between an interventionist and noninterventionist attitude, its disposition toward divorce was far from predictable. Would the
Church continue to adhere to the Vatican II model, or would it re-
vert to its traditional interventionist mode? After all, the divorce
referendum presented for the first time in history an opportunity
for the Irish people to vote in favor of legislation that was contrary

to Church teaching. How then would the Church defend its theological stance and what sorts of arguments would it use to present its traditional teaching in an increasingly secular society? Would it privilege the law of God or of science?

The same year (1985) that the bishops spoke with more than one voice on the liberalization of the contraception legislation, the hierarchy issued its definitive pastoral letter on marriage and the family, *Love Is for Life*. Here again the bishops reiterated the distinction between law and Catholic teaching. They stated: "The Catholic Church teaches that remarriage following divorce is impossible; but it does not follow from this alone that the laws of the State must embody this principle. Legislators have many considerations to bear in mind when they are drafting or enacting legislation. . . . We do not ask that Catholic doctrine as such be enshrined in law. We recognise that morality and civil law do not necessarily coincide."[19]

Similarly, in April 1986, when the bishops' delegation met with Garret FitzGerald for consultations about changes in the status of divorce, they reaffirmed their formal commitment to the distinction between law and Catholic morality.[20] Testifying to how far the position of the hierarchy on moral questions had come to deviate from its pre-Vatican II interventionist stance, the hierarchy's spokesman, Bishop Cassidy, emphasized that "the Taoiseach [prime minister] had not sought the advice of the Catholic bishops on whether or not to hold a referendum. . . . *Nor would the episcopal delegation give advice on a matter which was entirely a political decision*" [emphasis mine].[21]

This position was reiterated the day after the referendum was announced. Appearing on RTE's "Today Tonight," Bishop Cassidy was emphatic that "*the Church will not participate in the campaign* as such because I don't particularly like the word campaign. Because I think it has, well, unhappy overtones. It suggests that we will be holding public meetings and other platforms and knocking at doors" [emphasis mine].[22]

Challenged by the interviewer, John Bowman, that "there are public meetings every Sunday at which people assemble, i.e., Mass, and the priest speaks from the pulpit," Bishop Cassidy responded that "inevitably it would have to be part of pulpit preaching. The pulpit will be used but not abused." But while adhering to a separation of church and state, the hierarchy did not abrogate its pastoral role "to teach Catholics the truth of the faith, teach her members what Christ taught about marriage, and to teach her members the social and moral implications of any piece of legislation, including divorce. . . . We don't dictate to people. We have no right to dictate but we have no option but to teach."[23]

So, while Bishop Cassidy stated definitively that the bishops would not participate in the campaign, that politics is the domain of politicians, at the same time, he reaffirmed their pastoral duty to alert Catholics to the moral and social implications of divorce. From the outset, therefore, there was clearly a tension in the hierarchy's position between political nonintervention and pastoral teaching. To see how this tension was played out during the debate, let us turn first to the bishops.

Bishops

Three days after the announcement of the government's divorce proposals the four Irish archbishops—Thomas O'Fee of Armagh, Kevin McNamara of Dublin, Thomas Morris of Cashel, and Joseph Cunnane of Tuam—issued a preliminary statement on behalf of the hierarchy in which they reiterated the noninterventionist position. They welcomed some of the proposed changes, those, for instance, that were aimed at supporting marriage, even though they found it regrettable that "they are linked with the introduction of a divorce law."[24] Nonetheless, they continued their remarks by asserting that "the fundamental law of the State is a matter for the people and it is right that the people should have an opportunity to speak on a matter of this importance."

Later in the campaign, the hierarchy as a whole, after its seasonal episcopal meeting at Maynooth College on June 11, fifteen days prior to polling day, issued a joint statement on the referendum and the specific divorce proposals. In their statement, envisaged by the hierarchy as providing the framework for individual clerical preaching on the amendment, the bishops acknowledged that legislators "have to take account of the convictions of those who do not accept the teaching of the Catholic Church. . . . They have to try to give citizens the maximum freedom which is consistent with the common good." And, importantly, they emphasized.

that: "The ultimate decision rests with the people."[25] At a press conference after their meeting, Bishop Cassidy clarified that a Catholic with an informed conscience could vote "yes" to divorce. He explained that if Catholics made a "reflective, prayerful, conscientious decision"—one which would "take full account of all of the issues involved . . . it must take into account those who will be the inevitable casualties of divorce"[26]—they would not incur moral fault. When asked by a reporter if the Catholic church was not imposing its views of marriage on non-Catholics, Bishop Cassidy insisted that the Church did not want "a theocracy or government by bishops and priests."[27]

Thus throughout the debate there appeared to be an attempt by the hierarchy as a collectivity to adhere to the noninterventionist stance that it espoused on the amendment. Not all of the bishops agreed, however, that the question of making changes in the divorce law was "entirely a political decision." Once again, as in previous debates, individual bishops deviated from the collegial position. Four days after the hierarchy issued its collective statement acknowledging the right of Catholics to vote with good conscience in favor of divorce, the existence of internal dissension within the hierarchy came to the fore. Bishop Dominic Conway of Elphin diocese cautioned people against interpreting the hierarchy's statement "too loosely." He stressed that Catholics could not vote as they liked, but, because it was a "serious conscientious decision," people needed to ask if the decision was "in accordance with the law of God."[28] Following this, the hierarchy's spokesman, Bishop Cassidy, emphasized that the original collegial statement was emphatically against divorce and pointed out that recognition of the right to vote according to conscience must not obscure the fact that the bishops had offered "positive guidance" on divorce.[29]

Statements issued by a number of other bishops preceding polling day and read to diocesanal congregations further highlighted intra-Church ambiguity and tension. Archbishop McNamara of Dublin, the largest and most urban diocese, was the most vocal opponent of divorce. Throughout the debate he repeatedly stressed that the introduction of divorce legislation had no basis in Catholic social and moral doctrine and could not be reconciled with "God's plan for the family and society, or with God's 'no' to divorce."[30] Other bishops, similarly reflecting the strong association in Irish society between Catholic teaching and civil legislation, found it necessary to emphasize that voting in favor of divorce, or the subsequent introduction of divorce, was contrary to Catholic moral teaching. Bishop Diarmuid O'Sullivan of Kerry stressed that "civil divorce and remarriage were against the teachings of Christ . . . if divorce were introduced, the words 'until death do us part' would mean in civil law 'until divorce do us part.' "[31] Or, as more forcefully phrased by Bishop Jeremiah Newman of Limerick: "Catholic opposition to this measure rests fundamentally on the law of God the Creator."[32]

The tension among individual bishops on the amendment was clearly foreshadowed in *Love Is for Life,* the pastoral letter on marriage issued by the hierarchy in 1985. In that document there is continuous vacillation between compassionate understanding of the problems encountered in modern marriage and rigid adherence to the indissolubility of sacramental marriage. Typically, the bishops acknowledged the relational and personal or self-actualizing elements of marriage—"there are few things in life more beautiful and more exalting than the experience of love between man and woman. . . . [Married couples] grow into one another's personalities."[33] At the same time, however, in a more legalistic mode, the bishops insisted that "the compassion of Jesus cannot be invoked as a reason for departing from his teaching on divorce. . . . The bond uniting married couples is a sacramental bond, coming from God alone. . . . no human authority, no State or civil court can put this bond asunder."[34] Significantly, the bishops concluded *Love Is for Life* with a blessing in the words of St. Paul: "We wish you happiness; try to grow perfect. . . . May the God of peace make you perfect and holy,"[35] an exhortation that captures the essential tension in the Church's position. It wants people to be happy and at peace, but ceaselessly urges them toward perfection.

Theologians

Paralleling the tension among the bishops on divorce was dissension among theologians as to the correct disposition for a Catholic to take regarding divorce legislation. The hierarchy's noninterventionist stance toward the amendment found support among those Irish moral theologians who subscribe to the post-Vatican II principle of church/state autonomy and who take a personalist rather than a legalistic view of marriage. Seeing marriage as an ongoing dynamic relationship rather than as a rigid formal contract, they acknowledge the validity of a moral case for divorce. Theologians such as Sean Freyne of Trinity College invoked Vatican II's Declaration on Religious Freedom, applied it to the moral sphere, and argued that the Church, if it is to be a living, vibrant church, must "engage positively with the spirit of the age."[36] Thus, Vincent MacNamara, lecturer in Theology at Saint Patrick's College, Kiltegan, a missionary seminary, pointed out that "while there is a Catholic position on various matters of morality, there is not a Catholic position about the issue of enshrining them in law."[37]

Sharing this perspective, Maynooth moral theologian Patrick Hannon argued that committed Catholics have options other than necessarily opposing the introduction of divorce solely because "in the Catholic view the truth about marriage is that it cannot be dissolved."[38] Emphasizing that a Catholic who conscientiously decides to vote in favor of divorce is not disloyal to the teaching of the Catholic church,[39] he advised Catholics that when examining the issue of divorce legislation they "should refrain altogether from considering the problem in the light of . . . religious beliefs and should instead view it in terms of the requirements of . . . the freedom of the individual, and . . . the common good."[40]

Highlighting that it is not always self-evident what constitutes the social good, Gabriel Daly, lecturer in theology at Trinity College, noted that arguments based on the common good should not assume that there is a priori agreement on what this means; thus it should not be uncritically accepted that legal provision for divorce will not serve the common good.[41] In trying to serve the social good, the question becomes not whether the state should "in all circumstances refuse to grant a civil dissolution of marriage,"[42] but, as Patrick Hannon suggested, "how best is the State through legislation to cope with the fact that some marriages break down irretrievably having regard to all the values at stake?"[43]

In contrast to these views, Irish moral theologians who are opposed to the legislative introduction of divorce[44] grounded their objections in the "express statement of Jesus," that once a marriage is validly contracted no human power can dissolve it. As Denis O'Callaghan of Maynooth College suggested, divorce makes adultery respectable: "The Catholic Church teaches that the unions of divorcees are adulterous, adulterous because one or other party is already bound by marriage vows. Therefore the legislators who introduce divorce into society facilitate adultery and give it respectability."[45]

Arguing that it is fallacious to think there is a distinction between being a Christian in private belief and being a neutral public legislator, O'Callaghan stressed that legislators are morally responsible for the consequences of their decisions.[46] Accordingly, as Brian Kelly from Kimmage Manor, a seminary for the Holy Ghost fathers, has argued, it is not permissible for any Catholic, either as a legislator or as a voter, to "abstract from his faith when deciding on any concrete course of action whatever."[47] He posited that in any discussion of public morality a central question is "How will the proposed action contribute to, or hinder the realization of God's kingdom on earth?"[48] Following this perspective, therefore, Joseph Cremin of Maynooth maintained that Catholics are "duty bound" to vote "no" to divorce "if they wish to act as Catholics who are loyal to their Church and its teaching."[49] The question of introducing divorce becomes a "choice between the Christian vision of life and the secular humanist vision of life . . . A middle ground where we can honour our Christian principles and yet enact secularist laws is an illusion."[50] In short, as Vincent Twomey, lecturer in moral theology at Maynooth College, argued: "Indissolubility is not merely an ideal and certainly not an unattainable ideal. It is the necessary moral norm for marriage as discerned by the right understanding of human sexuality and confirmed as such by Our Lord Jesus Christ."[51]

Dissent within the Church

The divorce debate clearly demonstrated the dissension within the Church regarding morality and the roles of church and state in protecting Catholic moral standards. Despite the official collective pronouncements of the hierarchy declaring nonintervention, it is evident that in actuality the bishops' stance was more nuanced and equivocal. It is clear, in fact, as manifested by the contraception, pro-life, and divorce debates that the deviation of individual bishops from the hierarchy's collegial position has become a characteristic of the polemics surrounding the Church's position on socio-moral issues since it first issued its public acknowledgment of the autonomy between law and Catholic teaching.

In spite of its internal dissension, however, the hierarchy's position during the divorce debate was distinguished in two fundamental ways. One, as a collectivity, the hierarchy maintained a much more open stance on divorce during the campaign than that taken a few years later by the United States Catholic Bishops on abortion. Importantly, the Irish hierarchy, in accordance with post-Vatican II principles of church/state differentiation and religious freedom, acknowledged the right of Catholics in good conscience to vote in favor of divorce, whereas the American hierarchy adopted the more conservative attitude of the individual dissenting Irish bishops. In a resolution on abortion issued in November 1989, the U.S. bishops declared that "no Catholic can responsibly take a 'pro-choice' stand when the 'choice' in question involves the taking of innocent human life."[52]

Once the American bishops took this conservative collegial stance, some individual bishops acted on it by invoking their ordained power to refuse Catholic politicians who avowed a pro-choice position access to the sacraments. Bishop Leo Maher of San Diego, for instance, wrote to California State Assemblywoman Lucy Killea, informing her that she could not receive communion/the sacrament of the Eucharist because of her pro-choice stance, while the Catholic director of an abortion clinic in Texas, Rachel Vargas, was excommunicated by Bishop Rene Gracida of Corpus Christi.[53] More generally, John Cardinal O'Connor and auxiliary bishop Austin Vaughan, both of New York, warned politicians that they risked being excommunicated for their pro-choice positions.[54] In Ireland, the last and only time that politicians were barred from the sacraments was in the early 1920s during the civil war when treaty opponents engaged in violence against the new Irish state.

The second fundamental feature of the hierarchy's stance during the divorce campaign was that the hierarchy presented a much more complex and ambivalent stance than did the Anti-Divorce Campaign. Unlike the single issue, ad hoc ADC, the Church is not a homogeneous structure. It is, as the tension and equivocality in the Church's position illustrated, a complex institutional actor in Irish society. And while the nuances in the Church's approach to divorce may indeed have been facilitated by the fact that the ADC was expressing the essential Catholic moral position on divorce, on the other hand, its official stance accorded with the Church's own continuing acknowledgment of church/state differentiation and the autonomy of law from Catholic morality.

The dissension within the Church on these questions during the divorce campaign, however, remains interesting. What are we to make of the dissent? And, furthermore, what are we to make of the fact that the dissent was tolerated? After all, throughout its history, the Church as an institution has been known for its suppression of dissent and its censuring of bishops and theologians who depart from strict orthodoxy.

In the last twenty years the Vatican has prohibited moral theologians who have posited progressive interpretations of Church dogma from teaching theology in Catholic universities and seminaries, most notably, Hans Kung for his questioning of papal infallibility, and Charles Curran for his views on moral and sexual ethics. In 1990, Archbishop Rembert Weakland of Milwaukee, known for his compassionate approach to the politics of the abortion question, was prohibited by the Vatican from receiving an honorary degree from the University of Fribourg,[55] while more generally, the Vatican has also reaffirmed that theologians should not make public their disagreement with official Church teaching.[56]

What then do we make of the dissent within the Irish Church, a collegial body for which dissent is uncharacteristic, on divorce legislation? And how should we understand its acceptance of different episcopal interpretations on an issue that is fundamental to Catholic moral and social teaching?

The hierarchy's toleration of individual bishops who dissented from the official collegial line on the amendment becomes understandable when we take note of two points. One, the dissent within the Church was not over Church dogma on divorce but whether and how this teaching should be given expression in the civil legislation of Irish society. This issue of the relationship between law and morality, while an important one, is obviously less fundamental to the Church than questions of doctrine and dogma. Moreover, members of the Church hierarchy have individual autonomy. Although the bishops constitute an institutionalized collegial body committed to acting as such, at the same time each bishop has sufficient independence and jurisdictional license to articulate a personal interpretation of nondoctrinal questions, including one as controversial as the role of the Church in the modern world.

Secondly, the dissension, whether it was deliberate or not, fell on one side only. In the sociomoral debates we have discussed here, the individual statements that departed from the collective hierarchical position erred on the side of traditionalism. One cannot but wonder whether statements that might have taken a more progressive stance than the hierarchy on divorce—one, for instance, arguing that divorce may serve the common good—would have been equally tolerated. Giving voice to those who posited the more conservative view allowed the Church to equivocate: to officially embrace the modern view of the functional differentiation of church and state and of the autonomy of law and morality, and at the same time, to amplify the traditional position, an interpretation that, although deviating from Vatican II thinking, was, importantly, directly supportive of Catholic dogma on the morality of divorce.

More interesting, however, to the thesis of this book is the view that the inner dissension was the inevitable result of the Church's grappling with its new role in society. Trying to adhere to Vatican II principles of church/state differentiation and religious freedom and, at the same time, attempting to execute its pastoral duty to discuss the moral and social implications of divorce legislation, the hierarchy can be seen as struggling to find its rightful place in an important public moral debate. The dissension thus may be the inevitable outcome of what happens when a well-established institution tries to adopt a noninterventionist disposition, when for hundreds of years it has defined its sphere of competence as extending to the political process.

In trying to find new ways in which to present traditional doctrine, it is not so surprising that the Church's splitting of its role between the conflicting demands of pastoral obligations and secular expectations led to diverse perspectives being articulated. The multiplicity of voices within the Church signified the real tension and awkwardness that the Church encountered in trying to negotiate between teaching Catholic morality and simultaneously respecting the differentiated autonomy of church and state. Confronted with the challenge of maintaining the relevance of doctrinal belief in an increasingly secular world that privileges science rather than dogma, the Church, in its vacillation between an interventionist and noninterventionist stance, thus reproduced the individual human dilemma of "What shall we do and how shall we live?"

Despite the sincerity of the hierarchy's avowed commitment to nonintervention in politics, its pastoral duty to address the moral implications of legislation meant that the bishops necessarily intervened in the legislative process. The hierarchy's noninterventionist stance thus had a certain artificiality. Yet, in a sense, this was the only feasible way by which issues of church/state autonomy could be resolved. From the perspective of the Church, any resolution of the dilemma posed by the Church's intervention in public debates had to be artificial. The execution of its legitimate pastoral role meant that it could not but tread on the legislative process.

Secular Discourse

As we have seen, one noteworthy feature of the divorce debate from the vantage point of Church discourse was the nuanced manner of the bishops' arguments as they sought to maintain a noninterventionist stance in the campaign while simultaneously delineating Church opposition to divorce. But along with the subtlety of its discourse, the content of the message itself was significant. Adding to the complexity of the Church's stance on the amendment was the nature of its arguments. Unprecedented for the Irish hierarchy, it relied heavily on secular, empirical arguments—a this-worldly, sociological discourse—in articulating its opposition to divorce.

In the Mother and Child debate we saw that not only was there no acknowledgment by the bishops of church/state autonomy or intra-Church dissent on questions of law and morality, but, importantly, the arguments that the hierarchy used were purely religious. The bishops authoritatively declared what was morally and socially acceptable behavior, singularly based on Church teaching and without the support of empirically grounded reasons. That was the only legitimacy necessary.

But while the Church's use of sociological or empirically based arguments was unheard of thirty or forty years ago in Ireland, a significant shift has occurred since then. No longer do the bishops declare that it is a mortal sin to oppose the Church's social edicts.[57] Complementing the change in its active adherence to church/state differentiation, the hierarchy has increasingly appropriated scientific argumentation to bolster its theological and moral teaching.

The Church's use of empirically grounded arguments first appeared in its pastoral letter on abortion issued in 1975, *Human Life Is Sacred,* and reemerged in the 1985 contraception debate. Paying homage to the authority of secular reasoning, the bishops invoked "the experience of other countries" to support their argument that permissive contraception laws and the availability of abortion hasten a society's moral decline.[58] Thus, with regard to abortion, in 1975 the bishops argued that "since the Abortion Act came into force in Britain in 1967, the number of abortions notified has risen steadily year by year, going from 25,000 in 1968 to 170,000 in 1973. *The figures speak for themselves*" [emphasis mine].[59]

In the divorce debate the hierarchy used a combination of religious and secular arguments. Importantly, however, the debate saw the hierarchy's most extensive use to date of selective sociological evidence to defend its opposition to divorce. In fact, the debate clearly demonstrated a parallel process apparent in the Church's self-presentation whereby the more the Church endorses the separation of church and state, the more it uses secular discourse in presenting its teaching. While the hierarchy specifically stated that it would not be campaigning against the amendment, it was also the occasion during which the hierarchy most visibly framed the articulation of its opposition to divorce within a sociological discourse. Its substantial emphasis on empirical reasoning thus distinguished the divorce debate as a significant marker in the evolution of the Church's public response to controversial moral issues.

Unlike the pro-life amendment, which the bishops regarded as "a matter of great moral seriousness" and accordingly emphasized "the clear teaching of the Catholic Church on the sacredness of human life" and "the sacredness of human life, as created by God in his own image" in calling for its endorsement,[60] the bishops argued that the divorce amendment should be assessed in terms of its societal consequences. Repeatedly invoking empirical evidence documenting the negative effects of divorce, Bishop Joseph Cassidy, the hierarchy's spokesman, typically contended that "divorce has very serious consequences for society . . . once divorce is introduced it is very difficult to restrict it. . . . *Take a look at the evidence . . . take a look at the evidence. Take a look at the evidence in any country in the world.* In 1983 for instance in America, there were 2.4 million marriages and there were 1.2 million divorces. That's one out of two. In Great Britain at the moment the figure is running two out of every five" [emphasis mine].[61] And while from a moral standpoint the bishops emphasized the sacramental indissoluble nature of Christian marriage,[62] they related this to its social and institutional meaning. Thus: "Divorce legislation immediately upturns the whole legal tradition and introduces a completely new legal definition of marriage. Marriage as a lifelong union becomes legally obsolete. A commitment for life is replaced by a legal commitment to stay with one's spouse unless and until one decides otherwise."[63]

Paralleling the arguments of the ADC, the bishops also highlighted the negative consequences of divorce for women and children. They argued, for example, that "children are the chief casualties and victims of divorce. There is strong evidence from the United States and other countries that children of divorced parents are prey to a cluster of psychological and emotional problems and personality disorders. Even the danger of the divorce of their parents produces a host of disturbed behavior patterns among children."[64] With regard to women, they argued: "There are many indicators that divorce favours men rather than women. One California study found in 1982 that men experienced a 42 per cent improvement in their standard of living following divorce, while women experienced a 73 per cent loss. . . . Divorce obviously increases the number of one parent families."[65]

Related to these effects, the hierarchy also drew attention, as did the ADC, to the financial costs incurred by the state resulting from the increased prevalence of marital breakdown and divorce. Thus: "Marital breakdown in many countries has become a massive social and national problem. . . . Between 1971 and 1976 the number of one parent families in Britain rose from 570,000 to 750,000, an increase of 32 per cent. A recognised authority on population trends . . . has no hesitation in saying that this increase was 'due largely to the big increase in the number of divorced lone mothers'. . . . In Britain, there are now well over 800,000 one-parent families, with 1,500,000 dependent children. . . . These children are now costing the Exchequer more than 180,000,000 pounds."[66]

The Church's use of a sociological discourse during the divorce debate, therefore, even though it was used selectively and in combination with religious reasoning, represented a major, far-reaching departure for the Church. Recourse to secular argumentation extended the relevance of the discourse not just for Catholic believers but also to include skeptical believers and non-Catholics alike. Appropriating sociology to legitimate traditional Catholic dogma may well hold appeal for the more educated middle classes, some of whom, while committed to Catholicism, dismiss Catholic social teaching as being outdated and irrelevant for contemporary living.[67] Access to a modern this-worldly anti-divorce discourse, however, enables them to rationalize their own opposition to divorce.

But while the new use of secular arguments by the Church can be interpreted as a genuine effort on the part of the hierarchy to accommodate to the changing needs of its constituency, it is also hard at times not to construe these changes in rhetoric as inconsistent and artificially grafted. After all, as discussed in the case of the ADC, the use of secular arguments implies the acceptance of scientific canons of evidence. The principle of science means that you are open to all evidence, both positive and negative, and that you are prepared to abandon theories or views that run counter to the evidence. Taken to its logical conclusion, the use of secular dialogue implies that you are prepared to argue rationally, and, if science produces results, you are prepared to accept them.

And so the use by the Church of sociological evidence implies that the Church would be open to revise its stance and abandon its objections to divorce if the case provided by the social sciences was compelling enough. But is this the case? Would the hierarchy really be prepared to actively advocate divorce on the strength of sociological arguments running counter to its morally grounded views on the subject matter?

A truly comprehensive answer to this question is beyond the scope of this work, as it would lead us to issues of post-Vatican II theology. But what is true is that, even though some Irish theologians linked the question of divorce to pragmatic considerations of the greater or lesser evil, this is a minority view. As documented,

the bishops construe the issue of divorce as a fundamental dogma
of the Church, and therefore, not amenable to pragmatic reasoning.
While there are nuances in the bishops' approach to the question of
the relationship between Catholic teaching and civil law, this is a
separate issue. What is unequivocal is their moral position that
"for those who accept the teaching of the Catholic Church, divorce
with a right to remarry is not merely not permitted, it is impossible.
For marriage is a sacrament and the sacramental bond can not be
put asunder."[68] It is doubtful, therefore, that the hierarchy would
have followed its sociological arguments to their conclusion.

After all, the Church's use of secular discourse has to be seen
against the backdrop of the bishops' self-proclaimed privileged
knowledge when it comes to issues of morality. For, as the bishops
have declared: "When the Church states her moral principles . . .
she appeals ultimately to the truth and love which Christ brought
into the world. She takes the Divine Teacher as her model. . . . she
speaks with the confidence that the inner force of the Christian
message will, by God's grace, and because of its sheer truth and
rightness, find an answering echo in the heart of man."[69]

One way of contextualizing the Church's secular discourse is to
explore the Irish people's response to it. What is striking here is
that there was, essentially, no public discussion of the Church's sociological emphasis. The bishops' arguments were criticized by history professor John A. Murphy[70] and their competence in speaking
on the amendment was questioned by some in the media.[71] Nonetheless, the sociological claims of the hierarchy were not directly
challenged during the debate either by advocates of divorce, expert
sociologists, or the daily newspaper editorials. No one questioned
the Church's dual arguments nor spoke of the incompatibility between its use of dogma and empirical evidence.

One possible explanation for the reticence in engaging the hierarchy on its use of secular argumentation is that people were simply taken aback by the novelty of the Church's sociological
emphasis. As a relatively short debate with lots of issues being argued, the nine weeks of the divorce campaign may not have been
enough time in which to reflect on the implications of the bishops'
stance. Another interpretation, however, and probably a more compelling one, is that people never really took seriously the hierarchy's
this-worldly discourse, seeing it as lacking autonomy from the

Church's moral position. It may well be that the Church was developing a new, even more differentiated position on issues of law and morality, but people appeared to treat its nonreligious pronouncements as though they were still doctrinally grounded.

By not taking the hierarchy's secular discourse at its face value, however, the Irish lost an important opportunity to engage the bishops in rational dialogue on morality and the relationship between law and Catholic teaching. Without examining the hierarchy's reasoning and seeing what avenues this may have opened, we are left in doubt as to the true significance of the bishops' arguments and how the hierarchy would go about resolving the tension between the various strands of its position on divorce. In the absence of an attempt to probe critically the bishops' stance, the inconsistency between their theological and sociological reasoning could not be explored. The hierarchy's position thus remains ambiguous. What is unambiguous, however, is that, left unchallenged, the two strands in the Church's discourse, its sociological and theological arguments, combined in a forceful case against divorce and, importantly, legitimated and reinforced the parallel arguments of the ADC.

In sum, the Church emerges from the divorce debate as a complex evolving institution, one that maintains its adherence to fundamental points of dogma but also tries to grapple with contemporary issues. As argued in this chapter, the tension emanating from its commitment to the autonomy of church and state coupled with its pastoral obligation to speak on the moral and social implications of legislation, leads both to dissent within the Church and to the Church's embracing of strands of discourse that are not necessarily compatible.

CHAPTER SIX

Newspaper Editorial Opinion

The three Irish national daily newspapers, the *Irish Independent,* the *Irish Press,* and the *Irish Times,* were united in supporting the government's divorce proposals. The consensus of editorial opinion was that divorce was a necessary response to the problems associated with marital breakdown in Ireland.[1] This position was articulated by the newspapers throughout the campaign and seemed relatively uninfluenced by issues of circulation, economics, or readers' attitudes, since it was maintained even when it became evident that the pro-divorce case was losing popularity.

Of the three papers, it was the least surprising that the *Times* supported the introduction of divorce. Founded in 1860 as the voice of Irish Protestantism to distinguish its interests as separate not only from those of Irish Catholic nationalists but from British Protestants, today the *Times* articulates an essentially liberal and secular perspective on current issues and events. It is not aligned with any political party and it appeals mostly to urban, educated, and upper middle class readers. Among the editorial guidelines of the *Times* is the objective of promoting a society "free from all religious bias and discrimination" and one where "minority interests and divergent views" can be reasonably represented.[2]

It was thus in keeping with the *Times'* editorial policy that it favored the introduction of divorce. More surprising was the pro-divorce stance of the other newspapers, the *Independent* and the *Press.* The *Independent* has the largest circulation of all the papers and tends to espouse the ideology of big business and the free market.[3] It is generally perceived as being broadly supportive of Fine Gael and the interests of large farmers who, along with other rural and urban middle class readers, constitute a significant portion of its readership. In the case of the divorce amendment, however, it was evident that the *Independent* favored Garret FitzGerald and his divorce proposals over and against land and property

interests, which, opponents of divorce had argued, would be endangered if divorce was introduced.[4]

The *Press* was founded in 1931 by Eamon de Valera as the authentic voice of what he perceived to be the values of Irish nationalism. It remains partially in the control of the de Valera family and,
while independent of the Fianna Fail party, continues to be generally supportive of their policies. The *Press* appeals to rural readers,
particularly to small farmers and to older people.[5] Yet, it too presented arguments clearly favoring the introduction of divorce.

While the Irish print media are fairly homogeneous in the sense
that they all subscribe to the values of democracy and capitalism,
each of the newspapers appeals to a relatively distinct type of
reader. As a small and geographically dispersed media market, the
Irish newspaper industry encounters high costs of production and
distribution and faces sharp competition from the popularity of the
British tabloid papers in Ireland. Nevertheless, the Irish papers, par
ticularly the *Times*, maintain a strong commitment to quality journalism and emphasize political and economic news and commentary in preference to human interest and sensationalist coverage.[6]
As Conor Brady, an editor at the *Irish Times,* has suggested: "The
fortunes of Ireland's newspapers are the fortunes of Ireland itself.
Their interests are inextricably bound up with those of the nation."[7] Accordingly, the newspapers present themselves as speaking
on behalf of the social, economic, and political interests of the Irish,
and their editorial opinions fall within such ideological parameters.

Despite the economic and sociological constraints of the small
market they serve, the Irish newspapers have, at least since the
1950s, been characterized by a relatively strong tradition of professional independence among journalists and editors. This was evident not only during the divorce debate. Going back to the public
controversy stimulated by the Mother and Child issue, it was noted
at the time that while the then Protestant-owned *Times* criticized
the position adopted by the bishops, the two Catholic-owned daily
newspapers, the *Press* and the *Independent,* did not defend the
bishops' actions.[8]

In more recent times, the independence of the print media was
highlighted by the stance they took regarding questions of women's
equality. As with the divorce debate, they departed from traditional
values and espoused a greater recognition of the role of women in

Irish society. During the late 1960s, the three national newspapers instigated analysis of the unequal position of women in Ireland. Through special "women's pages," women editors and journalists provided critical information and commentary on discrimination against Irish women and led the way in challenging traditional assumptions that women had no role to play in the public sphere.

While the special focus on women was pioneered by the *Times*, it is noteworthy that the *Press*'s coverage of women's issues is regarded as having been the most revolutionary. One Irish feminist argues: "But it was the women's page of the Irish Press and its editor Mary Kenny which for most people revolutionised the concept of women's journalism in Ireland. After five years with the *Evening Standard* in London, Mary Kenny returned to Ireland in 1969 to be women's editor of the *Irish Press*. Two action-packed years of fearlessness in writing and speaking about what she considered to be the ills of Irish society made her a legend in her own time. Her name became synonymous with women's liberation in Ireland, the cause of women always being uppermost in her mind. She alienated herself from people in all sections of Irish society."[9] There is some evidence, therefore, that the print media in Ireland are not afraid of taking issue with popular beliefs and assumptions.

Let us now focus on the divorce debate and see how it was that the newspapers expressed their support for divorce. My concern is not with the newspapers' reporting of the campaign in general but with the editorial arguments that were articulated, including both formal editorials and opinion pieces by regular columnists.[10]

A variety of themes were evident in the editorial columns of the three newspapers. Some of the arguments put forward were directly supportive of the government's proposals; some were indirectly supportive insofar as they expressed general criticisms of the nature of Irish society and the strong association between law and Catholicism, whereas others directly challenged the arguments of the anti-divorce campaign.

Arguments Supportive of the Proposals

All of the newspapers acknowledged that divorce has negative consequences and would have some destabilizing effects on society, despite what, they pointed out, were the strong religious traditions in

Ireland and the emphasis on family values. At the same time, however, the papers framed divorce as a necessary response to the increasing pervasiveness of marital breakdown. The *Times* stated: "Of course divorce brings enormous problems. The question of where the children go, the mental distress and the emotional upset which the breakup of a parental home brings, are evident in all modern societies. There can be equivalent distress and mental consequences when marriages are held together purely out of economic necessity or fear."[11] The *Press* similarly wrote: "divorce, like surgery, is not something to be welcomed—it signals the formal end of what was once a warm, happy and loving relationship. . . . divorce inevitably leaves behind victims, bitterness and disillusionment. . . . To say all this, however, is not to deny that there now exists in this State a serious situation of marital breakdown."[12] In line with Garret FitzGerald's argument, therefore, the editorials saw divorce not as a libertarian civil right but in its broader societal context, as the most practical way to deal with a social problem of increasing magnitude.

Additionally, all of the papers stressed the restrictive nature of the specific proposals. They emphasized that the criteria for granting a divorce were sufficiently restrictive so as to attenuate some of the more negative consequences associated with "California style divorce." The *Press,* for example, which devoted the least amount of editorial opinion to the divorce amendment and was more reserved about the introduction of divorce than were the other papers, clearly saw the proposals as being restrictive. It pointed out that "the present proposal from the government at least has the merit of being limited and restrictive. . . . The proposals put forward by the government are restrictive, too restrictive some will claim. It is a good failing—at this stage, it is right that the intention should be to hasten slowly. The warning about opening the floodgates needs to be taken seriously. If there is to be divorce, then it should be available only when it is clear that a marriage has broken down beyond repair. A separation of five years would seem sufficient evidence of that."[13]

Moreover, as the campaign drew to a close, Tim Pat Coogan, the nationally known and well-respected editor of the *Press,* delineated in his weekly column personal reasons why he was going to vote in favor of the amendment. Here he emphasized the pervasiveness of the problem of marital breakdown, noting that "very few families in Ireland today, my own included, remain unaffected by this sadness," and he argued that "laws have to be changed sometimes to reflect changes in society."[14]

The *Times* and the *Independent* similarly stressed the limited and restrictive nature of the government proposals, and they argued that this restrictiveness would ensure that no major societal upheaval would ensue. The *Independent* argued: "This is an extremely limited form of divorce, but it is divorce nevertheless. It will certainly not open up the floodgates, because the conditions for obtaining a divorce are so severe that only a fraction of those looking for divorce will qualify."[15] In underscoring the restrictiveness of the proposals, the *Times* criticized the government's conservative approach but interpreted it as necessary to achieve the success of the amendment. It stated: "The Government may be criticised for taking an extremely conservative approach; for aiming to build the precise and very limited grounds for possible divorce into the Constitution itself. It is regrettable that the terms should be so tightly drawn but it may well turn out to have been necessary to do so in order to achieve the success of the referendum."[16]

Unlike the marginalization of Northern Ireland in the campaign arguments of the government and of the pro-divorce lobby as a whole, each of the newspapers accentuated the relevance of the future of Northern Ireland to the debate. They claimed that a refusal to legislate for divorce would constitute a mirror-image of the lack of compromise by the Protestant Northern Unionists and would be supportive of a partitionist attitude. As the *Times* argued: "The truth is that everything we do in the Republic matters in the North, and has its effects. . . . We have in so many ways disregarded the North in our law-making and in our general demeanor. . . . A duty lies on us all to think of others beyond our State boundaries. The decision in this referendum will undoubtedly influence people in the North of Ireland. . . . It is reasonably certain that a 'no' vote would cause Unionists to repeat with satisfaction their charge that Home Rule is Rome Rule."[17] According to the *Independent*, "The outcome of the referendum will also have a profound effect on our relationship with Northern Ireland. If we believe in peace and reconciliation . . . then we cannot escape the implications this has on the restructuring of our laws and on society."[18] Taking a sober view, the *Press* asked, "While no one would suggest that a Yes vote, however large, will persuade hardline Unionists to see the South in a new light, will rejection serve to bring the two parts of this island closer together, or push them further apart?"[19]

In directly advocating the introduction of divorce, therefore, the newspaper editorials stressed the practical necessity of some form of divorce, the restrictiveness of the proposals, and the significance of the referendum on North/South relations.

Irish Cultural Values

Spanning a broader perspective, the newspapers also commented on the strong Catholic tradition in Irish society, and they appealed to the Irish to embrace the values of tolerance and pluralism. Importantly, the editorials acknowledged that for many people the divorce question was as much religious as social. They highlighted, nonetheless, that it was not a "sectarian issue,"[20] nor was it a church/state clash, notwithstanding that the hierarchy differed from the government in their assessment of the social effects of divorce.[21] In this context, the soundness of Garret FitzGerald's Catholicism was emphasized. On polling day, the *Times* stated: "Today we are being asked to prove . . . that we can deal fairly with minority rights. In this case it is not a matter of Protestant versus Catholic, for it is evident that the great mass of those who advocate divorce are Catholics, and *led by a Taoiseach* [prime minister] *whose Catholicism has never been in doubt,* whose faith in the Irish people in all its manifestations is heartening" [emphasis mine].[22]

In what can be seen as a way of trying to persuade Catholics and others into the realization that Catholics could deal with the introduction of divorce, the *Times* variously pointed out that the majority of those who advocate divorce are Catholics; that Catholics in the North do not need legislation to keep them true to their faith; that conservative Catholics are willing to listen to minority voices; and that other Catholic nations have faced up to divorce.[23] It was conceded, nevertheless, that many Catholics would not be able to vote for something they believed to be socially and morally wrong.[24]

The *Independent* noted that "in this country many deputies [parliamentarians] have an allegiance to a Church which forbids divorce" and that "many members (but not all) of the Catholic

Church . . . will not be able to bring themselves to vote for a measure which they believe to be wrong—on moral and social
grounds."[25] It challenged the entitlement of the Catholic church,
however, "to bind the consciences of the legislators—in this case
the people themselves—in their determination of this issue." Accordingly, the *Independent* stated: "In our view, any Catholic
should be free to support these proposals without compromising
his or her conscience, and we sincerely hope that . . . the Catholic
bishops will make this absolutely clear."[26] When the hierarchy issued its collective official statement regarding the referendum in
mid-June, the editorials in the *Independent* and the *Press* did not
comment on it. The *Times*, however, accentuating a key point of
the hierarchy's argument, stressed that Catholics were free, in conscience, to vote "yes".[27]

Columnists at the *Times* were critical of the power wielded by
priests and bishops in influencing state legislation on divorce.
Among other points, it was argued that the "priests are the front-
line troops in preaching against the kind of change in the status of
marriage envisaged by the Government"[28] and that the Catholic
bishops want the state to "play sheepdog to the episcopal shep-
herds and their Catholic flock,"[29] while Mary Holland concluded
that "the Church's arguments, spoken and unspoken, will carry
considerable force."[30]

Nonetheless, the right of the hierarchy to articulate its social
and moral objections against divorce was accepted in the editorials as being reasonable, and the hierarchy was complimented for
how it conducted itself during the debate.[31] The *Times* even commended the bishops for the cogency of their arguments,[32] while at
the same time reminding them of the nonconfessional stance they
articulated on law and morality to the New Ireland Forum. The
Press and the *Independent* similarly commended the bishops for
the role they assumed, writing that "the Catholic Hierarchy can
take a great deal of credit for the measured manner in which they
have presented the Church's view, and other Churches too have
been constructive in their contributions to the debate,"[33] and that
"in a vigorous and fair campaign waged by the hierarchy, we feel
that the Church has discharged what it considers to be its moral
duty with scrupulous adherence to the commitment its bishops
gave . . . to the Forum."[34]

Maurice Hearne, a columnist who writes for the *Independent,* highlighted the Church's own distinction between matters of church and state, and he criticized his colleagues in the media for not giving greater coverage to statements by Church officials on this issue. Indeed, he was particularly critical of the "misguided libertarianism" of one of his co-columnists in the newspaper, Conor Cruise O'Brien, for his belief that religion should have no role in public affairs.[35] In a second piece, Hearne further articulated the theme of the appropriateness of the Church to pronounce on matters that are considered by it to have a moral dimension. At the same time, however, he pointed out the need for a separation between church and state and elaborated on the positive implications of guaranteeing religious freedom. Thus, Hearne argued that "the Catholic Church is the spiritual home of most of the people in this State. They have the right to expect that the laws which govern them will broadly reflect the standards of moral behavior expected of them. . . . [but] . . . we Catholics must realize that guaranteeing freedom of religion and freedom of conscience for all in our civil law guarantees our right to be Catholics, guarantees our right not to divorce and remarry if we believe that to be wrong. [Therefore] . . . in [voting yes] I am satisfied that I shall have in no way compromised either my conscience or my Catholicism. Perhaps I shall have enriched both."[36]

Related to this, the editorials defined the move to introduce divorce as a good thing, fitting this theme into a critical commentary on the nature of Irish society. Some of the social and cultural traits of the Irish came in for strong criticism, well summarized by one columnist's headline: "Tolerance is admirable but it is not our style."[37] The papers condemned the allegiance to a confessional ethic and the commitment of the Irish to being a "deviant" exception relative to other Western societies.

The newspapers differed in their emphasis on this theme—it was particularly evident in the *Times*—but an appeal to a national societal ideal was identifiable in all. In presenting this ideal, echoing a theme of the pro-divorce lobby, they questioned the extent to which democracy, realism, pluralism, tolerance, and maturity pervaded Irish society. The following excerpt from the *Times* typifies the kind of statements made in this context: "Growing up can bring strain and stress. So it is with the Republic as it faces a problem that most of our fellow European States have come to terms with: divorce. . . . No people can draw a curtain around itself and maintain a static society. To some extent we all have to live and move with the modern, complex and wicked world."[38]

The importance of according minority rights was also stressed. In this context the editorials emphasized that as a nation with a turbulent history and different religious traditions, Ireland should not continue to maintain a sectarian approach to divorce legislation. The *Independent*, for example, in a front page editorial on the day preceding polling day, stated, "we feel it is our duty to point out that we live in a pluralist nation, that our laws must reflect that pluralism and must not be seen to reflect only the confessional ethic of the majority in the socio-moral domain."[39]

Similarly, the *Times* and the *Press* exhorted the Irish people to show their true decency, generosity, and tolerance. The *Times* wrote, "It has been a decent State since its inception. . . . It has been a decent State and perhaps an innocent one. It has also been a generous State and the present referendum calls for an especial turn of generosity. It is time to free us from the concept that everyone must hold to one cultural or religious pattern."[40] The *Press* wondered, "will it be an Ireland of tolerance and generosity, ready to accommodate the differing views and traditions of people of all religions and none?. . . . is there not an obligation on all of us in the South to be seen to be scrupulous in according . . . respect and recognition of the rights of the minority in this jurisdiction?"[41]

Although these arguments were different from those discussed earlier in that they did not stress the practical need for divorce or the restrictiveness of the government proposals, they clearly supported change. Significantly, the editorials placed the move to introduce divorce in the context of praising the Irish for their generosity and decency. While the editorials in part castigated the Irish for their lack of tolerance, at the same time they spoke to feelings of grandiosity among the Irish, suggesting that they, indeed, are an exceptional people; exceptional not solely for prohibiting divorce but, more positively, for their record as a civilized nation. The message thus conveyed was that the Irish should demonstrate their civility by voting in favor of the amendment.

Arguments Challenging the Anti-Divorce Position

As well as articulating a range of both practical and idealistic arguments in favor of divorce, the editorials challenged the arguments invoked by opponents of divorce. They were critical of the negative social consequences that anti-divorce campaigners argued would follow its introduction. The *Times* stated: "So there was a Celtic Twilight all along; and some of the anti-divorce campaigners have been living in it. For they talk of a country—or rather a State—into which the introduction of divorce will bring a variety of hitherto non-existent evils. But if they looked at the real Ireland in the clear light of day they would see a society as prone to social ills as any other in Europe: poverty, crime, drug addiction, alcoholism, class divisions, urban dereliction. . . . All these problems have arisen, in a supposedly homogeneous, egalitarian society, governed by Christian moral principles. Has it occurred to those who like to moralise that the problems can only have been worsened by attempts to ignore them?"[42]

This editorial continued to undermine the anti-divorce position by arguing that the existing problem of marital breakdown and the absence of divorce already gives rise to many negative consequences. Thus: "On the specific question of marriage breakdown: it exists on a wide scale and must be faced up to. . . . We already have thousands of cases of 'divorce Irish style', where the man simply packs a suitcase, goes to England and, if he wishes, obtains a divorce there—leaving his unfortunate wife still legally married in Ireland. We have other thousands living in their own Celtic Twi light, in stable and fruitful unions unrecognised by Church or State, and beset by intense anxiety over such questions as property rights and the illegitimacy of their children."[43]

The *Press* pointed out that, other than divorce, there are many things the state can do to help marriages under threat, such as the provision of counseling and conciliation services and the amelioration of the family courts system. Nevertheless, echoing the arguments of the *Times,* it also asked: "But what can be done for those whose marriages have broken down irretrievably and where the partners have formed other relationships and new families are involved? Many of the victims of such breakdowns are in their twenties, with their whole lives ahead of them. Should they be refused the right to try to find happiness with another partner? Should those who have formed stable second unions be refused the right to legitimise their status and that of their children?"[44]

In particular, the editorials took issue with what the anti-divorce lobby argued would be the negative economic effects of divorce. Instead, the editorial line posited was that the economic consequences of divorce had to be an improvement over the existing financial circumstances of those whose marriages have broken down. The *Independent,* for example, argued that economic rights would be enhanced with divorce: "In view of the proposals being made [in regard to succession rights] it seems to us that the rights of the first family, far from being adversely affected will in fact be considerably enhanced when set against the existing circumstances of dependent spouses and children of marriages which have irretrievably broken down."[45] Similarly, the *Times* stated: "The specter of dispossession, while departed husbands invest new, young wives with the worldly goods due to a first wife and family, is a powerful argument. But how real is it? Can the circumstances of a divorced wife be any worse than so many of those who now suffer in the shadow of Irish marriages which have ceased to exist in all but name? Deserted wives whose husbands provide no maintenance for them while running a new home elsewhere; deserted husbands whose meagre wages are insufficient to provide adequately for young families; spouses who have calculatedly stripped whatever family assets exist."[46] Dick Walsh, the political editor of the *Times,* framed his criticisms more sharply. He argued: "To many of those who own property—and in most cases, the property is land—women are still the means by which the family line is maintained and, with it, the grip on the family's property. And where our old hunger for land has been succeeded by jealously guarded ownership, fear of losing the land is a potent weapon. The anti-divorce campaigners have seized it and are wielding it with zest. Playing on the fears of some and the greed of others, the argument is both crude and false."[47]

The editorials also criticized the anti-divorce campaigners' use of statistics in presenting their case. In particular, they challenged the comparative framework adopted by opponents of divorce, arguing that the societies compared were cultures dissimilar to Ireland. The *Independent,* for example, stated that "it is disingenuous to ignore the experience in Italy, an overwhelmingly Catholic country . . . where divorce rates have not risen. . . . In Spain, another Catholic country . . . the demand has been far less than anticipated. There has been a similar experience in Northern Ireland where divorce was introduced";[48] while the *Times* asked, "can anybody argue that Malta, Paraguay (ruled by a vicious dictator) and Argentina (where change is possible under the courageous new democratic Government) rank among the happiest countries?"[49]

Finally, although the editorial commentary did not focus specifically on women and the implications of divorce for their economic and social status, one editorial in the *Times*, remarking on the conduct of the divorce debate, noted that much of the terminology used was "demeaning of women, as if they were chattels."[50] John Healy, a columnist with the *Times*, similarly denounced opponents of divorce for targeting women's fears, noting, "Fifty-one per cent of the constituency are women. . . . They have been treated to the politics of fear. . . . It costs nothing to vote—and if there is a lingering doubt about the legal or financial effect of divorce a 'No' vote will put things beyond yea or nay. It protects their own marriages and self-interest is a strong interest."[51] In challenging the anti-divorce case, the editorials thus took issue with the sociological and economic thrust of the arguments articulated by opponents of divorce.

Evaluation of the Discourse

The preceding discussion is based on a comprehensive and exhaustive review of all twenty-eight editorials and twenty-three column pieces on the amendment featured in the national newspapers during the divorce debate. Although the fervor differed from one paper to another, the editorial opinion was consistently pro-divorce, from reaction on April 24 following the government's announcement of the referendum to polling day on June 26. This was true of the more urban and liberal *Irish Times*, and true for the *Press* and the *Independent*, which have a greater rural and more conservative readership.

It was also true of the daily provincial newspaper, the *Cork Examiner*, where a review of its seven editorials on the amendment found the paper acknowledging the restrictiveness of the proposals. While it did not call for the endorsement of the amendment, it emphasized the personal nature of the question and, calling for a reasoned debate, encouraged the electorate to make an informed decision on all aspects of the issue.[52] It was also significant that weekly provincial newspapers, even in electoral constituencies that overwhelmingly rejected the amendment, did not argue against divorce.[53]

It was clearly the case, therefore, that the national papers, all with a substantial rural readership, actively encouraged divorce and while the provincial press did not advocate it, neither did they actively oppose it. And although the national newspapers had ample opportunities to revise their editorial stance in favor of the status quo as opinion polls indicated declining support for divorce, none of them did so. In the case of the amendment, it was clear that the print media's commitment to societal change superseded economic considerations favoring an editorial line more in accordance with the traditional, and what turned out to be the majority, view.

In this context it is also important to remember that the national, Dublin-based newspapers were far from being out of touch with grassroots thinking and attitudes around the country. The urban/rural divide in Ireland, while an interesting one—it is more appropriately thought of roughly in terms of east of the Shannon (modern)/west of the Shannon (traditional)—is not similar to the urban-rural divisions characteristic of some other Western societies. In a country that, after all, has a population of only three and a half million people, the boundaries are less well defined, with a significant portion of those who reside in Dublin and other urban areas themselves coming from rural backgrounds. And, as voting trends on the amendment indicated, support for divorce was evenly split within Dublin as well as not showing a significant difference between urban (47 percent) and rural (42 percent) areas.[54]

While Dublin-based, each of the newspapers has a nationwide circulation, thus keeping them sensitive to the interests and concerns of various constituencies. One further way in which the national papers keep in touch with grassroots sentiment is through regular reports from around the country, demonstrated during the divorce debate by the *Times,* which featured reporters' "notebooks" detailing attitudes and opinions from different counties. Of all the papers, the one most closely linked with rural interests is the *Independent;* yet it was clearly committed to the passing of the amendment.

That the national newspapers argued in favor of divorce, therefore, confirms the expectation that in Ireland, as elsewhere, the mass media articulate a modern, secular voice.[55] The stance adopted by the newspapers on divorce highlights once again the complexity surrounding the divorce issue in Ireland. On the one hand, the Church and the Anti-Divorce Campaign argued against divorce substantially on sociological grounds, whereas the national print media unequivocally endorsed change. And, as we shall see in the next chapter, television, while it tried to probe both sets of arguments, inadvertently appeared to favor the status quo.

Clearly, the issue of the impact of the print media in shaping people's attitudes on the amendment is beyond the scope of this study. Although the duration of the debate saw a significant decrease in support for divorce, it may well be that more people would have voted against the amendment had the newspapers not adopted the unequivocal pro-divorce stance that they did. Any assessment of the influence of mass media on attitudinal or behavioral change has to take account of a wide range of dynamically interrelated variables and the sociohistorical context within which the media operates.

What is within the realm of this book, however, is an attempt to contextualize the arguments of the print media. How radical or nontraditional was the editorial stance? Were the editorials sufficiently forceful to shift moral opinion? Or was there something restrictive or constraining about the discourse that limited its power to convince people to go against Irish traditional values and vote for divorce?

One way of providing such a context for understanding the reach of the editorials is to consider the arguments articulated by one Irish columnist, Conor Cruise O'Brien. Internationally known writer, former government minister, self-declared agnostic, and divorced, O'Brien writes a weekly column for the *Independent.*[56] During the divorce campaign he wrote two forceful critiques of the Catholic hierarchy's position in which he directly challenged the legitimacy of the hierarchy to teach on the morality of marriage and divorce: "My basic objection to what you have to say is that you don't know what you're talking about. I don't mean that abusively

or petulantly; I mean it literally. You are a group of celibates, assuming yourselves to be authorities on married life: the condition
which you are unanimous in having rejected for yourselves
personally."[57] And O'Brien suggested further that the traditional
antipathy of the Church toward sexuality still existed even though
now it was disguised. He argued:

Traditionally, the attitude of the Irish Church towards sexuality has been
one of morose suspicion, bordering on downright hostility. It is no longer
a la mode for Churchmen to expose such feelings publicly, but the tradition was so strong, and entered so deeply into the training of the priest-
hood, that it would be surprising if the feelings associated with the
tradition had altogether vanished. Now in terms of that tradition, the sexual aspects of marriage are inherently distasteful: weaknesses of the flesh,
consequences of the Fall. . . . People don't talk like that anymore, do they?
No indeed, but the fact that they don't *talk* like that anymore doesn't necessarily mean that they have stopped feeling like that. I wonder what you
feel about that? You never tell us what you *feel*, of course, only what you
think and what you think we should think [emphasis his].[58]

In a later article, O'Brien raised questions about the waning
spiritual authority wielded by the hierarchy over Catholics regarding moral matters. Underpinning his remarks was the contention
that contrary to the Church's official position emanating from Vatican II, the Irish hierarchy did not recognize the autonomy of
church and state, did not believe in tolerating religious freedom,
and were under siege by modernity. O'Brien argued that the bishops were making recourse to the coercive apparatus of the state as
a way of enforcing Catholic morality. The thrust of his argument
was that "if Catholic lay people will not do your bidding, of their
own free will, they must be *made* to do your bidding, by the secular
courts and police. And if the civil and criminal laws of our Republic should be changed, in such a way that they cease to be available
for the enforcement of your particular teaching on divorce, then
you predict every manner of moral disaster for our people, helpless
as they will then apparently be before the inroads of the permissive
society" [emphasis his].[59]

O'Brien concluded by drawing parallels between the stance
adopted by the hierarchy during the divorce campaign to that of the
bishops regarding Charles Stewart Parnell's liaison and his fall

from political grace in the final years of the previous century: "Your tune still runs: 'You must decide according to your conscience. But we are the people who can tell you what your conscience ought to be telling you.' "[60]

As these quotations demonstrate, O'Brien sharply attacked the position of the hierarchy on divorce and, more fundamentally, challenged their legitimacy to have an informed opinion on marriage or to speak publicly on such matters. Clearly, however, the forcefulness of O'Brien's arguments would have been deflected by his maverick status in Irish society; they were the sorts of arguments the Irish people would have expected him to articulate.

But where O'Brien's remarks are very useful is in contextualizing the tone and arguments of the other editorial and column opinions. Whereas O'Brien's discourse was provocative and challenging, the other arguments were comparatively tame and deeply grounded in the prevailing cultural norms. His was the only opinion that was in any way radical; the kind of discourse we can imagine to have been forceful enough, if taken seriously, to shake deeply entrenched moral views. In comparison, the rest of the media analysis stayed firmly embedded within societal expectations and standards of what could be critiqued.

Yet, it is quite understandable that the editorials lacked the radical fervor of O'Brien. It is clearly not the role of the mainstream media to be revolutionary or to challenge existing social or cultural paradigms a la Cruise O'Brien. The jarring, provocative, and disturbing features of O'Brien's columns derived from his meta-analysis and criticism of Irish society and the Catholic church. But such meta-analysis is not what regular newspaper editorials are about. Media narratives crystalize, probe, and at times extend our views, but they rarely dismantle the values and meanings current in any given society. When we pick up a daily newspaper we do not expect to confront revolutionary fervor; we anticipate rather a continuation of "business as usual" or the "normalcy" of daily life. This clearly tempers the role of mass media as promoters of radical shifts in public opinion, particularly on such bedrock cultural issues as divorce. The arguments of O'Brien attest to that.

There is no doubt, however, as to the sincerity behind the editorials of the three national newspapers in arguing for the adoption of divorce and for rational evaluation of the arguments involved.

Their message of liberalism, pluralism, and modernity came across loud and clear. But what was the impact of this message? Did it sway people to vote for divorce? It may well have. Despite the rejection of the amendment, the editorials may have had some impact in preventing the level of support from slipping further. But they may also have had the opposite effect. Paradoxically, the print media's progressive pro-divorce message may have fostered complacency. Assuring people that they live in a modern, decent state where the secular media take a liberal stand on traditional moral issues, the editorial discourse may have served as a safety valve for the articulation of antitradition sentiment, but at the same time not been forceful or radical enough to challenge that tradition and thus tempt people into using the privacy of the polling booth to endorse change.

CHAPTER SEVEN

Television's Framing
of the Debate

In this chapter, I turn to television's coverage of the divorce debate, and specifically focus on RTE's preeminent current affairs program, "Today Tonight." I will bring to life some of the real drama and immediacy of the divorce debate and explore how it was that RTE dealt with the regulatory constraints of impartiality, objectivity, and fairness that apply in Ireland, as in other Western broadcast environments, to television's coverage of controversial public issues.[1]

Anchored by four well-known broadcasting personalities, all of whom have careers independent of the program,[2] "Today Tonight" programming, in the words of media sociologist, Mary Kelly, "has come to play an accepted and central role as a major source of information, comment and communication about Irish society."[3] Audience ratings consistently rank it as the most popular current affairs program on either radio or television, and its varied audience, drawn from all sectors of Irish society, frequently comprises one-third of all Irish households.[4]

Broadcast twice weekly for forty minutes during prime time, at 9:20 P.M. following the main evening news, "Today Tonight" provides critical, hard-hitting, investigative journalism on current political, economic, and social issues. In terms of scope, content, and format, it would be most closely approximated in American television by ABC's "Nightline with Ted Koppel," though "Today Tonight" has a more significant time slot and, with four anchors, less emphasis is placed on any single one of the individual interviewers. A typical "Today Tonight" program focuses on one or two current topics and is broadcast live without an audience from the television studios located at RTE's Dublin headquarters. It is usual for "Today Tonight" to present a background filmed report on the question at issue, followed by a panel discussion or one-to-one interviews representing partisan and expert opinion.

During the divorce campaign "Today Tonight" transmitted eight programs on the amendment, five of which were ranked in the top three most watched of all television programs for their respective broadcast week.[5] Beginning on April 23 with live transmission of FitzGerald's press conference announcing the referendum and separate studio interviews with William Binchy and Garret FitzGerald, until it concluded with a program that sought to elucidate nationwide popular opinion on divorce two days prior to the referendum (June 24), "Today Tonight" tried to present a variety of viewpoints on the issues raised by the amendment. Thus, departing from its usual format, two of the programs on "Today Tonight" were "outside broadcasts" featuring audience participation and a panel discussion on divorce, one broadcast from the Great Southern Hotel in Galway (June 3) and the other from the Imperial Hotel in Cork (June 10). Another program featured a discussion by a panel of politicians representing each of the parliamentary parties (May 22), while at the outset of the debate, the views of individual politicians and a number of committed partisans were presented (April 24).

Let us now turn to one such program and see how it was that "Today Tonight" broached the divorce question. What kinds of questions did the interviewers ask, and how did they cope with the responses offered? For my analysis, I focus in some depth on one "Today Tonight" program in which the two main protagonists, Garret FitzGerald and William Binchy, were interviewed.

On June 17, nine days prior to the referendum, "Today Tonight," in the fifth of its eight programs on the amendment, pitted the arguments of the two main players in the debate against one another, presenting separate one-to-one interviews with William Binchy and Garret FitzGerald.[6] Introducing the program, the authoritative voice of "Today Tonight" anchor/interviewer and political science professor, Brian Farrell, demarcated the oppositional poles on the amendment, stating in his customarily clipped tone: "William Binchy puts the case for a 'no' vote in next week's referendum. The Taoiseach, Dr. Garret FitzGerald, argues for a 'yes' vote to allow limited civil divorce."[7] After a brief summary of the background to the referendum, a reminder of the content of the government's specific divorce proposals, and an update on the latest opinion poll findings, John Bowman interviewed William Binchy and was followed by Brian Farrell interviewing Garret FitzGerald.

The Challenge to the Anti-Divorce Case

John Bowman, an interviewer with a self-assured manner, began the interview suggesting to William Binchy that the gap in support for the amendment, while narrowing, was still wide. Disagreeing, Binchy replied that, in addition to the polls, he found significant support for the anti-amendment position from his canvassing experience around the country, and he rejected Bowman's challenge: "Aren't you preaching to the converted at these meetings?" stating, "the trend is clearly downwards and the reason why that trend is going downwards is the arguments have been listened to. . . . This is not restrictive divorce and it will involve injustice to the first family." Then asked by John Bowman about "accusations of scaremongering," Binchy rejected this and elaborated that the practical economic implications of divorce were "indeed scary."

Importantly, Bowman then asked Binchy: "Are you against divorce itself absolutely or are you against the terms of this proposed amendment?" To this Binchy replied, "Well, if somebody can show me a divorce law that can work and adequately protect the first family and children, I would be in favour of it." In turn, Bowman challenged: "But does the present situation protect the first wife and family? The absence of law can also lead to a lack of protection for individuals." Responding, Binchy conceded the point but then, negating his hypothetical support for divorce that would protect women and children, went on to argue that "one thing that can be said about the present law is that marriage as a lifelong commitment is protected by it."

This point was pursued by John Bowman, who contended that lifelong marriage is not protected "since marriage doesn't last for a lot of people. Second liaisons are set up and second families are set up." Nonetheless, to this question and in the subsequent exchange, Binchy persisted: "Marriage as a lifelong commitment is protected by the law to this extent that those who enter marriage find that that commitment is supported in the area of maintenance payments . . . succession rights. If one has the right to remarry, that means the right to establish a second family, and the reality of life is that, unfortunately, if a man enters into a second family, his salary doesn't increase, doesn't double. It is just one salary . . . and the one salary has to cover two families."

BOWMAN: But that is so in the present situation where in the absence of legislation second liaisons are set up and the first spouse may be abandoned.

BINCHY: No, the whole point about the thrust of the present law is that the present law protects and aims to protect and actually seeks to protect the first wife in those circumstances by protecting her maintenance, her family home, and her succession rights . . .

BOWMAN: But what about the right of the wife who is abandoned now? She might also aspire to the right to remarry, to seek happiness in a second legitimate union. Aren't you denying, isn't your lobby denying her that right?

BINCHY: No. The situation is that those who marry in the sense of entering a lifelong commitment bind themselves by that commitment . . .

BOWMAN: But the marriage may have evaporated. It isn't there. The husband has gone off to Australia with another woman. Hasn't she the right to seek a second legal union?

BINCHY: Well if one says in isolation that a particular person, take a deserted wife . . . or indeed a battered wife . . . where our sympathy would go out in those circumstances to the individual concerned. One then has to say could one introduce a law that would cover that type of case and exclude the undeserving case where, let us say a deserting husband or a wife-battering husband sought a divorce. . . . in no country in the world has there ever been a successful attempt to separate what one could call deserving from undeserving cases. Even the notion of a deserving case is difficult to define. But the interesting thing to notice about this amendment is that whatever attempts one might imagine that could be made to distinguish between deserving and undeserving cases, this amendment doesn't do so at all. This amendment would allow a deserting husband, a wife battering husband, a husband who leaves the home for no good reason . . . the right to obtain a divorce and remarry against the wishes of the other spouse.

From this issue, Bowman then moved to the question of nullity (a civil or ecclesiastical procedure that renders an existing marriage void on the grounds that it was not validly contracted), but, here again, as the following dialogue demonstrates, Binchy gained the upper hand.

BOWMAN: What about nullity? Part of your group suggests that nullity is the answer. Now other critics say that nullity is a fiction, a cop-out. It suggests indeed to the children of that first liaison that they are illegitimate, that the marriage never existed.

BINCHY: Right. Well, of course, part of our group does not suggest that. Our position on nullity—

BOWMAN: Spokesmen for your group have suggested that.

BINCHY: No, John, that is not so. That has been said by those who are putting forward the divorce argument. That has not been said in fact by those on our side.

This exchange then led John Bowman to suggest that the ADC was in conflict with the Catholic church.

BOWMAN: So you're critical of the nullity provisions presently from the Catholic church?

BINCHY: Oh, no. That's not the position at all. There is such a concept as nullity which operates in respect of marriages that are invalid from the start. There is such a provision in Irish law, in State law . . .

Binchy's response here brought forth an elaborated exchange between Bowman and Binchy on the validity of the concept of nullity. The exchange clearly underscored the difficulties that "Today Tonight" interviewers had in penetrating Binchy's arguments and, in particular, the difficulties they encountered in adequately responding to his legal articulateness.

BOWMAN: In what sense are they invalid?   If the state recognizes that there was a marriage, however inadequate, however poor, there was a marriage.

BINCHY: Well John, if a brother married his sister because let's say in circumstances where a child was adopted and they weren't conscious of that, you would agree that the marriage was not a valid marriage. If a person aged fourteen years went into a marriage that marriage would not be a valid marriage.

BOWMAN: But it would have been a marriage. If they had children. . . . it would have been a marriage.

BINCHY: It would be a marriage but it wouldn't be a valid marriage in any country in the world . . .

BOWMAN: But there would be cases, for instance, where there was a marriage, where there was a Church annulment, where there were children and where there would be second liaisons blessed by the Church. Now in

Irish law such liaisons are bigamous. Shouldn't the Gardai [police] be in
there arresting them?

BINCHY: No. I think you wouldn't send the Gardai in there.

BOWMAN: But this is the anomaly of the present time.

BINCHY: No, the anomaly . . . I think you are misunderstanding really
the position on the ground in terms of nullity . . . There is widespread lack
of appreciation . . .

BOWMAN: But the grounds are different.

BINCHY: No, in fact, the grounds are not different. That's the interesting thing. There is complete misunderstanding about this . . .

Following this, John Bowman moved the discussion from his
earlier question about the difference between the Church and the
ADC on nullity to the similarities between the ADC and the Catholic
church on the question of divorce. Importantly, he asked Binchy
whether the ADC's view coincided with the Catholic church.

BOWMAN: In this campaign does your view coincide with that of the
Catholic hierarchy?

BINCHY: Well, I think the appropriate person to ask that to would be a
spokesman for the hierarchy. If I read the Catholic statement of last week
correctly, I think it is 100 percent against divorce on the social issues—

When Bowman persisted that the hierarchy also stated that Catholics could vote "yes" in good conscience, Binchy replied: "That's
true. That's on the theological question. . . . Now I, of course,
would only speak on the social data and the sociological area."
John Bowman continued, however, "Aren't the arguments that you
are putting forward in a way perfect for those who consider themselves Catholic and who want to have a lifelong marriage. . . . But
aren't you attempting to impose them on society at large?" to
which Binchy responded: "Well, I think that's a mistake, frankly,
John. I think that the arguments I would make against divorce and
the implications of this amendment are in terms of the injustice, the
clear injustice which it would cause to the first family. . . . *It has
nothing to do with religion*" [emphasis mine].

The interview then turned toward its conclusion with a discus-
sion of the implications of the defeat of the amendment on North-
South relations and to the role of the judiciary in granting divorce.
Again, with these questions, John Bowman was not able to match

Binchy's argumentative style and command of the issues, well illustrated by the authoritative way in which he dealt with Bowman's challenging questions on the North:

BOWMAN: But if you are moving towards a constitution which we would hope would be applicable to the whole island of Ireland, are you saying that there should be no divorce anywhere in Ireland?

BINCHY: No, absolutely not. That certainly would not be my position because—

BOWMAN: Why not?

BINCHY: Because I am not addressing the position north of the border. I am addressing the position in this country, which is south of the border, the twenty-six counties.

BOWMAN: But isn't that partitionist then?

BINCHY: No, John, because I will be quite happy to tell you my views on a united Ireland and how I would feel that the question of North/South relations would be resolved in the area of divorce. I'd be delighted to tell you my views but, that is, I would suggest to you, for another program.

BOWMAN: But the constitution has Article Two and Three in it as well. Surely our whole aspiration, our whole political culture, is also one to encompass Northern Ireland if possible?

BINCHY: Well, if you ask me my personal views on the question of North/South relations, the kind of society that I would like for North/South relations, I would like to see a federal society in this country in which the values of those in the North would be reflected in the laws of those in the North, the values of those in the South would be reflected in their laws. But that, I would suggest to you, is a comment on my view of the question of the unification of this country rather than the social question which is what the voters will be voting on on the twenty-sixth of June.

As demonstrated by this interview, Binchy was asked several challenging questions. Importantly, John Bowman attempted to explore the inconsistencies in the ADC's agenda—the current anomalies presented by Irish law and, more significantly, the denominational nature of the ADC's position. Binchy's preemptive style, however, and his tendency to redefine the questions asked did not allow for an in-depth exploration of these key issues. His forceful style was all the more significant given that he was featured on "Today Tonight" several times during the debate; unlike Garret FitzGerald, who was interviewed twice, Binchy appeared on five of the eight programs.

Binchy's presentational style was also adopted by other ADC spokespersons. Interviewing the ADC's Joe McCarroll, "Today Tonight" presenter Pat Kenny similarly tried to penetrate the ADC's objection to the principle of divorce. But, as with Binchy, McCarroll too was able to deflect attention to the economic effects of divorce.

KENNY: Let's get it quite clear. You're against any divorce, not just this bill as it is drawn up. . . . your basic point is no divorce no matter how tight, how restrictive, how conservative it might be.
McCARROLL: Yes, I believe that divorce is unjust. . . . The most important clause is the one that was included about adequate provision for women and children. . . . Now that means that if a person had no money at all when they divorced their wife and children. . . .[8]

In sum, the ADC's case as it was presented on "Today Tonight" appeared free of any ambiguity or contradiction. Forcefully reiterating a set of linear arguments, Binchy framed the anti-divorce position in simple, straightforward, concrete terms and was able to stifle any suggestion that it might be otherwise.

The Challenge to the Pro-Divorce Case

After a preliminary question to Garret FitzGerald, "Why do it [hold a referendum] and why now?" Brian Farrell, in his no-nonsense style, challenged FitzGerald that he had changed his mind regarding the effects of divorce. Farrell said, "You're saying to the Irish people vote 'yes,' and nine years ago . . . you were the person who said divorce is bad for children, you were saying that economically, biologically, women are vulnerable if you introduce divorce?" On the defensive, FitzGerald replied that he had been misquoted and what he had said was that, as is still the case: "I don't believe, contrary to other people whom I respect, that there is a civil right to divorce. I believe it is a social issue." Pursuing this issue, Farrell asked: "What about the argument of those who are opposed. . . . if you introduce divorce you change the whole nature of marriage for everybody, not just for that minority, and secondly, that in terms of these people you are not making their life necessarily any easier, because, after all, some may not want a divorce;

it may be forced upon them?" Responding, FitzGerald argued that "the situation is not quite" as depicted by Farrell. FitzGerald explained: "On the question of [divorce] being forced upon them, for a great majority of the people concerned the choice will either be a joint one or one acceptable to both. There will be some cases of disagreement, but remember, that in such cases the partner who doesn't want the divorce, who says the marriage hasn't failed, who believes that there is a chance of reconciliation will put that case to the judge. And unless the judge is satisfied that that partner is wrong and that the marriage has failed . . . constitutionally, a divorce cannot be given."

FitzGerald was then challenged by Farrell that divorce brings about negative economic effects. "What about," Farrell asked, "the rights of the first family, that after all, and there is evidence in virtually every country where divorces occur, families are hit, family finances are hit?" In reply, FitzGerald pointed out how the form of divorce proposed would improve the financial situation of wives and elaborated that it would give them economic compensation for their contribution to the marriage. Farrell further challenged him, saying, "But couldn't one argue that all of these extra protections could be brought in by legislation without ever introducing divorce?" FitzGerald replied that "there is a constitutional doubt about whether you can without changing the constitution."

The other question relating specifically to the proposals referred to their unrestrictiveness. "Your opponents have said that the failure line you are adopting in regard to divorce is less restrictive than that available anywhere else in the world. Floodgates?" Farrell asked. Responding that "well, of course, that's absolute nonsense," FitzGerald continued by emphasizing the restrictiveness of the divorce criteria. Farrell's rejoinder to FitzGerald's elaborated remarks, however, was to suggest the possibility of a loop-hole in the criteria as had been suggested by a prominent anti-divorce member of FitzGerald's cabinet. "What about the point of your cabinet colleague, Mr. Cooney, who says that couples will be coercing the courts to give them divorces?"

This exchange then facilitated an easy transition to a central theme highlighted by "Today Tonight" throughout its coverage of the debate, that of conflict and divisiveness. Underscoring the intracabinet and intraparty divisions regarding the amendment, Farrell, showing his academic sense for political intrigue, wondered, "But if, Taoiseach, if all your points of view are so reasonable, if they are so pervasive, if it's so much in the public interest, how come you could not persuade your cabinet colleagues in total to go along, and your party colleagues?" When FitzGerald responded that the question of divorce was one of individual conscience and therefore he accepted individual politicians' decision not to support the amendment, Farrell then challenged him, saying, "Isn't this whole referendum going to be, isn't it already, very divisive? Haven't we seen a division between urban and rural people, between young and old, between those who are very much committed to the concept of living in a society with an overwhelming Christian ethos and those who seek some other kind of society?" FitzGerald argued that the latter division didn't exist because "the vast majority of our people are practicing Christians who believe that marriage is indissoluble. But there is a minority of people who don't have that conviction that in special circumstances they should abstain from a further marriage. . . . And the question is are we willing to cater for that minority." In turn, Farrell suggested, "Wouldn't those who are opposed to your proposals say that what you are doing is you're catering for a very small minority by introducing divorce which will expand that minority?"

This exchange led to the accentuation of another theme of conflict, that of church/state divisions. FitzGerald invoked the experience of divorce in Northern Ireland in order to illustrate his point that the extent of divorce in a society depends on its values, saying, "It is true that in countries very unlike ours, countries where you do not have the vast majority of the people practicing Christians, certainly divorce has tended to expand . . . But . . . I know from ecclesiastical sources in the Roman Catholic church that while divorce exists in Northern Ireland and there are quite a large number of divorces, amongst Catholics in Northern Ireland there are very few divorces." Farrell, however, reminded FitzGerald, and the audience, that he was at odds on this point with the Irish Cardinal, Thomas O'Fee: "But you're quoting anonymous ecclesiastical sources. Now, the highest ecclesiastical source in the Roman Catholic church . . . tonight he is speaking about the plague of divorce. He's saying, here we are, four hundred and fifty years after the Roman Catholic church was prepared to break with England on the basis of a royal divorce, here you are proposing to introduce divorce."

In response, FitzGerald once again distinguished between his personal belief in indissoluble monogamy and his role as a legislator to cater to the needs of people in the society, an argument that was challenged by Farrell, who said, "Equally isn't there a balance of judgment here that some people would say that you may be seeking the pluralist society, you may end up with a permissive society?" FitzGerald rejected this claim by again referring to the low rate of divorce for Catholics in Northern Ireland and by emphasizing the restrictiveness of the divorce procedure being proposed. In response to this, Farrell alluded to another division in Irish society, an economically based one, pointing out, "But you've emphasized the difficulty, you've emphasized the involvement of the courts and the involvement of the lawyers. Doesn't that add up to saying that this is a procedure which really is for the middle classes, only for those who can afford it?" The interview concluded with Farrell raising the political impact of the possible defeat of the amendment and equating the outcome of the referendum with FitzGerald's political future. "If you lose this referendum," Farrell said, "what effect is that going to have on you politically? At least politically embarrassing?"

In this interview with FitzGerald we see the main themes that characterized "Today Tonight's" campaign coverage as the interviewers asked several questions challenging the validity of the pro-divorce case. As is well illustrated by this exchange, "Today Tonight" emphasized the divisiveness regarding divorce, the unrestrictiveness of the proposals, and their economic costs. It was the stress on conflict and divisiveness, however, that constituted the primary frame of the representation of the debate as presented by "Today Tonight."

Already in the first program broadcast on the referendum, John Bowman, interviewing FitzGerald, repeatedly confronted him with the "deep divisions" within his own party and highlighted this by quoting statements from dissenting members of his parliamentary party. Although FitzGerald reiterated his acceptance of party members deviating from support of the amendment on account of personal conscience, Bowman wondered about "party members campaigning against party policy" and stressed that during the campaign "we are going to get two Fine Gael voices."[9]

For its part, "Today Tonight" ensured that the audience/electorate did hear two Fine Gael voices during the campaign, featuring, for example, Alice Glenn, the outspoken dissenting Fine Gael parliamentarian on its second program.[10] In two further programs, Brian Farrell alluded to the "great deal of dithering on the part of Fine Gael" and the "division in the ranks of the government,"[11] while the final program preceding the referendum featured Fine Gael's chairperson being challenged by "Today Tonight" reporter, Gary Agnew, that his nonparticipation in the campaign was contrary to party policy.[12]

"Today Tonight" also emphasized interparty conflict. Again, in the first program, John Bowman suggested to FitzGerald that he could be accused of making a "political football" out of the divorce campaign by not trying to reach full agreement with Fianna Fail on the divorce proposals before publishing them.[13] In three subsequent programs, "Today Tonight" drew attention to the "neutral" strategy officially adopted by Fianna Fail, even though many of its spokespersons, including those who appeared on "Today Tonight," articulated an anti-divorce stance, thus reinforcing the interparty divisions on the amendment.[14] During one program, Brian Farrell commented on Fianna Fail's "strategic opposition" by observing that this was "the first time on any major issue facing the Irish people in the last fifty years that Fianna Fail did not have a position."[15]

Nevertheless, despite the official nonparticipation of Fianna Fail in the debate, "Today Tonight" included a Fianna Fail representative in three of its programs.[16] It is arguable, indeed, that "Today Tonight" legitimated the party's contradictory stance during the campaign by featuring Fianna Fail members on its anti-divorce panels. This strategy, however, further enabled "Today Tonight" to highlight the interparty political divisions as well as the conflicts between pro- and anti-divorce campaigners and thus fit well with its conflict motif.

Farrell's remarks to FitzGerald accentuating his deviation from Church officials on divorce also fit a broader pattern whereby "Today Tonight" emphasized the Church's opposition to the government's proposals and to divorce in general. From the beginning of the campaign, "Today Tonight" highlighted church/state divisiveness and the "confusion about the moral responsibility for conscientious, practicing Catholics" with regard to voting.[17] It was apparent that the underlying assumption of "Today Tonight" was the traditional view that the state should support and reinforce Church teaching. Accordingly, it presented the government's attempt to introduce divorce as oppositional to this.

At the government's press conference announcing the proposals, "Today Tonight" reporter Una Claffey asked FitzGerald whether he was aware of what role the Catholic church would assume in the campaign. When FitzGerald replied that it was a matter for the Church to express its theological and sociological views to its own members, Claffey pushed FitzGerald to know whether the Catholic church "will involve itself in an actual campaign against the referendum."[18] Later that same evening during his studio interview, FitzGerald was once again asked about the Church's involvement in the campaign. In a tone of challenging definitivity, John Bowman stated, "Presumably the Church will oppose this . . . they have said so from the beginning."[19]

In several programs, the "full, outright opposition of the Catholic Church" to the government's proposals was mentioned by "Today Tonight" interviewers,[20] with Pat Kenny insisting to pro-divorce activists that they would "be up against priests in the pulpit every Sunday pointing out the moral . . . and the sociological implications of divorce."[21] In its campaign review program, "Today Tonight" reiterated the points of difference between church and state on divorce. Featuring an excerpt from an interview with the hierarchy's spokesman, Bishop Cassidy, the hierarchy's mistrust of the proposals was once again underscored when Una Claffey asked, "The Taoiseach [FitzGerald] has given guarantees that [a liberalization of divorce criteria] will not be the case. Do you not accept that?" Bishop Cassidy replied, "I accept the word of the Taoiseach, but even the Taoiseach, with due respect, cannot foresee what a future Oireachtas [Parliament] will do."[22] The theme of church/state conflict thus extended the focus on political conflict, as "Today Tonight" appropriated the range of divisions brought to the fore by the amendment and used them to challenge the legitimacy of introducing divorce.

Evaluation of the Framing of the Debate

Although I have considered here just one episode of "Today Tonight," the exchanges quoted demonstrate rather compellingly that the hard-hitting journalism was intended to penetrate aggressively the arguments of the protagonists in the divorce campaign. In fact, "Today Tonight" probed the two sides much more than did the print media, who, despite their strong endorsement of divorce, did not refer to the inconsistencies in the anti-divorce discourse. Furthermore, it is clear that "Today Tonight" attempted to conduct itself in an impartial manner. And yet, it is also true that what resulted from the coverage was a reproduction of the conflict and inequalities that characterized the debate as a whole. Focusing on government dissent and highlighting pro-divorce fragmentation, "Today Tonight" underscored the narrow base of institutional support for the proposals and appeared to do more damage to the pro-divorce position, despite its efforts to maintain impartiality.

Why was this? What might account for the undermining of the pro-divorce case? To understand the framing of the debate by "Today Tonight" we have to consider the regulatory environment in which it operates. Like in other Western societies, broadcasters in Ireland are bound "in a matter of public controversy or a matter which is a source of current public debate, [that] information, news or a feature presented about it, is presented . . . objectively, impartially and . . . fair to all interests concerned."[23] This, essentially, enjoins broadcasters to provide a balanced representation of an inherently unbalanced reality.[24] During times of sensitive moral or political debate, precisely when feelings of partisanship run high among the public, broadcasters are constrained to represent impartially the questions at issue.

Obviously there are different ways of trying to achieve impartial coverage. One way is to adopt a behaviorist approach using objective criteria such as equal time and equal representation. Another way is to take a more subjective interpretation that aims to achieve greater substantive completeness by, for instance, allowing more time for more complex arguments. Throughout the debate, "Today Tonight" was acutely aware of its regulatory constraints—all the broadcasters with whom I spoke emphasized their professional commitment to fair coverage—and it sought to maintain impartiality in several ways.

Departing from its customary recourse to expert opinion, "Today Tonight" did not interview either a sociologist or an economist on any of its programs, despite the frequent references to sociological and economic data. And despite the frequent references to the post-divorce experience in England and America, neither was an "expert" familiar with the post-divorce experience or culture of either of these countries interviewed. When I discussed the absence of such interviews with "Today Tonight" personnel, anchor/presenter Brian Farrell stressed that in any campaign situation, "Today Tonight" has to be careful in ensuring that no "set-up" pieces are featured because they might indirectly favor one side.

For the same reason, no "human interest" background material was included, based, for instance, on personal experience of desertion or separation, nor was there a report documenting the social or economic consequences of marriage breakdown in Ireland.[25] "Today Tonight" thus excluded experts and background reports as a way of eliminating potential sources of bias in its coverage of the campaign, and it was also careful to balance pro-divorce politicians with those opposed to the amendment.[26]

But because such strict standards of impartiality were adhered to by "Today Tonight," the representation of the two cases came across very differently and very unequally. It is quite understandable that, when confronted with such a tense debate, "Today Tonight" favored objective, behaviorist standards, but this led to a variety of problems. "Today Tonight" immediately ran into the problem of an unequal number of groups and spokespersons on the two sides. Thus the same individual spokespersons from the ADC appeared more frequently than did individual pro-divorce spokespersons.

Reflecting the greater organizational cohesiveness of the ADC and the organizational differentiation of the pro-divorce lobby, William Binchy was featured on five programs, and a second anti-divorce spokesperson, Joe McCarroll, appeared on three, whereas key pro-divorce people such as Garret FitzGerald and DAG chairperson Jean Tansey each appeared on only two of the eight programs transmitted. Similarly, nobody from the DAG was interviewed in the television studio on a one-to-one basis, whereas from the ADC, William Binchy was interviewed alone twice and Joe McCarroll was featured alone once.[27] Consequently, while the audience was exposed to a range of different pro-divorce spokespersons, Binchy achieved greater exposure because of his repeated individual appearances on behalf of the ADC. This raises the possibility that Binchy's recurring appearances perhaps enhanced his legitimacy and identifiability with the audience, and thus strengthened the appeal of the anti-divorce message.

"Today Tonight" was itself concerned about Binchy's greater exposure. Midway through the campaign, as a senior broadcaster told me, "Today Tonight" "tired of interviewing Binchy," asked to interview Des Hanafin, the ADC chairman, instead. The ADC refused this request, and "Today Tonight" decided then not to feature any representative from the ADC on the planned program. Reviewed at a routine meeting of an RTE steering committee specifically established to monitor RTE's coverage of the campaign, the decision by "Today Tonight" was overruled. RTE executives feared that charges of partiality would be incurred if Binchy, as the ADC representative, had not been included on the same program that was to feature pro-divorce speakers. "Today Tonight" broadcasters, therefore, could not do anything to circumvent the ADC's decision to have Binchy as their primary spokesman, underscoring the fact that, during controversial debates, in addition to the routine organizational and economic constraints, broadcasters' professional autonomy is further curtailed by statutory regulations.[28]

More important, however, adoption of behavioral criteria by "Today Tonight" did not allow for differences in the unequal nature of the opposing arguments. Journalistic preoccupation with themes of conflict meant that "Today Tonight" found the government a much easier target than the ADC. The range of dissenting opinions openly acknowledged by FitzGerald facilitated broadcasters' use of frames of conflict. Constituting better—that is, more dramatic—television, "Today Tonight" interviewers were well able to exploit the divisiveness and conflict caused by the initiative to introduce divorce.[29]

The preference "Today Tonight" showed for themes of conflict was accentuated by the fact that in the case of the divorce campaign, FitzGerald was presenting something new; in arguing for the introduction of divorce, he was arguing for societal change. Binchy, on the other hand, was defending something that was already well embedded in the culture. In arguing for change, Fitz-Gerald put forward complex views, but, as abstract arguments, they were easier to dispute than the straightforward concrete arguments of William Binchy and the ADC. In sum, the pro-divorce discourse, both in terms of its complexity and its divisiveness, was much more accessible to dramatic journalism than was the anti-divorce case.

But if, as we have seen, behavioral criteria do not result in impartiality, then what can broadcasters do? If they use other means, such as incorporating expert analysis or allowing more time in which to flesh out complex arguments, they run a greater risk of incurring charges of partisanship from aggrieved parties. Therefore, while subjective criteria might be more successful in capturing the complexity of the issues raised by controversial debates, objective criteria have the advantage that they seem, at least on the surface, to be less biased. As we have seen with coverage of the divorce debate, however, using objective standards of impartiality, "Today Tonight" reproduced the conflicts and inequalities of the campaign and in doing so inadvertently undermined the pro-divorce case. Ultimately, the representation of the debate by "Today Tonight" shows the great dilemma that broadcasters encounter, no matter how great their commitment and sensitivity to impartiality and fairness, in presenting controversial issues in a substantively balanced manner. And, finally, it also illustrates the futility in thinking that legislative requirements mandating objectivity can override successfully the differentiated complexity and inequalities that inhere in controversial public issues.

CHAPTER EIGHT

Values in Tension

In modern times, from the secularization of marriage and the introduction of restrictive divorce to the no-fault divorce reforms of the 1960s, the evolving emphasis on marriage as a contract has paralleled economic rationalization. For most Western societies, there was a processual inevitability between changes in the economic, political, and moral domains. Cultural modernization was virtually an invisible process with a trend toward increasing secularization evident only retrospectively. Changes in modern divorce law, occurring in circumstances that did not require constitutional change and electoral approval, were achieved independent of public debate. Framed primarily by legal and political elites, there was little discussion of cultural considerations and implications.

Ireland, for various reasons, is different. Rather than liberalizing its marriage law, it took the opposite path and in 1937 proclaimed a constitutional ban on divorce. Ireland's cultural exceptionalism can be traced to its colonial history and the peripheralization of the Irish economy, which resulted in the retardation of Ireland's economic development. It also reflects the special status of the Catholic church in Ireland, which, as well as being a source of moral guidance, is a symbol of national identity. A "natural" progression, therefore, did not occur in Ireland between economic and cultural change. While economic rationalization took effect from the late 1950s, in the moral domain, Ireland in the late 1980s still resembled a traditional society as indicated by its prohibition of divorce and abortion and the restricted availability of contraception. Cultural change and the question of divorce thus became a matter of deliberate and self-conscious decision-making as the Irish sought to define what values they wished to privilege.

The idea behind this book has been that analysis of this deliberate engagement in moral discourse would provide insight into issues of values and morality in Ireland as well as into how people in general deal with morally charged questions. This is particularly so since the Irish debate took place in the 1980s, a moment in which the ideology of rationality and progress was being reevaluated and challenged in the West. Compelling claims that societal fragmentation is the twin of secularization and empirical findings locating the negative consequences of divorce pose a strong challenge to previously accepted assumptions regarding the desirability of modernity.[1] In this final chapter then, I will first summarize the central points that emerge from analysis of the Irish debate and conclude with some thoughts on the tension in values between tradition and modernity.

The Multifaceted Nature of the Discourse

Our exploration of the arguments put forward during the divorce debate has illustrated the complexity of the discourse and the various strands and frames of reference that surrounded discussion of this morally charged question. What stands out is the range of different perspectives that was articulated. This study reemphasizes the fact that in order to understand public dialogue one has to look at it from a variety of perspectives, since what is emphasized in the discourse and what is presented as being important changes as actors, venues, and stages change.

Newspaper editorials, for example, conveyed the idea that there was solid, widespread support for divorce. All three national dailies—the *Irish Independent*, the *Irish Press*, and the *Irish Times*—argued that divorce was a necessary response to the increasing incidence of marital breakdown, and, delineating numerous reasons why the amendment should pass, they urged their readers to vote "yes." Appealing to the decency of the Irish people, the editorials argued for a pluralist society that would recognize minority interests and, emphasizing the restrictiveness of the proposals, maintained that divorce would not cause societal upheaval.

Also favoring change, trade unionists and socialist politicians framed their support for divorce in the language of individual rights. Arguing that the right to divorce is a universal and basic civil right, they contended that its denial was undemocratic, discriminatory, and sectarian. This rights discourse on divorce was in many ways similar to the language of individual rights that pervades American moral debates. But unlike the situation in the United States, however, in Ireland a discourse of individual rights is not commonly used; it is found only in particular cultural pockets. Consequently, the notion of a "right to divorce" was, in fact, challenged by Garret FitzGerald and other prominent advocates of divorce, who instead framed the issue in the context of the social good. And while some pro-divorce activists referred to the right to divorce, it was never really a theme of their campaign. The inaccessibility of an individual rights discourse, however, severely restricted pro-divorce campaigners' ability to reach a broadly differentiated public with a commonly shared abstract notion that, once in use, has a very practical and well-understood meaning.

Ambiguities in the Church's stance during the debate gave lie to popular assumptions that the Catholic church bears all responsibility for the cultural peculiarities of the Irish. Not only did the bishops declare their official nonparticipation in the campaign, but they acknowledged that Catholics in good conscience could vote in favor of divorce. But, in expressing its pastoral views on the amendment, the hierarchy, in addition to its moral reasons, gave substantial emphasis to selective sociological data delineating the negative effects of divorce and thus framed its theological opposition to divorce within a secular framework. However, rather than being exploited by pro-divorce activists or the Irish people, the Church's secular voice went unchallenged during the campaign. The Church's dual arguments, therefore, paralleled and reinforced the ADC's practical, empirical arguments as well as the other-worldly, moral cum religious objections that shadowed the ADC's economic discourse.

One could well believe from some of their pronouncements that neither the Church nor Fianna Fail were involved in the debate at all. But, despite their official nonparticipation in the campaign, the contribution of both was significant. As well as articulating opposition to divorce, their well-organized respective "machines" provided an important campaign infrastructure to the canvassing efforts of the Anti-Divorce Campaign. It facilitated the communication of the anti-divorce message at the local grassroots level, allowing arguments against divorce to be differentially presented in view of the specific concerns and interests of the different communities.

Unlike the print media, which emphasized arguments in favor of divorce, television highlighted the crisis and conflict stimulated by the divorce initiative. Broadcasters' preferences for drama and dissension led "Today Tonight," a program renowned for its critical journalism, to emphasize the fragmentation in the pro-divorce ranks and the divisions within the government and Garret Fitz-Gerald's party on the amendment. Notwithstanding its efforts to maintain impartiality, "Today Tonight" reproduced the conflicts and inequalities of the campaign, and, adhering to a behaviorist interpretation of objectivity, its coverage seemed to undermine the pro-divorce case.

All of the players in the cast of the Irish divorce debate, therefore, presented various strands of argumentation, ones that were not always consistent or coherent. Neither simple or straightforward, the discourse included a range of nuanced and often polarized arguments.

Concrete Discourse about Lofty Issues

Since the 1940s and 1950s there has been a shift in the discourse used in sociomoral debates in Ireland. Most discernible in the statements of the Catholic hierarchy, post-Vatican II arguments have become more this-worldly, suggesting, perhaps, that people want to adopt a stand grounded in pragmatic reasoning rather than in faith or dogmatic assertion. This study affirms that while issues of values may be abstract and philosophical, arguments for and against them, especially those that appear to be effective, tend to be grounded in very concrete realities. The defeat of the divorce amendment may well be attributed to the ADC's this-worldly discourse—its mundane, prosaic, concrete arguments about economics and the basic flaws in the design of the proposed legislation. On the surface at least, the anti-divorce position was couched in concrete terms. Although that is not all that went on, the ADC, as we saw, emphasized the practical, down-to-earth consequences, not the moral or social philosophical implications of introducing divorce.

The ADC's pragmatic and economic arguments were solidly grounded in Irish cultural and historical realities, which have made economic security a priority concern. A central theme of Irish history, the motif of economic dispossession, is enhanced in contemporary times by the downturn in the Irish economy and the reemergence of unemployment and emigration as primary social problems. In emphasizing the economic costs of divorce, therefore, the ADC spoke to a basic cultural preoccupation with economic interests and to the status of married women, the majority of whom are economically dependent on marriage.

In contrast, FitzGerald's discourse was very different. Compared to Binchy's pragmatic economic discourse, FitzGerald's argument that divorce would serve the social good and his invocation of the notion of indissoluble monogamy sounded abstract, hollow, intellectual, and detached. The pro-divorce arguments were removed from everyday realities and, relative to those of the ADC, seemed downright esoteric. Unable to rely on an economic discourse or to use practical notions of individual rights, advocates of divorce were unable to demarcate clear-cut, straightforward reasons for favoring divorce. While FitzGerald's and the pro-divorce message as a whole was reasonable and well-intentioned, it lacked a concrete base. The sort of practical discourse that is necessary to challenge social and economic arrangements was demonstrated by trade unionists who couched the right to divorce in concrete terms comparable to the well-understood right to work.

Clearly, it would be an injustice to see the Irish divorce debate purely in terms of economic arguments, just as it would be an injustice to see the American abortion or Equal Rights Amendment (ERA) debates in a similar light. In all cases, questions of morality, traditional values, and gender relations are, to a greater or lesser extent, at issue. Nevertheless, what is true is that on the most apparent level, these debates in both Ireland and America had a very concrete character.

A central theme in the anti-divorce discourse was: Who benefits? Whose economic interests would divorce serve? The cultural and moral significance of introducing divorce legislation was, apparently, reduced to a question of economic allocation. Partly at issue in the ERA debate were concerns about the costs of paying women equal pay for equal work if the amendment was enacted. Those who opposed ratification wondered who would provide the additional money necessary if the gender wage differential was eliminated.[2] As with the Irish divorce debate, the ERA controversy raised fundamental questions about spousal economic responsibility and the dilemma of converting nonmonetary domestic activity into quantifiable rewards. Similarly, alongside arguments of individual rights to privacy and reproductive choice, one of the frameworks within which the ongoing American abortion debate is couched is whether taxpayers should underwrite the costs of abortion for low-income women.

The cost-benefit criteria of economic analysis thus seem to provide a readily accessible framework for dealing with the complexity of lofty moral principles. While I do not want to claim that moral issues become reduced to questions of material interests, yet, in a world that privileges rationality, nonmaterial values seem to be more easily dealt with if couched in economic language. The discourse of economics thus provides the contemporary metaphor for values.

Toleration of Contradictory Discourse

The debate on divorce was a heated one characterized by the exchange of polarized arguments. But, although argumentation was at the center of the debate, the main protagonists seemed willing to embrace quite contradictory strands of discourse. This was illustrated particularly well in the case of the arguments of the ADC and the Church. As I documented, both the ADC and the hierarchy relied heavily on secular reasoning, emphasizing the empirically grounded, negative economic and sociological consequences of divorce. But they also expressed adherence to the principle of lifelong marriage and thus opposed divorce on moral grounds.

To use a distinction borrowed from the philosopher of science Imro Lakatos,[3] it could be argued that the hard core objections of the ADC and the Church to divorce were grounded in moral and religious doctrine. These were the immutable objections, those not susceptible to argumentation. The positive heuristic used by the ADC and the Church, the set of reasons and arguments grounded in empirical evidence, was couched in the contingent realms of economics and sociology. On the basis of their dual approach, the ADC and the bishops were able to draw force from two powerful, yet in many ways antithetical, traditions—those of religion and social science—which when juxtaposed in the case of the divorce question were clearly in tension.

The logic entailed in the this-worldly social scientific argument is that if there is empirical evidence indicating that divorce has positive effects, then those who subscribe to the empirically grounded claims should be prepared to reevaluate their position. With economics as the criterion for assessing whether or not divorce should be introduced, the decision is one grounded in evidence and empiricism. Prior to knowing the evidence, one can equally favor or oppose divorce, but once new evidence becomes available this should have a significant bearing on one's disposition. The "tyranny of facts," for better or worse, is what empirical discourse is all about.

This is not so in the case of other-worldly, moral cum religious arguments. If you adhere to a moral position then whether you favor divorce or not becomes a matter of doctrine, and doctrine is not amenable to empirical validation. If morally one is opposed to divorce in principle, then no amount of empirical evidence in its favor can change your mind. Accordingly, regardless of how restrictive the form of divorce proposed or how few its guaranteed economic costs, those who oppose divorce in principle must oppose divorce in any form. It should be clear, therefore, that one cannot argue against divorce with any degree of consistency using both empirical and moral grounds. The two types of arguments, to paraphrase Ludwig Wittgenstein, pass one another by.[4]

What is of particular interest here is that the tension in the Church's and the ADC's strategy of drawing their arguments from two quite incompatible traditions was tolerated throughout the campaign. It was never addressed or challenged. Reflecting perhaps that the Irish were simply taken aback by the rationality of a discourse they expected to be primarily moral and dogmatic in character, this reticence may also say something important both about Irish society and, more generally, about the broader question of how issues of values are debated in modern societies. This tension and its acceptance also prefigures the tension between tradition and modernity, a theme to which I shall return in the second part of this chapter.

The case of the Irish. From the narrower Irish perspective it is important to note that, despite the tensions, economics and religion together constitute the bedrock of Irish culture. The Irish worldview invokes both traditions simultaneously. It is a view in which traditional other-worldly and modern this-worldly values are embraced side by side. This worldview and the tension it embodies is crystalized by the divorce debate itself. It is well illustrated by the fact that a divorce referendum was held in Ireland, that economic and practical arguments were the primary reasons articulated by those who opposed divorce, and that the amendment to introduce divorce was defeated. Highlighted by this is the dynamic, dialectical relationship, if you will, in the way in which religious and economic values hit off one another in Irish society but then coalesce into a unified force.[5]

The dialectical relationship between religion and economics is also illustrated by the predicament of the pro-divorce activists. Arguing for legislation that posed a possible challenge to the religious tradition impinged on their ability to use an economic discourse, since one validated the other. So, while the pro-divorce lobby used economic arguments, it did so cautiously and in defensive response to the economic arguments of its opponents. The ADC and the Church, on the other hand, were free to use economic arguments, because at the background to their economic objections to divorce was moral opposition to the legal dissolution of lifelong marriage.

The divorce debate also exemplifies how economic discourse becomes liberated from religious strains. This was illustrated in particular by the secular this-worldly arguments of the Catholic hierarchy during the debate. Rather than simply declaring their disapproval of legislation as they did in the 1940s and 1950s, the hierarchy attempted to adhere to a noninterventionist approach where issues of legislation and Catholic teaching interface, while at the same time expressing its views on the moral and social implications of the proposed changes. As we saw in the divorce debate, the hierarchy did not officially campaign against the introduction of divorce, but in executing their pastoral obligations the bishops articulated their reservations about the proposals. What was especially new and significant about the hierarchy's discourse was its heavy reliance on sociological and economic arguments. But the move toward secular arguments was only partial, however, since religion still appeared to be needed in the background to provide legitimation.

Reasoning about values in contemporary times. The tension between the two strands of discourse, religious and economic, is not a uniquely Irish phenomenon, although it may be accentuated in the case of the Irish. What is at issue here is the fundamental tension in how people argue about values, and this applies equally to

Ireland, the United States, and all other societies. Values are so fundamental and so deeply embedded that for the most part they are
not consciously acknowledged; they are the cultural bedrock or the
"givens" of a society.

Ultimately, values and moral or religious beliefs are beyond reason; "values are irrational, thus undebatable via rational discourse
and the rules of logic."[6] We cannot rate the greater validity of one
value compared to another. Normative judgment cannot be supported or refuted in accordance with scientific criteria. We can
evaluate the greater efficiency of the means used to achieve a certain end, but we cannot rationally decide whether the objective
itself is worthwhile. Science is meaningless, as Max Weber, following Tolstoy, told us, because "it gives no answer to the only question important for us: "What shall we do and how shall we live?"[7]

Nevertheless, we live in a world where reason is paramount. How
then can we defend and argue about values when they are "incomprehensible" and "rationally indefensible?"[8] One way to deal with
questions of values in a rational society is to split off the two
realms—the hard core of immutability from the positive heuristic of
contingency—and draw on both, but simultaneously keeping them
apart. This is what opponents of divorce did when they buttressed
the hard-core religious objection to divorce with the this-worldly
reasons of economics and sociology. This strategy clearly proved
very effective but at the price of inevitable contradiction or slippage.

What is significant, nonetheless, is that the Church and the ADC
were able to exploit the premium on rationality and empirical evidence in today's society by using empirical evidence to argue
against divorce. And, importantly, they used this secular discourse
to challenge the very idea of progress represented by rationality,
which, increasingly, is being challenged by the cumulating empirical evidence demonstrating the negative consequences of divorce
and other modern phenomena. Conservative groups, therefore,
who are committed to particular moral views can now draw on rational evidence to argue against the rationalization of morality.

The Call for Divorce as Paradigm Shift

While, for many Western societies, divorce was the result of an almost invisible process as cultural change followed on the heels of economic rationalization, this wasn't true of all European countries. Strongly Catholic societies similar to Ireland such as Italy, Spain, and Poland, all, unlike Ireland, have divorce but, significantly, in each case divorce was introduced in circumstances of societal upheaval.

Catholicism and the link between church and state has played a historically dominant role in Spanish politics,[9] with the Church and Catholicism serving as "the principal ideological pillars"[10] of General Franco's revolutionary fascist dictatorship. Conventions and laws restricting divorce and other rights, which had been established in the Church-backed 1881 civil code, reemerged during Franco's authoritarian rule.[11] After Franco's death in 1975, feminist-led campaigns for the reform of laws prohibiting contraception and divorce and, subsequently, abortion rights took hold.[12] Popular revolt against Franco, which was also, in part, a revolt against the Church-supported laws his regime enforced, helped facilitate the legalization of divorce in 1981 and, in 1985, abortion.

"Progressive" legislative changes in Poland also coincided with the disruption of a prevailing social and political order.[13] With the imposition of communism after the Second World War, the Catholic church became associated with an obsolete capitalist regime. Attendant on this, its teaching was also regarded as obsolete for the new social structure, at least by those in power, the Communist party elite, who introduced permissive divorce and abortion laws. And, paradoxically, although Poles used their Catholicism and participation in church ritual as a way of showing their defiance against the communist state, they also readily availed themselves of state-sponsored divorce and abortion services, even though this was contrary to Church teaching.[14]

The path taken by Italy is somewhat different. Until the 1970s when reforms took place, the laws in Italy regarding divorce, abortion, and contraception dated from the fascist period of the 1930s. An explanation of the "delay" in the occurrence of reform would seem to be grounded in the intricacies of Italian political culture. Notwithstanding Mussolini's exaltation of woman as heroine and the transmitter of Italian greatness, Fascist policy, supported by Church teaching, was aimed at repressing women's participation in the public sphere.[15] Italian women managed to remobilize in the late 1960s, however, at the same time that major economic changes were occurring in Italy and when demands for social reforms were taking place in other Western societies. Dissatisfaction with both the Left and the Right stimulated a vigorous Italian women's liberation movement, which supported the male-initiated divorce reforms and subsequently campaigned for changes in the abortion and rape laws.[16]

Despite strong and persistent opposition to such reforms by both the Church and the Christian Democratic party, the campaigns were ultimately successful, with the existing restrictive divorce law liberalized in 1974 and abortion legalized in 1978. Therefore, although religion is a highly salient force in Italian politics, it is tempered by Italians' opposition to the legislative remnants of Fascism and by their increasing disapproval of the alignment of the Church with the Christian Democratic party. Because Italians believe that one can simultaneously be both a "good Catholic" and a "good communist," popular majorities of "good Catholics" support ideas, such as divorce, that are opposed by the Church.[17]

It is clear from our very brief review that in each instance divorce was introduced into these Catholic countries in the wake of some societal disruption. The end of the Franco regime in Spain coincided with moves to legalize divorce and abortion, while the imposition of communism in Poland brought about the formal establishment of secular laws that were contrary to Church teaching. The changes in Italy, although they did not coincide with the end of Fascism, can be seen in part at least as opposition to its legislative and cultural remnants. One way in which to deal with a cultural lag, therefore, or with issues of traditional morality, is to effect change through a dramatic break with the existing authority structures represented either by the state or the church or both.

In *The Structure of Scientific Revolutions,* Thomas Kuhn introduced the notion of a paradigm, an overarching set of postulates that serve to provide meaning or a backdrop for ordinary scientific activity.[18] Since a paradigm provides an overarching worldview for the scientific community, it tends to remain stable until it is overthrown in scientific revolutionary time by an incommensurable rival. One way to appreciate the task of the pro-divorce forces in Ireland is to see them as promoting, to use Kuhn's terminology, a paradigmatic shift, and one in nonrevolutionary times to boot.

The attempt to introduce divorce in Ireland took place in a society in which the relationship between religion and politics, church, state, and people, was a remarkably integral one, representing a deeply grounded consensual affirmation of Ireland's identity as a special Catholic nation. Unlike the European Catholic countries, the Irish did not have to contend with internal revolutionary Fascist or Communist regimes, and their secession from British domination was achieved through rebellion rather than through revolutionary force.[19]

Moreover, unlike most other European countries, Ireland also was spared the tragedy of World War II.[20] Demonstrating, in part, its independence as a national entity distinct from Great Britain, Ireland remained neutral during the war.[21] But, while it was spared the atrocities of the war, it was also deprived of the postwar societal renewal and restructuring that took place. It did not get to experience the new social patterns that emerge during wartime: the expansion of women's entry to the paid labor force, for example, and the long-term implications of this both for women and for the society as a whole.[22] The changes that occurred in Ireland at this time—rural depopulation, for instance—were "grounded in the dynamics of the country's post-independence history,"[23] and thus lacked the same potential for sweeping societal change as that which the total disruption of war brings.

Comparing Ireland with other European Catholic countries, therefore, puts the Irish case in perspective and shows the enormity of the task faced by FitzGerald. It also highlights the inevitable tensions in the pro-divorce discourse. On the one hand, FitzGerald and other advocates of divorce had to be innovative, challenging, bold, and nontraditional, but on the other, they had to be concerned with issues of legitimation. They had to argue for change without the aid of a postrevolutionary new order. How do you argue for change and still maintain credibility within the prevailing structures of meaning and discourse? FitzGerald's attempts to push for a distinction between the public and private spheres and for a new definition of the social good, which was autonomous of Catholic morality, can be seen in this context.

In arguing for the introduction of divorce, its advocates were confronted with the problem of trying to gain legitimacy for an

agenda that directly challenged the tradition of Irish identity as
Catholic. The very idea of wanting to introduce divorce was contrary both to Catholic teaching on the indissolubility of marriage
and to cultural values that expect that Catholic teaching should be
supported by civil legislation. Advocates of divorce thus had to
convince the electorate that they were in fact, "good Catholics," as
FitzGerald tried to do from the outset by reiterating his personal
commitment to indissoluble monogamy, and, at the same time, they
had to convince people that it was necessary to break the ties between legislation and Catholic morality.

The problem and the enormity of the task of implementing a
shift in values, particularly in societies where it is not accompanied
by "upheaval," is, I hope, clear by now. While it is not impossible
to effect change in the absence of societal disruption caused by revolution, war, or some other force, it makes the task more complicated and enables various anomalies to develop.

Far from being a uniquely Irish problem, an even stronger case
of intracultural anomalies is provided by Switzerland. A much
more economically advanced society than Ireland, the economic
changes set in motion by its earlier industrialization enabled Switzerland to achieve a highly rationalized economy, internationally
distinguished for its banking and manufacturing power. Like Ireland, Switzerland is also a homogeneous society with a relatively
tranquil history that has precluded internal revolutionary wars or
participation in World War II. And just as Ireland can boast of being the "Island of Saints and Scholars," the Swiss pride themselves
on their special status as a center of global diplomacy.

It may not be accidental, therefore, that greatly at odds with its
economic and international reputation, the anomaly in Swiss society was in the domain of women's rights. Swiss women were not
allowed to vote at the Federation level until 1971 and in two regions could not vote at the cantonal level until as recently as
1988.[24] Similar problems and paradoxes are also illustrated by recent events in Belgium. Before Parliament's liberalization of the
1867 abortion law could be enacted, King Baudouin I, declaring
that he as a Catholic could not in good conscience sign legislation
permitting abortion, had to abdicate power for a day so that the
law could take effect without his signature.[25]

Comparative Issues

I will highlight two examples of cross-cultural issues, describing how the issue of women's rights is similarly framed in two different societies and how the Catholic church as an institution assumes different roles in different societal contexts. It is significant that, when it comes to questions of gender and women's rights, some of the Irish arguments find interesting parallels in the American context. Appeals to the notion of women as victims is a case in point, a theme evident in the Irish divorce debate and one that also characterizes contemporary American debates. Whether arguing against divorce, abortion, or women's equal participation in the workforce, all of which are seen by their opponents as exploitative of women, the rhetoric of women's victimization is invoked in attempts to restrict women's independent status and their liberation from domestic dependency. Argued by those who want to maintain traditional gender roles, and often with men in the vanguard, the motif of women's victimization is a sexist and exclusionary argument used to perpetuate the idea that women are naturally and inherently unsuited to certain social roles.

Whereas the women's victimization motif shows how the same arguments are used in Ireland and America, also of interest from a comparative perspective is the different response of the Catholic bishops in the two countries to relatively similar moral issues. The stance of the Irish bishops regarding divorce compared to the stance of the United States Catholic bishops on abortion shows how the same institution can behave differently in different countries. In spite of the strong tradition in America of a separation between the spheres of church and state, the American Catholic hierarchy appears of late to be taking a more interventionist approach with legislators on the abortion issue.[26]

For the first time in the history of Irish society the divorce amendment challenged a fundamental doctrinal position of the Catholic church, an institution accustomed to having its moral and social teaching enshrined in the constitution and laws of the Irish State. When confronted with this unprecedented occasion, the hierarchy stated that it would not campaign against divorce, and, while it expressed its sociological and theological objections to divorce, it also acknowledged the right of Catholics in good conscience to vote for the amendment. And while some bishops took a more conservative line than others, neither the electorate nor the politicians whose initiative it was to propose the amendment were in any way threatened that favoring divorce legislation would preclude them from being considered good Catholics.

Adopting a much more conservative stance than their Irish co-bishops, on abortion, American bishops not only warned Catholic politicians of the dangers of "going to Hell" for their pro-choice views but some went so far as to excommunicate Catholics for their position. The response of the American Catholic hierarchy to the ongoing abortion controversy may suggest that the Church as a whole is gradually becoming more conservative as the Vatican under Pope John Paul II seeks to recoup its greater centralized authority, which was attenuated somewhat in the wake of the Second Vatican Council and its acknowledgment of religious freedom. Or, it may simply illustrate that the American Church is different from the Irish one, thus underscoring the different forms the universal Catholic church assumes in different sociocultural contexts.

Limited Power of Media Regarding Moral Discourse

The dynamic processual relationship between mass media and readers or audiences is a complex one, and this seems to be especially the case when it comes to moral questions. In the case of the Irish divorce amendment, the national print media were all clearly and consistently pro-divorce. The only deviation was arguments by Conor Cruise O'Brien, someone who was even more radical than his media colleagues and provocative in pushing for change. Yet the majority of people voted against the amendment. While the shift in public opinion might have been greater had the newspapers not been so unequivocally in favor of change, the fact remains that the editorial arguments were not able to sustain the support for divorce evident at the outset of the campaign.

It is clear, however, that moral choices are qualitatively different from commodity choices. Moral claims are not as easily evaluated as consumer promotional claims. Worldviews and values that have been inculcated over generations are not likely to be influenced by a spate of media articles in the same way that opinions on political candidates or consumer goods might be. For one, where moral questions are concerned, people are more likely to seek guidance from traditional institutions such as church or family than from the mass media.[27] And even though the media articulates a secular and often critical perspective on cultural values and social relations, this is not, nor is it expected to be, a revolutionary voice. Encountering the same problem of legitimation as does any other group who wants to argue for change, the power of the media to inform moral choices clearly recedes in comparison to authoritative moral institutions such as the Church.

Importance of Communicative Style

We started our summary with the simple but important point that discourse on moral issues is complex and multifaceted. It has to be studied from a range of different perspectives in order that the various strands of argumentation put forward by different players and in different contexts can be appreciated. I want to end this summary with an equally simple and important observation. Discourse about moral values may well be lofty matter, but, nevertheless, its effectiveness and impact is still anchored in issues of primacy, charisma, exposure, and agency. Questions of legitimacy extend beyond the themes of discourse to the credibility, leadership, and self-definition of the speakers.

While as Prime Minister Garret FitzGerald had national legitimacy, in the circumstances of the divorce debate, arguing as he was to introduce divorce, his credibility was under question. In contrast, William Binchy, who until the divorce debate was a relatively unknown public figure, presented as the more compelling speaker. Aside from the nature of Binchy's discourse, his charisma was enhanced by the focus, clarity, and precision with which he articulated the ADC's arguments, compared to FitzGerald's seemingly abstract and convoluted manner.

The organization and choice of spokespersons is also important. This takes on increased significance in light of the reliance on television to act as a conduit of arguments to the public domain. From the Irish debate and television's representation of it using objective criteria of impartiality, it is clear that a group arguing for a particular agenda is at a greater advantage if it is represented by one primary spokesperson than by a range of speakers.

Also relevant to the successful outcome of a public campaign is the issue of who sets the agenda. The person or group who succeeds in taking the initiative in establishing the salient questions at issue as opposed to defending arguments put forward by others is, clearly, at an advantage. This was highlighted by the economic discourse of William Binchy and the ADC. Although the ADC was in the initial position of responding to the government's proposals, it, not Garret FitzGerald and the pro-divorce lobby, succeeded in framing what became the central questions in the debate. They were also able to set the agenda on television both with their economic discourse and with William Binchy's superior competence over the "Today Tonight" interviewers in discussing legal points.

Finally, who is perceived as agent and the importance of this in establishing control over the discourse was also demonstrated by the role of organized women in the debate and their absence as activist issue definers. Women cannot rely on others to present their interests but need to define and defend their interests themselves. With the pervasiveness of such themes as women's victimization and the ever-present threat of a backlash against women's independence, the importance of organized women counterarguing and affirming their emotional and intellectual strength assumes greater urgency. Women need to maintain constant vigilance against encroachments on their rights, because once they lose gained ground— as when reproductive laws are deliberalized, for instance—it becomes very difficult to reclaim lost rights. Unless women, whether they are Irish or American, engage actively in public discourse against encroachments on their autonomy, it is likely that the theme of women's victimization will continue to be argued by those who wish to maintain women's traditional status and the structures that uphold that dependence.

Tradition and Modernity

Viewing modern society as uniquely different from previous forms of social organization, sociologists have explained social change in terms of a linear process of societal development, arguing, as does Reinhard Bendix, that modernization "refers to all those social and political changes that accompanied industrialization in many countries of Western civilization. Among these are urbanization, changes in occupational structure, social mobility, development of education."[28] Clearly linking changes in social relations and the social structure to industrialization, economic rationalization, and economic progress, modernization theorists, although not Marxist in conceptualization or intent, suggested a direct, inevitable, and almost natural relationship between economic transformation and social development. Thus Neil Smelser defined the structural changes associated with economic development, saying, "with respect to technology, there is a change *from* simple and traditionalized techniques *toward* the application of scientific knowledge; . . . . In agriculture, the change is *from* subsistence farming *toward* commercial production of agricultural goods. . . . In ecological arrangements, there is movement *from* the farm and village *toward* urban centers" [emphasis in original].[29]

Openness to the spiral of changes stimulated by industrialization became the hallmark of modern societies and distinguished them from traditional societies, where, it was argued, economic, social, and cultural change was resisted because of the supremacy of religious, familial, and noncontractual values.[30] Although the degree of "economic backwardness" of a given country was recognized as significantly affecting the nature of its industrialization and subsequent development,[31] nevertheless, it was still maintained that as backward economies gradually embraced industrial technology, the constitution of their social structure and culture would converge along lines already established in other modern societies.[32]

In short, modernization theorists posited an immanent, atemporal pattern of synchrony between the economic and cultural spheres of society. Moreover, as well as postulating synchrony, the modernization thesis also had an evaluative component, conceptualizing modernization as desirable, progressive, and superior to traditional forms of social organization. With a premium placed on an ever-expanding rationality, tradition, or delayed modernization, was seen as retrograde.

From this perspective, Ireland presents as an interesting deviation and challenges the thesis of synchronic modernization. While it has a modern economic and social structure, traditional values continue to be institutionalized in the cultural sphere as demonstrated by the prohibition of divorce and abortion. Ireland, therefore, is an unevenly modernized society.[33] As a peripheralized colonial economy, it did not experience industrialization and did not undergo economic change when other Western societies were in the process of industrializing. Post-independence nationalist sentiments seeking economic self-sufficiency further retarded its economic development until the late 1950s, almost one hundred years later than the apex of industrialization in America and most of Western Europe. Nevertheless, once economic rationalization and growth did occur, in a relatively short span of time, Ireland, as discussed in chapter 2, presented many of the economic and social characteristics associated with modernization. Although comparatively poorer than other Western countries, it is a modern, economically developed, urbanized, consumer society with high levels of participation in education, politics, and mass media.

And yet, at the same time, directly challenging the synchrony postulated by the modernization thesis, Ireland's economic and social modernization is not matched by cultural modernization. Its prohibition of divorce and abortion and the affirmation of the values that their absence represents demarcates Ireland as a traditional society and highlights its cultural deviation from other Western countries. This is the interesting anomaly presented by Irish society and its continuing prohibition of divorce despite having a modern economic and social structure.

Modernization theorists, however, could well explain this puzzle by framing the absence of divorce as a historical lag.[34] It could be argued that just as Ireland experienced a lag in economic development relative to other Western societies, the absence of divorce may also be seen as a temporary setback. Delayed economic modernization may account for the attendant delay in cultural rationalization. In this reasoning, the absence of divorce is simply a cultural lag that will eventually be resolved once divorce is enacted. Indeed, it can be argued that the move to introduce divorce and the holding of the referendum in themselves constitute evidence that Ireland is on its way to full modernization and an integration of the economic and cultural spheres. It would be tempting then to conclude this book by equating the failure of the divorce referendum with a missed opportunity by the Irish to become a fully modernized society. On this view, the rejection of divorce is certainly aberrant and may be seen as regressive. Individual autonomy, a core value of modernity, is clearly restricted in Irish society.[35]

But we can imagine also another ending to our story. As we recall, an essential aspect to the modernization thesis was the assumption that increased rationality and progress was desirable if,
in fact, not synonymous. In light of this then, let us consider the
social reality that the Irish confronted as they deliberated on the
divorce question. Crucial here is the fact that the divorce referendum occurred in the late 1980s, a time when the desirability of modernity and the equation of rationality with true progress is
challenged with empirical evidence to the contrary.

In its range and scope, modernization, clearly, has brought many
unprecedented benefits for individuals and societies: economic
prosperity, progress in scientific and technological knowledge and
its impact on medical and other spheres, extensive participation in
education, increased leisure time, and appreciation of nonmaterial
values and quality of life issues. At the same time, however, the cu-
mulation of evidence documenting a broad range of societal problems, including ever-widening gaps in economic equality both
within and between nations and ecological disruption and environ-
mental damage, challenges the superiority of instrumental reason,
the hallmark of modernization.

Confronted with the mixed consequences resulting from an emphasis on economic growth and individual autonomy, the implications of modernity are being subjected to greater critical scrutiny.
Unlike at the turn of the century or in the 1960s when the more
progressive divorce legislation was introduced, what was particularly relevant to the Irish divorce debate was evidence that the
stress on progress and rationality has led to anomie, fragmentation,
meaninglessness, and the absence of clear, communal values.

Importantly then, because of the lateness of Ireland's modernization relative to other Western societies, its deliberations on divorce occurred in a context in which the effects of modernization
were already known.[36] Whereas Ireland's economic development
began at a time when the "positive" characteristics and effects of
economic modernization were already well in place in other Western societies, evidenced by high standards of living, disposable
personal income, and the glamour and sophistication of a consumer lifestyle, the divorce amendment was introduced at a time
when some of the "negative" effects of divorce have been documented and the premises of cultural modernization as a whole are

being challenged. For all its creative potential, modernity and the autonomy of the individual has clearly come at the price of societal fragmentation and "human dislocation and suffering."[37] To some, divorce may not seem such a good thing, or, at best, it may seem that its overall value to individuals and society is ambiguous.

This then is the context in which the Irish confronted the question of whether or not to introduce divorce and complete the process of societal modernization. While strands of anti-modernism have always been a feature of modernizing societies,[38] the context and timing of the referendum gave the Irish good grounds for being wary of divorce, the exemplar of cultural modernization, "as a threat to an existing pattern of meanings and values."[39]

Given this background, therefore, Irish opposition to divorce may be seen not as a temporary lapse on the road to fully fledged modernization but rather as an innovative, postmodern way of dealing with the threat of anomie and cultural fragmentation. In the same way that postmodern architecture combines stylistic elements of various eras, the Irish rejection of divorce may also be seen as an attempt to create an alternative solution, one that by selectively upholding traditional values alongside economic and social modernization sustains at the same time the coherence to life associated with tradition. Rather than introducing divorce and then having to confront its costs, the Irish, it could be argued, chose, more or less consciously, to formally retain the values underpinning lifelong marriage. Not convinced about the benefits of modernity, progress, and rationality, in this scenario, that the Irish voted against divorce can be construed as a more or less deliberate attempt to preserve the cohesiveness of private and social life.[40]

On this second view, the "Irish solution" to the issue of divorce with its forged juxtaposition of culturally disparate elements may be seen as anticipating things to come. As other societies grapple with the conflicts, tensions, and the legacy of modernity, they too may find that some sort of previously unanticipated mix of economic rationality alongside the retrieval of the remnants of tradition may prove to be the response necessary to stave off increased public dissatisfaction with the costs of rationalization.

Whether we construe the divorce debate from a modernist perspective as a lost opportunity by the Irish to integrate economic and cultural development and achieve parity with the rest of the

Western world by introducing divorce or, in postmodern terms, as an innovative way of preempting societal anomie, ultimately, debates about moral issues do not occur in a vacuum. Whichever way we construe the debate, its outcome had a direct and tangible effect, whether positive or negative, on the lives of all the Irish people. While the retention of certain traditional values might provide solace and comfort for those at the center, the majority who oppose divorce and value the conflation of private and public morality, for those at the margins—in particular, those who seek legal recognition of a failed marriage or of a new relationship, or those who cannot afford a costly legal separation or foreign divorce—it is the retention of an obsolete, regressive, and essentially hurtful way of dealing with marital breakdown. But such a trade-off, perhaps, is inevitable when debates focus on the negative consequences of modernization, without, at the same time, fully confronting the negative consequences of tradition.

Marriage Breakdown in Ireland

The constitutional ban on divorce in Ireland has not prevented marriage breakdown. Significant numbers of people experience the breakdown of their marriage even though, in keeping with the official view of the sanctity of marriage and the family, this was not officially recorded for many years. For the first time in the history of census taking in Ireland, the 1986 census gathered information on the de facto as opposed to the de jure status of the ever-married population. Statistics showed that approximately 37,245 people were separated, which represented about 6 percent of the total number of marriages contracted. More women (22,607) than men (14,638) reported being separated, and the majority of separated women were between the ages of thirty-five and forty-four and live in the Dublin area. (*Census '86: Summary Population Report Ireland*, vii-viii)

Foreign Divorce

In the absence of Ireland's own divorce provision, there is some recognition of foreign divorces. Prior to legislation enacted in 1986 (the Domicile and Recognition of Foreign Divorces Act), a wife's domicile was dependent on her husband's, and consequently a foreign divorce was only recognized if both spouses were domiciled in the country in which it was granted. The current situation means that a foreign divorce is recognized if either spouse was domiciled in the country in which it was granted.

Legal Separation and/or Civil Annulment

Couples whose marriages break down and whose economic circumstances allow them may make recourse to the Irish judicial system in order to secure a judicial separation or a civil annulment or, independently of the courts, to make a private separation agreement. A judicial separation, was, up until revisions in the law in 1989, fault based, requiring that the defendant be guilty of either adultery, cruelty, or unnatural practices. A judicial separation removes the obligation on the plaintiff to live with his/her spouse, but it does not dissolve the marriage, and consequently neither party is free to remarry. Importantly, the Judicial Separation and Family Law Reform Act, 1989, permits the equitable division of the separating couple's assets, including the family farm, at the time of separation.

With a decree of nullity, a marriage is rendered void under the grounds of lack of capacity, nonobservance of formalities, and absence of consent at the time of, or antecedent to, the marriage. Events and experiences after the marriage are relevant only if they can be shown to point to defects that were already present at the time of the marriage. If a marriage is annulled, the individuals involved are treated as if they were never married. Accordingly they are free to remarry, the parties lose succession and maintenance rights regarding each other's estates, and, prior to the enactment of the Status of Children Act, 1987, children of annulled marriages were declared illegitimate thus losing any legal entitlement to their parents' estate.

In addition to the options of judicial separation and civil nullity, spouses who choose to separate also have the option of making a separation agreement, which is legally valid without the expense of going to court. Such an agreement does not affect the validity of the marriage, and the separated parties are not free to remarry. Few whose marriages break down, however, apply either for a judicial separation or for a civil nullity. Between 1973 and 1983, for example, there were 339 petitions to the High Court for a judicial separation and 145 nullity petitions (see *Report of the Joint Committee on Marriage Breakdown*, 132-33).

Ecclesiastical Annulment

More popular than a legal separation or a civil annulment is for couples to seek an ecclesiastical annulment. These are granted by a tribunal of the Catholic church under canon law. An annulment may be granted under one of three broad categories: (1) because of an impediment, such as impotence, because of having been underage at marriage, or because of the existence of a previous valid marriage; (2) because the proper formalities were not observed—the marriage did not take place before a properly authorized priest in the presence of two witnesses; or (3) because the consent was defective (Catholic Press and Information Office, 1986). A church annulment says that a valid marriage between the couple never took place— the marriage is nullified—and, accordingly, those granted a Church annulment are then free to (re)marry within the church. In many cases, however—up to three-quarters—the nullity decrees issued by the Church are subject to a "vetitum" which prohibits one or both of the partners from (re)marriage. The Catholic hierarchy estimates that less than one half of one percent of all marriages in the Catholic church in Ireland are declared invalid. Between 1976 and 1984 there were 5,885 applications for ecclesiastical annulments, of which 828 were granted. (ibid., 11-12). Nullity applications are clearly increasing. For the statistical year November 1, 1985 to October 31, 1986, the total number of applications for nullity received was 733. Of a total of 189 decisions, 164 cases were given a nullity decree and 25 were denied. In 163 cases a "vetitum" was imposed on one or both parties (see *Irish Catholic Directory,* 1987, 349). For the statistical year November 1, 1989 to October 31, 1990, the total number of applications for nullity received was 1,043. Of a total of 250 decisions, 216 were given a decree and 34 were denied. In 192 cases a "vetitum" was imposed on one or both parties (see *Irish Catholic Directory,* 1991, 351). Many of the nullity applications submitted are not admitted to a formal investigation because they are subsequently withdrawn, because they lack a prima facie ground of nullity, or because the tribunal may lack legal competence to try the case.

The regulation of marriage in Irish society gives rise to an interesting anomaly related to the fact that more Church annulments than civil annulments are granted. Some of those who receive a Church annulment but who do not have a civil annulment subsequently (re)marry in Church. In Irish law a marriage that takes place before a priest or pastor is considered a legally valid civil marriage. Accordingly, individuals who have received a Church annulment and who (re)marry in Church simultaneously contract a valid civil marriage that is recognized by the state. But because the state does not recognize church annulments, one or both of the partners, as the case may be, by contracting a second civil marriage, commit bigamy. The state tends to turn a blind eye to this, however, by not prosecuting the guilty parties. Nevertheless, from a legal point of view, the state recognizes only the first marriage of the parties to the second marriage. Consequently, the partners in the second marriage would not have succession rights to each other's estate, nor, if this union in turn broke down, legal entitlement to maintenance or deserted spouse's benefits.

State Protection of Women in Marriage

Despite the fact that the constitution pledges to guard the family with special care and states that mothers will not be obliged by economic necessity to work outside the home, it does not include any directives as to how this should be achieved. Within marriage, for example, a spouse is not required by the constitution to maintain economically the other spouse or the children of the marriage. It was only through legislation enacted in 1964 (the Succession Act) that married women's succession rights were legally recognized. The relevant legislation provides that if a spouse dies without leaving a will, the spouse remaining can claim all the estate if there are no children and two-thirds of it if there are children, with the children claiming the remainder. Even if a will is made, the legislation states that the spouse and children always have precedence over any others named in the will. Under the Married Womens Status Act, 1957, a wife can apply to a court to have her interest determined in any property held by her husband or held jointly.

State Protection in the Case of Marital Breakdown

While the legal protection of women in marriage may present as more rhetorical than practical, their protection in the case of marital breakdown is even more precarious. Desertion of one spouse by the other is the most common form that separation related to marriage breakdown assumes in Ireland. Yet, up until 1970, deserted spouses did not have any economic protection. Then, a means-tested allowance for deserted wives was introduced. In 1973, a deserted wife's benefit was also instituted, which applies to deserted wives if either they or their husbands have made sufficient social welfare insurance payments prior to the desertion. If a deserted wife is receiving any maintenance payments from her husband and if she is under forty and has no dependent children, she is not eligible to receive desertion benefits. Moreover, the legal entitlements apply only so long as the deserted wife is not cohabiting with a partner and so long as the deserting spouse did not have "just cause" for leaving. In 1986 there was a total of 10,610 women receiving a state social welfare payment for deserted wives (see tables 8.31 and 8.34, *Ireland: Statistical Abstract,* 1986). It is noteworthy that under the Social Welfare Act, 1989, in part as a response to the plight of the deserted husband that was highlighted by the divorce referendum debate, a means-tested allowance for all lone parents was introduced.

Research on the social characteristics of deserted wives who receive the deserted wives social welfare payment provides an interesting snapshot of who these women are (Ward, 1990). The majority of the recipients were under forty years of age; their average age at marriage was 23.2 years (with that of their husbands 25.1 years, both of these figures being below the national average), and for almost half of them, the separation occurred within seven years of marriage. Eighty-five percent had dependent children living with them, and 35 percent of these had three or more children. The majority of deserted wives came from a poor socioeconomic background. Twenty-five percent were married to unemployed men, 22 percent to skilled manual workers, and 20 percent to unskilled or semi-skilled workers. Only 3 percent were married to farmers, and 9 percent were married to professional/managerial men (ibid., 48-9).

Other legislation has also been enacted in recent years to help redress some of the economic losses attendant on marriage breakdown. In 1976, the Family Home Protection Act was the first piece of legislation introduced into Ireland that was designed to give some protection to a spouse who had no proprietary rights in the property in which she/he lived. This law ensures that the family home and its contents may not be sold, leased, or mortgaged without the written consent of both spouses. A deserted or deserting spouse, therefore, cannot sell the family home without the consent of the other spouse. Prior to the passing of this act, it was possible for the spouse who solely owned the property in which the family lived—the husband, most usually—to sell, lease, or mortgage the home without the consent of the other spouse. In practice, this meant that wives in particular were vulnerable to their husbands' decision to sell the home without providing the family with alternative accommodation.

Legislation (the Family Law [Maintenance of Spouses and Children] Act, 1976) also enables one spouse—the wife, most usually—to receive maintenance payments if it can be shown that the other spouse has failed to provide proper maintenance for the spouse and any dependent children of the marriage. In deciding whether to issue a maintenance order, the court takes into account the income, earning capacity, property, and other financial resources of the spouses as well as their financial responsibilities and imposes on the defaulting spouse a court order requesting compliance with a specified income payment to the dependent spouse and children on a regular basis. Until the Judicial Separation and Family Law Reform Act, 1989, no maintenance order could be made for the support of a spouse who had deserted and continued to desert the other spouse. The court also had the discretion to deny an order to the applicant spouse if that spouse had committed adultery (see Ward, 1990, 2-5).

At the same time as a wife applies for maintenance, it is also common for her to apply to have the husband barred from the family home (ibid., 27). This is enabled by The Family Law (Protection of Spouses and Children) Act, 1981 whereby a barring order may be granted to one spouse that excludes the other spouse from entering the family home. This is issued if there are reasonable grounds for believing that the barred spouse poses a threat to the physical safety or welfare of the applicant spouse or to the children.

Aside from desertion benefits, therefore, there are a number of avenues open to people whose marriages have broken down, which they can pursue in order to receive some economic compensation from their spouse. The cost of legal proceedings, however, is suggested as being a deterrent to people seeking a remedy for their problems through the courts. While there is a free civil legal aid scheme in operation since 1980, its means-tested criteria and the tendency for offices to be located only in large urban centers means that for many people, particularly poorer people in rural areas, professional legal advice is inaccessible. For those who are granted maintenance orders, the low amounts of money awarded and the high rate of default on payments means that "a large majority of wives granted maintenance orders cannot be assured of either an adequate or a secure income. Many of them and their children will end up dependent on social welfare eking out a minimal existence. Unless the wife had independent means or secures employment, long-term reliance on state support seems an inevitable consequence when couples separate" (ibid., 46-7).

Therefore, despite the formal provision of legal entitlements to desertion and other forms of maintenance payments, their implementation and the actual benefits that result appear to fall short of the economic needs of many of those whose marriages break down, most particularly economically dependent women.

Divorce and the Protestant Churches

Catholic/Protestant divisions in Ireland are not just confined to Northern Ireland. A small minority of Protestants—3.4 percent—live in the Republic. What then was the position of the Protestant churches on the amendment?

Unlike the Catholic church, all the Protestant churches accept the need for civil divorce as a response to the problem of marriage breakdown. They maintain a much clearer distinction between private morality and public legislation. Accordingly, they oppose the constitutional ban on divorce even though, like the Catholic church, their theological teaching proclaims the lifelong nature of marriage. As Bishop Walter Empey of Meath and Kildare diocese stated on "Today Tonight" the evening following the announcement of the referendum, "We do not marry divorced persons, but we feel that divorce is a response to marital breakdown ("Today Tonight," Apr. 24).

The divorce debate coincided with the annual General Synod of the Church of Ireland (the Anglican church) and with the annual Presbyterian General Assembly. Both churches used the opportunity presented by their respective meetings to express publicly their support for the form of divorce proposed by the government. Robert Eames, the primate of the Church of Ireland, argued that, with the escalation in the number of marriages breaking down, divorce with the right to remarry was necessary. Stressing the Church of Ireland's commitment to the sanctity and stability of marriage and the family, he emphasized that there was no conflict between the church's advocacy of the sanctity of marriage and providing couples with an opportunity to end the human misery they may encounter through a complete failure of their marriage (*Irish Times*, May 21, 1986, 1,6).

Against a backdrop of ongoing vigorous ecumenical relations between the Catholic hierarchy and the Church of Ireland, the Church of Ireland Archbishop of Dublin, Donal Caird pointed out that the divorce referendum should not be seen as a contest between itself and the Catholic church but as a difference in their social philosophies (*Irish Times*, May 15, 1986,

7). Its official newspaper, however, the *Church of Ireland Gazette*, criticized the absolute opposition of the Catholic church to the amendment. Other Church of Ireland bishops reaffirmed the distinction between church discipline on marriage and state legislation as a response to marital breakdown, with one, Bishop Empey of Meath and Kildare, arguing that no one church had a monopoly on morality: "we have to nail the lie that permissiveness flows from the Church of Ireland" ("Today Tonight," May 22, 1986).

Presbyterian ministers pointed out that their church had "a long tradition of recognising divorce as a last resort" and argued that divorce was a civil right that should be available to all citizens (*Irish Times*, June 6, 1986, 8). In sum, for Protestants, as stated by the Irish Council of Churches, a representative body of all the major non-Catholic denominations in Ireland, although divorce should not be an "easy option," the state has a duty to legislate for the irretrievable breakdown of marriage (*Irish Press*, June 11, 1986, 4).

Interviewees

Activist leaders
William Binchy, Anti-Divorce Campaign (ADC)
Jean Tansey, Divorce Action Group (DAG)

Political Party Press Officers
Tony Heffernan, Workers' Party
P.J. Mara, Fianna Fail
Stephen O'Byrnes, Progressive Democrats
Cathleen O'Meara, Labour
Peter White, Fine Gael

Catholic church
Brendan Comiskey, bishop, Diocese of Ferns

Print media
Vincent Browne, *Sunday Tribune*
Nick Lundberg, *Irish Catholic*
Michael O'Toole, *Evening Press*

RTE *personnel*
T.V. Finn, director general
Bob Collins, director, television programs
Tony Fahy, director, audience research unit
Eugene Murray, managing editor, "Today Tonight"
John Bowman, interviewer/anchorperson, "Today Tonight"
Brian Farrell, interviewer/anchorperson, "Today Tonight"
Pat Kenny, interviewer/anchorperson, "Today Tonight"
Gary Agnew, reporter, "Today Tonight"
Rhona O'Byrne, administrator, "Today Tonight"

Notes

Epigraph: Max Weber [1919], "Science as a Vocation," 152-53.

ONE Introduction

1. See Glendon, 1987, table 2: "Grounds for divorce in Nineteen Countries," 68.

2. In England, for example, a mutual consent divorce is available only after a two-year separation, and a unilateral divorce is available only after a five-year separation period. France requires six years' and West Germany three years' separation in the case of unilateral divorces. Additionally, similar to the Irish proposals, each of these countries also has a "hardship" clause, which allows the courts to dismiss a petition if the divorce would cause exceptional hardship (Glendon, 1987, 68-75).

3. The poll was conducted at the end of April by the Market Research Bureau of Ireland (MRBI) in association with the *Irish Times*, in which it was published on May 5, 1986 (See table 1). An RSI/*Sunday Press* poll published on May 11 similarly indicated that, excluding don't knows, 58 percent were in favor of the amendment.

4. After 1983 pro-divorce opinion wavered somewhat, ranging from 42 percent to 52 percent, and at the beginning of 1986, support again passed the majority threshold with 52 percent of those polled favoring the ban's removal. These figures are taken from various MRBI polls. The 52 percent figure comes from the MRBI poll published in the *Irish Times*, Feb. 2, 1986. In addition to the question regarding the removal of the divorce ban, pollsters also asked whether their interviewees favored the introduction of divorce in certain unspecified circumstances. When this question was first asked in 1983, 66 percent agreed, and by February 1986, 77 percent of those surveyed stated that divorce should be permitted in certain circumstances. (See MRBI, Apr. 1986, chart E.)

5. The 1986 Census, not available at the time of the referendum, was the first in Ireland in which information on ever-married persons was collected on the basis of de facto rather than de jure marital status. Of a total of 37,245 people who were separated, representing 6 percent of the ever-married population excluding the widowed, 54 percent had some form of legal or other separation; 31 percent were deserted; 12 percent had a divorce from another country, and 3 percent had annulled marriages. See Central Statistics Office, 1989a, vii-viii. Prior to the 1986 Census, official estimates of marital breakdown were based on 1983 Labour Force survey data, which suggested that 37.5

thousand people were separated. One indirect indicator of the incidence of marriage breakdown in Ireland is the number of women receiving Deserted Wife's Benefit: In 1986 it was 6,165, whereas in 1982, it was 3,416 (Central Statistics Office, 1989b, table 8.31).

6. 62 percent of the electorate voted on the amendment. An MRBI/*Irish Times* poll published on the day before the amendment indicated that excluding don't knows, 45 percent intended to vote in favor and 55 percent to vote against the amendment (See table 1).

7. See Max Weber's essay "Science as a Vocation" [1919], and his discussion of social action, 24-26, in *Economy and Society.*

8. See in particular Alexander, 1983; Schluchter, 1979, 1981; and Sica, 1988.

9. See Bellah et al., 1985; Sennett, 1978; and Lasch, 1979, for discussions of the impact on individuals and society of the rigid separation of the public from the private spheres of life in American society.

10. The first quote is from Riane Eisler, 1977, xiii. She argues that "In essence, our laws determine how we may or may not relate to other people. . . . in their explicit or implied definitions, laws also help determine how other people shall view us, and even how we shall view ourselves" (ibid.). The second quote is from Glendon, 1987, 10. Glendon adopts a cultural approach to understanding abortion and divorce in Western law. Drawing on the work of the anthropologist Clifford Geertz, Glendon argues that different legal systems differ in the "stories they tell," the "symbols they deploy," and the "visions they project" (8). Lawrence Stone's (1990) history of divorce in English law similarly demarcates the relationship between changes in societal values and changes in the law on marriage and divorce.

11. See Kelly, 1984.

12. Max Weber [1904] 1949, 81-84, discusses this in his essay " 'Objectivity' in Social Science." He states: "In the *method* of investigation, the 'guiding point of view' is of great importance for the *construction* of the conceptual scheme which will be used in the investigation. In the mode of their *use*, however, the investigator is obviously bound by the norms of our thought just as much here as elsewhere. For scientific truth is precisely what is *valid* for all who *seek* the truth" [emphasis in original].

13. See Paul Rabinow's (1977) personal reflections regarding the problems encountered by researchers as outsiders studying a culture different from their own. Following Paul Ricoeur, he defines the problem of hermeneutic understanding as "the comprehension of the self, by the detour of the comprehension of the other. . . . The self being discussed is perfectly public. . . . it is the culturally mediated and historically situated self which finds itself in a continuously changing world of meaning" (5-6).

TWO Irish Cultural Themes

1. See Hayes-McCoy, 1976, for an extensive discussion of the Tudor Conquest of Ireland.

2. The proportion of Catholic land fell from 59 percent in 1641 to 22 percent after the Cromwellian settlement to 14 percent after the Williamite war (Corish, 1985, 123).

3. Beckett, 1966, 159.

4. Corish, 1985, 123.

5. See Maureen Wall's review of the penal laws. Catholic land ownership fell to about 5 percent under the provisions of the penal code (Corish, 123).

6. Corish, 1985, 124.

7. Ibid. 131.

8. Ibid. 130-31.

9. Ibid. 161.

10. Ibid. 192-94; Inglis, 1987, 135-38.

11. Inglis, 1987, 166; Corish, 1985, 226.

12. Corish, 1985, 232.

13. Ibid.

14. In particular, see the survey research findings of Maire Nic Ghiolla Phadraig, 1977; Breslin and Weafer, 1985; and Mac Greil, 1977. Mac Greil (454) notes that: "There is sufficient evidence to indicate a relatively high degree of authoritarianism among the respondents. . . . The scores for 'pro-establishment' and 'religious fundamentalism' subscales are particularly high, which seems to indicate a highly conservative and religiously "dogmatic" type of mentality." A more general discussion of Irish legalism is also presented in Inglis, 1982, and Inglis, 1987, 14-32. For a good discussion of issues of law and morality in Irish society from the perspective of a political philosopher, see Clarke, 1985, particularly 60-68 and 112-35.

15. Gallagher, 1981, 715.

16. Bellah et al. (1985) provide the most interesting discussion of the centrality of a discourse of individual rights in America. Also, Glendon (1987, 38, 134) argues that "the right to privacy, which is so bound up with individual autonomy and isolation, has become one of the most absolute rights known to the American legal system. . . . In American constitutional law . . . the expressed rights to individual liberty and equal treatment are dominant."

17. Although the Civil Rights Association established in Northern Ireland in 1967 was forceful in bringing world attention to the discrimination against Catholics in the North, it is not customary for people in the Republic to articulate arguments regarding their entitlement to certain civil rights.

18. Most Irish people can probably relate a personal story documenting that the reason for their achievement in some sphere of their lives was attributed by somebody to the power of God or prayer. An example of this is provided by the well-known and popular Irish radio and television personality Gay Byrne in his recent autobiography. In recounting the joyous reaction of his mother to his brother's success in landing a clerical position in Guinness's brewery, which at that time was unprecedented for a Catholic, Byrne states that his mother dropped to her knees praising God (1989, 26).

19. For example, 72 percent of the Irish think that adoption of an EC charter of fundamental social rights is a "good thing" (*Eurobarometer Trends 1974–1990,* table B19).

20. See Hechter, 1975, and Crotty, 1966 and 1986, for an extensive discussion of the impact of colonialism on Irish economic development.

21. Crotty, 1966, 29-30.

22. See the discussions in Kennedy, 1973, 19-40; and Crotty, 1966.

23. Crotty, 1986, 47-48.

24. Kennedy, 1973, 88-89. 82 percent of holdings were under fifteen acres.

25. Lee, 1973, 11-12, 16-18.

26. Beckett, 1966, 336.

27. Ibid. 343.

28. Kennedy, 1973, 27.

29. Lee, 1973, 2-3.

30. Ibid. The number of holdings decreased from 691,202 in 1841 to 570,338 in 1851 (Beckett, 1966, 348). About 7 percent of farmers had leases. The rest were tenants from year to year, holding their farms on a verbal agreement with their landlords, which could be ended by either side with six months' notice. For a general discussion of the Irish economy immediately after the Famine, see Lee, 1973, 1-35; Lyons, 1973, 34-70; and Beckett, 1966, 336-75.

31. Whyte, 1966, 6-23.

32. Beckett, 1966, 407. The terms of repayment were 3.25 percent per annum over sixty-eight and a half years. See also Lyons, 1973, 218-19. After Irish independence, the Land Act (1923) provided for the Land Commission to compulsorily purchase all land still owned by landlords.

33. Inglis, 1987, 193-94; Corish, 1985, 192.

34. Lee, 1973, 4.

35. Kennedy, 1973, 139-72.

36. Ibid. 145-47.

37. Ibid. 151.

38. Ibid. 149-54.

39. There is much anecdotal and literary evidence about the workings of the dowry system in Ireland. It is generally accepted that the formal dowry system ended around the late 1940s. The anthropologist John Messenger (1969), however, states that this practice was still to be found in the Aran Islands, off the west coast of Ireland, in the 1960s. Messenger states: "Numerous factors are weighed by the representatives of the future spouse before a match is consummated. Uppermost in the minds of the relatives of the man is the size of the dowry that the woman will bring to the marriage" (70).

40. Kennedy, 1973, 155.

41. Lee, 1978, 39.

42. Lee, 1978, 37.

43. O'Tuathaigh, 1988, 149.

44. Brown, 1985, chapters 1-5. Other comprehensive accounts of the early decades of the Irish state can be found in Lyons, 1973, part 3A, chapters 1 and 2; and in Lee, 1989, chapters 2-4.

45. Boylan et al., 1988, 162.

46. I am paraphrasing a defining speech of de Valera's broadcast on St. Patrick's Day, 1943. For its full text see Lee, 1989, 334.

47. See Whyte, 1980, 60; and Brown, 1985, chapter 4.

48. This is a popular claim of Irish folk-politics. For corroborating academic acknowledgment, see Lee, 1989, 334.

49. This famous radio speech of de Valera's was broadcast to the United States on St. Patrick's Day, 1935. Printed in the *Irish Press,* March 18, 1935, 2. Brown (1985) quotes this, 151. For a biography of de Valera, see Earl of Longford and Thomas P. O'Neill, 1970. *Eamon de Valera.* Importantly, his biographers comment that: "In all that concerns faith and morals he [de Valera] might fairly be called docile. In such matters he was prepared to accept unreservedly the teaching of the Church. . . . For all his acknowledged piety he could never be defined as a clerical statesman" (xxii).

50. See Whyte, 1980, 60.

51. 1937 speech of de Valera broadcast on Irish Radio and relayed to America explaining the provisions of the constitution. Published, on its forty-ninth anniversary, in the *Irish Press,* June 24, 1986, 9.

52. Grogan, 1967, 171. See also Whyte, 1980, and Keogh, 1986, for an analysis of the Catholic influence on the constitution.

53. Article 44, Section 1.2, until it was deleted in 1972, stated: "The State recognises the special position of the Holy Catholic Apostolic and Roman Church as the guardian of the faith professed by the great majority of the citizens."

54. Article 41, section 1, and section 3, subsections 1 and 2.

55. *Constitution of Ireland,* 1937. Article 41, section 2, subsections 1 and 2. Article 40 recognizes personal rights, but these refer to property and reputation.

56. Inglis, 1987, 188, 187-214.

57. See Manning, 1978, for a discussion of women in post-independence Irish politics, and for an account of Irish women's suffrage, see Cullen-Owens, 1984.

58. The marriage bar was repealed in 1973 although teachers were exempt from this as of 1958.

59. Since the Act of Union, which in 1801 imposed the union of the Irish parliament with that of England into the United Kingdom, Irish couples seeking divorce could petition the House of Lords at Westminster. As of 1879 two procedures had to be followed: (1) a common law separation granted by the High Court, and (2) a private parliamentary divorce bill had to be approved, which settled property and financial matters and provided for the right to remarriage. This was the situation the newly independent Irish government inherited in 1922. The Upper House of Parliament, the Senate, was the equivalent of the British House of Lords except it did not have the same restrictions or regulations on bills. See Fanning, 1983.

60. A comprehensive discussion of this is provided by John Whyte, 1980. See chapters 2 and 4-10 especially.

61. See Whyte's (1980) detailed discussion, 120-302, and Fanning, 1985.

62. Letter from Archbishop McQuaid to John A. Costello, April 5, 1951, summarizing the objections that they had already communicated to the Fianna Fail government. Quoted in Whyte, 1980, 143.

63. Letter from the Bishop of Ferns, James Staunton, who was the secretary to the hierarchy, to Prime Minister John A. Costello, October 10, 1950. Published in Whyte, 1980, 424-25.

64. Fanning, 1985.

65. Letter from Archbishop McQuaid to Prime Minister John A. Costello, April 5, 1951. Published in Whyte, 1980, 446-48.

66. Kennedy, 1973, 95.

67. For a good review of this period, see Brown, 1985, 241-311.

68. See Peillon, 1982, 156-64.

69. Brown, 1985, 242. Michael Hout (1989, 1) compares the changes that took place in Ireland between 1959 and 1973 to the "kind of economic miracle now associated with Southeast Asia." However, as O'Hearn (1990, 604) reminds us, Ireland, along with Spain, Greece, and Portugal, "are all poor regions of the European periphery with a standard of living far below the rest of the continent."

70. As well as Brown, 1985, for an extensive discussion of these changes, see the essays in Litton, 1982, and Clancy et al., 1986.

71. Rottman and O'Connell, in Litton, 1982, 67.

72. Sexton and Dillon, 1984.

73. For example, between 1971 and 1983, support for retaining the constitutional ban on divorce decreased from 79 percent to 47 percent (MRBI surveys, various years).

74. An instance of this is provided by a 1972 referendum in which 84 percent of the electorate who voted endorsed the removal of the special position of the Catholic church from the constitution.

75. Gardiner, 1988, 14. In the national election of November 1992, women won 12 percent of the parliamentary seats.

76. MRBI, 1987a, table 1C/1. Fogarty et al., 1984, however, paint a somewhat different picture, finding that 43 percent of women compared to 58 percent of men are "interested but not active in politics" (table 35d).

77. For instance, the Women's Political Association is a non-party voluntary organization founded in 1970. With branches in Dublin and around the country, it organizes seminars on women and politics, and canvasses for women electoral candidates.

78. See, for example, the data in Fogarty et al., 1984, tables 17b, 21e, 22e, and 34d.

79. Fogarty et al., 1984, tables 34d and 17b.

80. In 1983, 32 percent females compared to 26 percent males, and in 1987, 32 percent females to 22 percent males expressed support for Fine Gael. No significant gender difference is apparent in support for the other parties. See MRBI, 1983, table 9; MRBI 1987b, table 5.

81. See Rose, 1975, for a brief overview of the women's movement in Ireland, and Levine, 1982, for a personal account.

82. For example, women are not specifically represented in government organized national wage agreement discussions, unlike the farmers, the trade unions, and the employers' federation, who are considered social partners.

83. My argument here disagrees with Beale's claim that it was "the women's movement which articulated most forcefully the arguments for individual freedom and personal choice" (1987, 13). Since the late 1960s, the Irish courts have recognized the right of married women to contraception, interpreted as part of a right to marital privacy; the right of women to serve on juries; the right of a mother to the custody and care of her illegitimate child; the right of women to independent tax assessment from their husbands (see McMahon, 1985; and Robinson, 1978). Much of the initiative for employment equality and anti-discrimination labor force legislation in the 1970s, including the establishment in 1977 of an Employment Equality Agency in Ireland, came from the EC.

84. *McGee* v. *Attorney General*, 1974. The case was argued by Mary Robinson, currently the president of Ireland. As a young senator, Mary Robinson was involved in introducing a number of bills, beginning in 1970, that aimed unsuccessfully to decriminalize contraception, and she has played a major role in initiating and leading debates in Ireland on contraception and divorce.

85. The Health (Family Planning) Act, 1979, section 4 (1) b (ii).

86. This was how Charles Haughey, then the minister for health responsible, described the new legislation.

87. The Health (Family Planning) (Amendment) Act, 1985. Nonetheless, contraceptives can still be bought only at a recognized medical establishment. What this means in practice is that supermarkets, record stores, and college campus shops, for instance, cannot sell condoms.

88. The Health (Family Planning) Act, 1979, section 10.

89. Riddick, 1990, 6. On his visit to Ireland, Pope John Paul II singled out the abortion question for special attention. See *The Pope in Ireland*, 1979, 80.

90. See Cooney, 1986, 61-71, for a description of the politics of the pro-life amendment referendum.

91. The amendment, Article 40.3.3, reads: "The State acknowledges the right to life of the unborn and, with due regard to the equal right of the life of the mother, guarantees in its laws to respect, and as far as practicable, by its laws to defend and vindicate that right." O'Carroll (1984) discusses the arguments articulated during the pro-life amendment debate.

92. In the American context, Kristin Luker (1984, 234) argues that: "Pro-life activists. . . . want a human life amendment to the Constitution (or a federal law) primarily in order to make a *moral* statement about abortion and only secondarily in order to prevent all abortions in practice."

93. In a subsequent referendum in Ireland in November 1992, the majority of the electorate voted to overturn the information restrictions and to uphold the right of a woman to travel abroad for abortion, while reaffirming opposition to the legal provision of abortion in Ireland. Every year, thousands of Irish women travel to England for abortions. In 1989, for example, official British statistics indicate that 3,721 Irish women had abortions performed. For a discussion of abortion-related events in Ireland see Riddick, 1988, and 1990. Jackson (1983) provides an interesting review of the history of "backstreet abortion" in Ireland.

94. See, in particular, the text of an address delivered by FitzGerald in 1976 and published in the *Irish Times*, April 29, 1976, 10. Following the RTE radio news interview with FitzGerald in September 1981 in which he reiterated this view, FitzGerald's commitment to effecting pluralism became popularly known as his "Constitutional Crusade."

95. Ireland's budget deficit constituted 8.3 percent of the Irish gross national product in 1986. Less than ten years earlier, in 1977, the deficit was 3.6 percent of GNP (*Ireland: A Directory*, 420)

96. For comments critical of Irish materialist values see, Lynch, 1989, 139-53; Daly, 1982; Lee, 1973, and 1989, especially 522.

97. *Eurobarometer Trends 1974–1990*, tables B26 and B27. The EC index is for the ten member countries, excluding Spain and Portugal, who joined in 1985.

98. *Eurobarometer Trends 1974–1990*, table B26.

THREE   Arguing about Divorce

1. The most prominent government dissenter was the minister for Education, Patrick Cooney, who represented Longford/Westmeath. The junior agriculture minister, Paul Connaughton, from Galway East, and two prominent Fine Gael backbenchers, Alice Glenn of Dublin Central and Oliver J. Flanagan of the midlands (Laois/Offaly), were also outspoken against the amendment. Both Glenn and Flanagan also opposed in 1985 legislation liberalizing the availability of contraception. Some other Fine Gael parliamentarians, while not publicly dissenting, did not actively campaign for acceptance of the amendment.

2. The DAG has a branch in all of the Dublin electoral constituencies, in all of the constituencies in the East and Midlands, in two of the nine constituencies in the Northwest, and in seven of the thirteen most southerly constituencies. Overall, its paid membership is 1,000 people, and at the time of the referendum, it had only one full-time paid employee. DAG's chairperson, Jean Tansey, joined DAG in 1984. She is an experienced campaigner having being involved in the Anti [Pro-Life] Amendment Campaign, the Labour Women's National Executive, and the Council for the Status of Women.

3. The ADC's organizing committee had nine members in all. Two of these were women.

4. At the time of the referendum, Binchy was also research counselor to the government-sponsored Law Reform Commission.

5. McCarroll has also written a book on divorce (1985). Bonar is a member of Family Solidarity and is also chairperson of a conservative group called The Responsible Society. She actively favored the pro-life amendment and later opposed the 1985 contraception legislation. Other members of the ADC organizing committee were Michael Lucey, the chairman of Family Solidarity, whose wife was one of the main spokespersons in the "Women Doctors for the [Pro-Life] Amendment" group and later became president of the Society for the Protection of the Unborn Child (SPUC); Jerry Collins, the PRO for

Family Solidarity, who was active in the pro-life amendment campaign; and John O'Reilly, who is the secretary of The Responsible Society.

6.While Family Solidarity was launched to the public in 1984, it held its first meeting in the fall of 1983. In an interview in the *Irish Times* (Dec. 14, 1984, 11), Family Solidarity's chairman, Michael Lucey, stated: "I have good reason to believe that the embryo of Family Solidarity predated the [pro-life] amendment." While Family Solidarity is officially a group independent of the pro-life movement, many of its founding patrons were active pro-amendment supporters. As well as opposing contraception, divorce, and abortion, Family Solidarity opposes government economic policies that in its view, discriminate against families. Its membership is constituted by people from both urban and rural backgrounds and from the middle class and working class socio-economic categories.

7. Although the political parties have branches at the local level, often two or more per parish, the members of these branches, especially in the rural areas, were not enthusiastic about campaigning for acceptance of the amendment, as many members themselves opposed divorce. This appeared to be particularly true for Fine Gael. Even those who favored divorce did not want to alienate supporters of their party who were opposed to divorce but overall were generally favorable to Fine Gael. Consequently, the pro-divorce campaign as a whole tended to be orchestrated from the national headquarters of the component groups in Dublin and did not have the same energy or resources invested in it as a normal general election would have.

8. Fianna Fail parliamentary party statement, Apr. 25, 1986.

9. Fianna Fail party political broadcast, RTE, June 23, 1986. Two well-known Fianna Fail parliamentarians who spoke in favor of divorce were Charles McCreevy, a deputy from Kildare, and David Andrews of Dublin.

10. FitzGerald's press conference was broadcast live on RTE's flagship current affairs program, "Today Tonight," April, 23, 1986. I taped and subsequently transcribed all of the "Today Tonight" programs relating to the amendment.

11. Between March 21 and April 7, 1986, Prime Minister Garret Fitz-Gerald and the minister for justice, Alan Dukes, held separate discussions with the leaders of all of the churches in Ireland—Catholic, (Protestant) Church of Ireland, Presbyterian, Baptist, Methodist, Quaker—and the Jewish Community. Their views were sought on various aspects relating to marriage, separation, and divorce. Earlier, FitzGerald had defended his decision to seek consultations with religious leaders, stating: "The necessity for such consultations is . . . self-evident in view of the role of the Churches in the solemnization of marriage. . . . It would be quite improper to seek changes in the law without seeking the Churches' views on the matter. . . . The correct procedure is to consult with the Churches as this is a matter on which Church and State are intimately linked" (*Parliamentary Debates,* Dail Eireann, Feb. 18, 1986).

12. The Protestant Church of Ireland recognizes the civil provision for divorce as a "last resort" in dealing with the problem of marital breakdown.

It reaffirmed this at its annual Synod in 1984. In contrast, the Catholic Church opposes divorce on both theological and social grounds.

13. *Parliamentary Debates*, Dail Eireann, May 14, 793.

14. Interviewed by Pat Kenny, "Today Tonight," Apr. 24.

15. Quoted in the *Irish Times*, June 13, 11.

16. *Parliamentary Debates*, Dail Eireann, May 14, 793. See similar remarks expressed by other Fine Gael members, in *Parliamentary Debates*, Dail Eireann, May 14, 953 (Mary Flaherty), and 1054 (Liam Skelly).

17. FitzGerald's press conference, "Today Tonight," Apr. 23.

18. Interviewed by Brian Farrell, "Today Tonight," June 17.

19. *Parliamentary Debates*, Dail Eireann, May 16, 1380.

20. Ibid., May 14, 856.

21. Stated by him on "Today Tonight," June 10.

22. Interview by John Bowman, "Today Tonight," Apr. 23.

23. *Parliamentary Debates*, Dail Eireann, May 16, 1380.

24. FitzGerald's press conference, broadcast by "Today Tonight," Apr. 23. The full text of the government's statement of intent with regard to marriage, separation, and divorce was published in the *Irish Times*, Apr. 24, 6.

25. Pat Kenny, "Today Tonight," asked this question. Featured on its transmission of Apr. 23.

26. *Parliamentary Debates*, Dail Eireann, May 16, 1390-91.

27. Alan Dukes, "Today Tonight," June 3.

28. Reported in the *Irish Times*, May 26, 1. Emphasis mine.

29. *Parliamentary Debates*, Dail Eireann, May 15, 1271-72.

30. Reported in the *Irish Independent*, June 16, 9. Emphasis mine.

31. *Parliamentary Debates*, Dail Eireann, May 16, 1462.

32. Jean Tansey, "Today Tonight," June 3.

33. "Today Tonight," June 19.

34. "Today Tonight," Apr. 23.

35. Interviewed on "Today Tonight," Apr. 24.

36. Interviewed on "Today Tonight," June 19.

37. Ibid.

38. Interviewed on "Today Tonight," May 22.

39. Interviewed on "Today Tonight," Apr. 24.

40. ADC press release, May 9.

41. Interviewed on "Today Tonight," Apr. 24.

42. ADC press release, May 9.

43. *Parliamentary Debates*, Dail Eireann, May 20, 1659, 1706; May 21, 1756.

44. Ibid., May 20, 1737-38.

45. ADC press release, May 9.

46. One of the characteristics of the anti-divorce activists during the campaign was a tendency to emphasize the factual and empirical basis for what they were arguing. As well as directly using empirical evidence, they also argued that they did not have a campaign "strategy." Rather, as Joe McCarroll stated ("Today Tonight," May 22), "We have only one [campaign strategy]

and that is information." Bernadette Bonar ("Today Tonight," Apr. 24), also stated: "I have no doubt that when [the Irish people] hear the facts, and let me repeat, when they hear the facts, and I hope they get them properly from both sides, that the people . . . will reject the amendment."

47. William Binchy interviewed on "Today Tonight," June 19.

48. ADC press release, May 9.

49. Padraig Faulkner, (FF), *Parliamentary Debates*, Dail Eireann, May 14, 927.

50. Ibid., 826. Another Fianna Fail parliamentarian, Sean Treacy, also invoked the image of Frankenstein in highlighting the negative effects of divorce. Quoting what Lord Campbell, the person who first introduced divorce into England in 1857, had to say about its results: "I have been sitting two days in the divorce court and like Frankenstein, I am afraid of the monster I have called into existence. There seems some reason to dread that the prophecy of those who opposed the change may be fulfilled by a lamentable multiplication of divorces and by the corruption of public morals." Treacy continued by appealing to those who wish to see divorce introduced to "beware the monster they are creating and which they cannot control" (ibid., May 15, 1102-1103).

51. The full text of this statement was printed in the *Irish Times*, May 21, 4.

52. This was the phrase he used when interviewed on "Today Tonight," Apr. 24.

53. ADC press release, May 9.

54. Ibid. The ADC also argued that divorced parents would lose their constitutional rights with respect to the rearing of their children. Binchy argued that the current "constitutional protection towards the family in the rearing of children and the education of children would be removed entirely," a consequence that he suggested had been overlooked by the government (interviewed on "Today Tonight," Apr. 24). The ADC contended: "Divorced parents would lose all their constitutionally protected rights to provide for the religious, moral, intellectual, physical and social education of their children" (ADC press release, May 9).

55. Quoted in the *Sunday Tribune*, June 22, 9.

56. Interviewed on "Today Tonight," June 19.

57. Interviewed on "Today Tonight," June 10.

58. Interviewed on "Today Tonight," June 17.

59. ADC press release, May 9.

60. Interviewed on "Today Tonight," June 17.

61. Interviewed on "Today Tonight," June 3.

62. ADC press release, May 9.

63. William Binchy, interviewed on "Today Tonight," June 3.

64. Bernadette Bonar, interviewed on "Today Tonight," Apr. 24.

65. ADC press release, May 9. Emphasis in original statement.

66. Joe McCarroll, interviewed on "Today Tonight," May 22.

67. ADC press release, May 9.

68. Similar remarks to those expressed by Woods were reiterated by other senior members of Fianna Fail (FF). For example, see Rory O'Hanlon, "Today

Tonight," May 22; Michael O'Kennedy, "Today Tonight," June 3; and Padraig Flynn, "Today Tonight," June 19. For further evidence of the legal/economic arguments, see also the contributions by FF members to the Parliamentary debate, especially, Padraig Faulkner, May 14, 923-25; Sean McCarthy, May 15, 1081; Noel Treacy, May 16, 1397-98, and Seamus Kirk, May 16, 1418-19.

69. *Parliamentary Debates*, Dail Eireann, May 14; 823-25.

70. Ibid., 825.

71. Ibid., 828.

72. "Today Tonight," Apr. 23.

73. "Today Tonight," Apr. 24. McCarroll also reiterated this argument, "Today Tonight," June 10.

74. ADC press release, May 9.

75. "Today Tonight," May 22.

76. ADC press release, May 9.

77. Family Solidarity, 1986, 4.

78. Interviewed on "Today Tonight," June 17.

79. The ADC were going further than the Catholic hierarchy, however, in explicating a demand that the state, on theological grounds, provide legal protection and support for lifelong marriage.

80. *Parliamentary Debates*, Dail Eireann, May 15, 1099-1102.

81. Ibid., 1241. See also Michael Barrett, (FF), *Parliamentary Debates*, Dail Eireann, May 21, 1938.

82. "Today Tonight," June 17.

83. *Parliamentary Debates*, Dail Eireann, May 16; 1380-81.

84. FitzGerald interviewed by Brian Farrell, "Today Tonight," June 17, and Binchy, interviewed by John Bowman, "Today Tonight," June 17.

85. *Parliamentary Debates*, Dail Eireann, May 16, 1363-64.

86. Jean Tansey speaking at a DAG press conference, May 21. Reported in the *Irish Times*, May 22, 7.

87. Jean Tansey, reported in the *Irish Times*, May 22, 7; and featured on "Today Tonight," June 3.

88. "Today Tonight," June 19.

89. Excerpts from DAG's first press conference were transmitted by "Today Tonight," Apr. 24.

90. *Parliamentary Debates*, Dail Eireann, May 15, 1091.

91. See, for instance, David Molony, ibid. May 15, 1132, 1232; and Bernard Allen, ibid., May 16, 1451.

92. The ICTU is a national federation that acts as an umbrella group for trade unions and has been formally committed to removal of the ban on divorce since 1982. Remarks by Donal Nevin, the general secretary of the ICTU, reported in the *Irish Times*, May 20, 1; *Irish Independent*, June 5, 9.

93. Remarks by Patricia O' Donovan, legislation and equality officer of the ICTU. Reported in the *Irish Times*, June 11, 6.

94. Reported in the *Irish Times*, June 25, 8.

95. This quotation is taken from its campaign literature on the divorce amendment. The goal of the Workers' Party is to create a democratic, secular,

socialist republic based on the unity of workers in the North and South of Ireland.

96. In 1978 the Matrimonial Causes (Northern Ireland) Act brought the divorce legislation in Northern Ireland into line with that operating in England and Wales, which in 1969 removed the fault clause.

97. Press conference broadcast by "Today Tonight," Apr. 23.

98. *Parliamentary Debates*, Dail Eireann, May 16, 1391.

99. Ibid., May 15, 1323-24.

100. Reported in the *Irish Times*, May 30, 1.

101. *Parliamentary Debates*, Dail Eireann, May 16, 1363.

102. "Today Tonight," June 10; *Parliamentary Debates*, Seanad Eireann, May 23, 1758-59.

103. "Today Tonight," June 17.

104. Tras Honan, *Parliamentary Debates*, Seanad Eireann, May 22, 1610.

105. *Irish Times*, May 30, 9.

106. Somewhat indicative of this is the fact that in a 1987 poll conducted in the Republic, only 33 percent of the respondents regarded the people of Northern Ireland as Irish. The poll also found 67 percent expressing an aspiration toward unification, while 56 percent regarded the Irish nation as constituting thirty-two counties. Additionally, 49 percent agreed with the statement that "northern Ireland will never be reunited with the South" (MRBI, 1987a, 47-51). Attitudes in the South toward the causes of the conflict in Northern Ireland are discussed in Dillon, 1990.

107. This is the aim of the Irish Republican Socialist Party, from which the IRA draws much of its support. The perceived support for the IRA in the Republic of Ireland tends to be exaggerated. It is true that in a 1981 general election in the South two IRA H-Block candidates were elected: Kieran Doherty in Cavan/Monaghan and Patrick Agnew in Louth, representing just over 2 percent of the total votes cast. That result does not reflect enduring support for the IRA but would appear to be more of an immediate demonstration of sympathy for the plight of IRA H-Block prisoners in Long Kesh prison, who in the early months of 1981 embarked on a long drawn out hunger strike in which several prisoners, including Doherty, died. More indicative of the level of support for the IRA in the South are the results from the most recent general elections in the Republic of Ireland. Sinn Fein, the political wing of the IRA, received in 1987 1.9 percent and in 1989 1.2 percent of electoral support (see Coakley, 1990, for a discussion of minor parties in Ireland). Also indicative of lack of support for the IRA are findings from an opinion poll conducted in November 1987 (MRBI, 1987b) regarding the Republic's Extradition Act. In the poll 40 percent agreed that the act should be implemented; 23 percent that it should be postponed until a future date; 20 percent that it should be scrapped completely; and 17 percent were undecided.

108. Various reports prepared for the New Ireland Forum documented the economic costs of unification. See in particular, New Ireland Forum, 1984.

109. *Parliamentary Debates*, Dail Eireann, May 16, 1363.

FOUR   Women and the Divorce Campaign

1. Lovenduski, 1986, 22. For a historical analysis of the evolution of Western divorce see, Phillips, 1988; and Stone, 1990.

2. Weitzman, 1985, 3.

3. Stone, 1990, 7.

4. Weitzman, 1985, 6-7.

5. Stone, 1989, 12.

6. Weitzman, 1985, 7.

7. Glendon, 1987, 66. See table 2, 68, and her discussion, 63-111.

8. See Arendell, 1986; and Weitzman, 1985. Importantly, however, Weitzman's much publicized contention that women suffer a 73 percent drop in post-divorce income has been challenged by other, more comprehensive, research data. See in particular, Duncan and Hoffman, 1985; and Hoffman and Duncan, 1988. The authors argue that "the economic consequences are serious, and gender-based inequities exist; but that the magnitude of the problem is not nearly as great as suggested by Weitzman" (641). Demonstrating instead that women's economic status fell an average of about 30 percent in the first year following divorce (Duncan and Hoffman, 1985), they "show that Weitzman's findings are almost certainly in error" (Hoffman and Duncan, 1988, 641).

9. Weitzman, 1985, 365, commenting on the members of the California Governor's Commission on divorce law reform.

10. Weitzman, 1985, 364.

11. Eisler, 1977, 11; Weitzman, 1985, 364.

12. Beckwith, 1985, 25.

13. For a review of the economic consequences of marital breakdown in Ireland, particularly the negative economic consequences for deserted women, see Ward, 1990.

14. MRBI, June 1986, table 1A. (See table 1).

15. MRBI, 1983, table 4. See also Fogarty at al., 1984, table 21e.

16. Aims culled from organizational materials of the CSW and advertisements published in Women's Political Association (Dublin Branch) Journal, 1988, 6, and 1987, 10.

17. CSW Press Statement, June 16. This was made available to me by the CSW.

18. Ibid.

19. Address by the economist Eithne FitzGerald to the CSW public meeting, June 24. This address was made available to me by the CSW.

20. Letter from Liz Sherry, CSW vice-chairwoman, Irish Times, June 26, 11.

21. The CSW has issued a two page "Charter for Women's Rights: Setting the Agenda for the '90s." Despite its title, however, it tends toward the delineation of various general demands regarding women rather than articulating women's specific "rights." Significantly, there is no mention of divorce, contraception, or abortion. See CSW's Council News, Sept. 1989, 4-5, available from CSW, Dublin.

22. "Today Tonight," Apr. 23 and 24.

23. The ADC stated, for example. "DIVORCED WIVES WOULD LOSE THEIR RIGHTS UNDER THE SUCCESSION ACT" [emphasis in original]. ADC press release, May 9.

24. Bernadette Bonar, "Today Tonight," Apr. 24. See also William Binchy, "Today Tonight," June 3.

25. Bernadette Bonar, "Today Tonight," Apr. 24.

26. Support for this claim was provided by the formation of a new women's group during the campaign, Women Against Divorce (WAD), esti- mated to have the support of about four hundred women from around the country. Commenting on its formation, journalist Mary Maher explained that these separated women opposed divorce because they saw it as the judi- cial system giving respectability to the husbands who had left them and set up new unions. Maher stated that WAD basically conveyed three messages: "men are rats; the Irish legal and judicial system cannot be trusted; and as sep- arated women themselves they felt that they and their children had been de- prived of a proper, good family life by the actions of irresponsible men" (Irish Times, June 25, 8).

27. "Today Tonight," June 19.

28. "Today Tonight," Apr. 24.

29. Mary McAleese, "Marriage still the best guarantee overall", Irish Times, June 20, 10.

30. "Today Tonight," June 19.

31. See, for instance, Denis Foley, Parliamentary Debates, Dail Eireann, May 14, 851, and Sean McCarthy, ibid., May 15, 1079-80.

32. Parliamentary Debates, Dail Eireann, May 16, 1371-79.

33. Parliamentary Debates, Seanad Eireann, May 22, 1607-15.

34. Alice Glenn, "Today Tonight," Apr. 24.

35. Parliamentary Debates, Dail Eireann, May 14, 843.

36. Ibid.

37. Family Solidarity, 1986, 3.

38. Family Solidarity, 1986, 2, 8; Bernadette Bonar, "Today Tonight," Apr. 24; Alice Glenn, Parliamentary Debates, Dail Eireann, May 14, 843.

39. See particularly Ginsburg's (1989) discussion, 214-18.

40. Ibid., 11.

41. Ibid., 215-18. The divisiveness caused by the issue of gender roles is also well illustrated by Rebecca Klatch's (1987) study, which draws attention to the differences existing among women of the New Right regarding the proper roles of women and men in society.

42. Barbara Ehrenreich, quoted by Mansbridge, 1986, 108. Emphasis in original.

43. Mansbridge, 1986, 100.

44. Just as Irish anti-divorce campaigners argued that divorce would sanc- tion men's repudiation of their wives and children, Ginsburg, 1989, 216, points out that right-to-life activists see abortion as liberating men from taking re- sponsibility for their actions and making a commitment to women.

45. These are the 1986 figures. The European figure is taken from Blackwell, 1989, table 3.8. It includes the population in private households only, which makes the usually quoted Irish rate of 21 percent for 1986 (based on the Irish Labour Force Survey that includes non-private households) increase to 26 percent. The EC average does not include Scandinavian countries, where the proportion of married women working is higher. The U.S. figure is from *Statistical Abstract of the United States: 1990*, table 634.

46. Consider the character Mary Kate in John Ford's well known film *The Quiet Man*, starring Maureen O'Hara and John Wayne. In Gaelic literature, the life of Peig Sayers (Sayers, 1936; 1974) embodies the courageous strength and wisdom of many Irish women.

47. "Men and Women in Europe in 1987," *Women of Europe* (Brussels: Commission of the European Communities), Supplement 26, 24.

48. See Chodorow, 1978, 93, 140, 169-70; and Gilligan, 1982, 151-74.

49. Women display greater religious orthodoxy and higher sacramental participation than men (Weafer, 1986, 516-17; Nic Ghiolla Phadraig, 1986, 151), place greater value on religion, and express greater confidence in the church. Sixty-seven percent of women compared to 55 percent of men see religion as a "very important" personal value (MRBI, 1987a, table 3B/3); 67 percent of women in contrast to 52 percent of men say they would "definitely miss" the Church (ibid., table 3A/1), and 59 percent of women compared to 45 percent of men say that they have a "great deal" of confidence in the Church (Fogarty et al., 1984, table 17b). Importantly, women also attribute greater influence than men to the Church's influence on their thinking and opinions about abortion (51 percent:43 percent) and divorce (44 percent:37 percent), MRBI, 1987a, table 1B/2. Of interest here, significantly more women (75 percent) than men (62 percent) supported the 1983 pro-life amendment, MRBI, 1983, table 1A.

50. Karen O'Connor of DAG, "Today Tonight," Apr. 24.

51. "Today Tonight," June 19.

52. Ibid.

53. Joan Tanooy, ibid., June 3.

54. Ibid.

55. This was pointed out, for instance, by the minister for justice, Alan Dukes, in his opening statement to the Dail on the divorce proposals (*Parliamentary Debates*, Dail Eireann, May 14, 797). This was also stated by the Workers' Party in their organizational literature and argued by one of their representatives in the Dail, Proinsias de Rossa, *Parliamentary Debates*, Dail Eireann, May 14, 1042-48.

56. Reported in the *Irish Times*, June 26, 1, 8.

57. Reported in the *Irish Press*, June 12, 4.

58. *Parliamentary Debates*, Seanad Eireann, May 22, 1448-63.

59. Ibid. Dail Eireann, May 15, 1270.

60. Ibid. Dail Eireann, May 16, 1404.

61. Ibid., 1410.

62. *Parliamentary Debates*, Seanad Eireann, May 22, 1556-67.

63. Ibid. May 23, 1744-61.

64. See, for example, an article by Nuala Fennell, "This change will be a change for the better," *Irish Times,* June 13, 12, and remarks by her reported in the *Irish Press,* May 22, 4; June 24, 4. See also report of remarks by Gemma Hussey and Monica Barnes, *Irish Press,* June 12, 4; and Catherine McGuinness, "Today Tonight," June 10.

65. *Parliamentary Debates,* May 15, 1117, 1122.

66. For instance, an outspoken supporter of divorce was history professor John A. Murphy, University College Cork, and a small number of academic sociologists collectively expressed public support for the amendment (see *Irish Press,* June 25, 4).

67. As a senator and lawyer, Mary Robinson has championed women's rights and family law reform for twenty years. During the divorce debate, controversy surrounded Mary McAleese on account of her role as interviewer for a video on divorce made by the Catholic hierarchy, for whom she was also a delegate at the New Ireland Forum. DAG accused her of changing her mind on divorce. See McAleese's response to the allegations in letters to the editor, *Irish Times,* June 5, 11; *Irish Independent,* June 5, 8; and *Irish Press,* June 12, 16.

68. Mary Robinson, "No constitutional protections endangered," *Irish Times,* June 2, 8.

69. Mary Robinson, "Family's rights not threatened by poll," *Irish Times,* June 3, 18.

70. Nell McCafferty, "Divorce, Dallas and Dail debates", *Irish Press,* May 22, 4. McCafferty also wrote a background article on the Divorce Action Group, *Irish Press,* Apr. 24, 15.

71. Nell McCafferty, "They want to abolish marriage," *Irish Press,* July 3, 10.

72. Mary Holland, "An issue the Liverpool boat can't carry away," *Irish Times,* June 25, 12.

73. See Nuala O'Faolain's columns in the *Irish Times,* June 6, 10, and May 16, 8.

74. Nuala O'Faolain, "Marriage did them and so will divorce," *Irish Times,* May 9, 10.

75. I am using this in the Gramscian sense. Importantly, in Gramsci's (1971) conceptualization, a historical bloc is not that of a homogeneous and unified group but connotes the collaboration of various social classes or social fractions that collaborate against external threats. As I mentioned in chapter 2, organized women do not constitute one of the national "social partners" in Ireland in the same way that employer organizations, trade unions, and farmers do. Individual women participate in public debates but do not represent a unified collective women's agenda.

FIVE   The Catholic Church and the Referendum

1. This is the figure for 1984, a decrease from 91 percent in 1974. Data collected in 1988–1989 suggest that the proportion of Catholics attending mass weekly is 82 percent. See Nic Ghiolla Phadraig, 1992. Ireland is 93 per-

cent Catholic, 3.4 percent Protestant, 0.06 percent Jewish, and the remainder is other/none/religion not stated. Only 52 percent of American Catholics report weekly church attendance (Hout and Greeley, 1987, 326), while church-going levels in Europe (25 percent) and Britain (14 percent) are significantly lower (Fogarty et al., 1984, table 1(ii)).

2. See especially, 108-36.

3. See McSweeney, 1980, for an excellent discussion of the revolutionary impact of Vatican II on the Church and on society.

4. McSweeney, 1980, 135.

5. *Pastoral Constitution on the Church in the Modern World,* II:4:76. This and other Vatican II documents I quote below are taken from *The Sixteen Documents of Vatican II.* See also *Declaration on Religious Freedom,* articles 6 and I:4:4.

6. *Declaration on Religious Freedom,* articles 2 and 3. On this point, see also MacEoin, 1966, 174.

7. *Declaration on Religious Freedom,* article 6. Recall that until it was deleted in 1972, the Irish constitution recognized the "special position" of the Catholic church.

8. Initiated by the then Fine Gael/Labour coalition government led by Liam Cosgrave, deliberations concerning this legislation provide a good example of the hegemonic power of the Catholic church: during the Parliament vote both the prime minister and one of his ministers voted against the government bill on grounds of conscience.

9. Irish Episcopal Conference, Nov. 25, 1973. Individual bishops subsequently expressed the view that the State should not enact legislation that is against moral law (Ryan, 1979, 120).

10. Irish Episcopal Conference, 1971.

11. Ibid., Apr. 4, 1978.

12. Ibid. Aug. 22, 1983 (1983b).

13. Archbishop Ryan, Sept. 1, 1983. Statement supplied by the Catholic Press and Information Office, Dublin.

14. Irish Episcopal Conference, 1983c.

15. Politicians participating in the forum such as Senator Mary Robinson of Labour and John Kelly of Fine Gael tackled the bishops' delegation on questions of minority civil and religious rights. See Irish Episcopal Conference Delegation, 1984.

16. Irish Episcopal Conference Delegation, 1984, 2.

17. See Bishop McNamara, *Irish Times,* Feb. 8, 1985, 9; Feb. 11, 1985. See also McNamara, 1985, 7, and additionally, the contributions of Bishop Newman of Limerick, *Irish Times,* Feb. 18, 1985, 7, and Bishop McDonnell of Killala, *Irish Times, Feb. 18, 1985, 7.*

18. University of Notre Dame theologian, Richard P. McBrien (*New York Times,* Mar. 12, 1990, A17) observes that with Pope John Paul II, the post-1978 Vatican's strategy is aimed at restoring the Church to its institutional authoritarianism that existed prior to Vatican II.

19. Irish Episcopal Conference, 1985, 56-57. In May 1986 the hierarchy reissued relevant sections of this pastoral (1986b).

20. Irish Episcopal Conference Delegation, 1986, 2.

21. *Irish Times,* Apr. 8, 1986, 1.

22. "Today Tonight," Apr. 24.

23. Ibid.

24. Irish Episcopal Conference, Apr. 26, 1986 (1986a).

25. Irish Episcopal Conference, June 11, 1986 (1986c).

26. As explained by Bishop Cassidy on "Today Tonight," Apr. 24.

27. Bishop Cassidy, RTE Evening News, June 11.

28. Bishop Conway of Elphin diocese, *Irish Times,* June 16, 9.

29. Bishop Cassidy, ibid., June 17, 6.

30. See reports in the *Irish Times,* June 6, 8; June 20, 8; and *Irish Press,* June 23, 4.

31. Reported in *Irish Press,* June 23, 4.

32. Reported in *Irish Times,* June 23, 8. See also the remarks of Bishop Thomas McDonnell of Killala, *Irish Times,* June 23, 8, and Bishop Brendan Comiskey of Ferns, *Irish Independent,* June 19, 9.

33. Irish Episcopal Conference, 1985, 1. See Freyne, 1986, for further discussion of this point.

34. Irish Episcopal Conference, 1985, 54-55.

35. Ibid., 92.

36. Freyne, 1986, 13.

37. MacNamara, 1986, 13.

38. Hannon, 1976, 470.

39. Ibid. 1986, 11.

40. Ibid. 1976, 473. See Hannon, 1992, for a more extensive discussion of issues of law and morality.

41. Daly, 1986, 25.

42. Ibid., 20.

43. Hannon, 1976, 440.

44. See here, for example, the discussion offered by Cremin, 1986; Kelly, 1976; O'Callaghan, 1986; Twomey, 1986a, 1986b; and Twomey et al., 1986. Denis O'Callaghan is former professor of moral theology and Vincent Twomey is a lecturer in moral theology at Saint Patrick's College Maynooth.

45. O'Callaghan, 1986, 13.

46. Ibid.

47. Kelly, 1976, 562.

48. Ibid., 563.

49. Cremin, 1986, 11.

50. Twomey et al., 1986, 8.

51. Ibid.

52. U.S. Bishops' Meeting, "Resolution on Abortion," *Origins,* Nov. 16, 1989, 19:24, 395-96.

53. See *New York Times,* Nov. 17, 1989, A18, for a report concerning Bishop Maher, and the *New York Times,* June 30, 1990, A7, concerning Bishop Gracida.

54. For reports on this see, respectively, *New York Times,* June 15, 1990, A1, A14; and *New York Times,* Feb. 5, 1990, B1.

55. In March and April 1990, Archbishop Weakland held "listening sessions" with Catholics in his diocese to hear their views on abortion. See his response to these sessions, *Origins*, May 31, 1990, 20:3, 34-39. Opposed to abortion, Weakland has criticized the tactics of the pro-life movement. In prohibiting Weakland from receiving the degree, the Vatican Congregation for Catholic Education noted certain positions of Weakland's "relative to the question of abortion which are not without doctrinal importance and which are causing a great deal of confusion amongst the faithful in the U.S." (See *Origins*, Nov. 22, 1990, 20:24, 387-89.

56. See a report on this by Peter Steinfels in the *New York Times*, June 27, 1990, A1, A6.

57. In 1944, for instance, the Archbishop of Dublin prohibited Catholics from attending Trinity College and declared it a mortal sin (Whyte, 1980, 306).

58. Text of Archbishop McNamara's sermon printed in the *Irish Times*, Feb. 8, 1985, 9.

59. Irish Episcopal Conference, 1975, 14-16.

60. Irish Episcopal Conference, Aug. 22, 1983 (1983b); Irish Episcopal Conference, Nov. 2, 1982; Irish Episcopal Conference, Mar. 29, 1983 (1983a). (The referendum was held on Sept. 7, 1983.)

61. Bishop Cassidy, "Today Tonight," Apr. 24, 1986. See also Irish Episcopal Conference, 1986b, sections 19 and 24-26; 1985, 60-67; and June 11, 1986 (1986c).

62. Irish Episcopal Conference, June 11, 1986 (1986c).

63. Ibid., 1986b, section 20; and 1985, 58.

64. Ibid., section 29. See also ibid., section 30; and 1986c; and Bishop Clifford of Cashel, *Irish Press*, June 14, 4.

65. Irish Episcopal Conference, 1986b, section 32. See also sections 35 and 37; and 1986c.

66. Irish Episcopal Conference, 1986b, section 45.

67. Weafer (1986, 516) notes that Catholic orthodoxy and practice in Ireland decreases with educational qualifications and is lowest in areas of highest population density.

68. Irish Episcopal Conference, 1986b, section 16.

69. Irish Episcopal Conference, 1975, 8.

70. See a report on Murphy's remarks in the *Irish Times*, June 10, 7.

71. John Bowman, "Today Tonight," asked Bishop Cassidy, "How good is your sociology?" (Apr. 24); Dick Walsh, *Irish Times*, June 19, 10, commented on the contradiction between the Church's opposition to civil divorce and its own annulment procedures; and columns by Conor Cruise O'Brien, *Irish Independent* (May 24, 8; June 21, 8) and editorials in the *Sunday Tribune*, (Apr. 27, 10; May 18, 10) challenged the right of the hierarchy to offer pastoral guidance on divorce.

SIX   Newspaper Editorial Opinion

1. This was also true of the Sunday papers: the *Sunday Independent*, the *Sunday Press*, and the *Sunday Tribune*.

2. Personal communication from Maev-Ann Wren, assistant editor, the *Irish Times*. In 1974 after more than a decade of editorial change and expansion, the directors of the *Times* established a nonprofit-oriented trust (Brady, 1985, 6). The articles of the trust require that no interest group or party or sectional interest shall have or shall appear to have majority control. In accordance with this principle, a board of trustees or governors drawn from academic, business, labor, and administrative fields was appointed. A very large proportion of its readers live in Dublin, belong to the professional/ managerial occupational categories, and are in the 25 to 40 age group (Brady, 1985, 6-7). The *Times* has a daily circulation of 93,827 readers (*Ireland: A Directory*, 211).

3. The *Independent* was historically the voice of the old Irish Parliamentary Party, which relayed the message of Charles Stewart Parnell throughout Ireland. Today, it is owned and controlled by Tony O'Reilly, the international businessman, and by business and professional associates of his (Brady, 1985, 6). It has a circulation of 149,620 readers (*Ireland: A Directory*, 211).

4. So strongly did the *Independent* support the divorce amendment that on the day before polling day it printed an editorial on the front page, entitled "Why we feel it is necessary to say 'yes' tomorrow." Earlier in the campaign it devoted a full half page to an editorial—"Why the amendment should pass"— in which it echoed the sentiments of Garret FitzGerald that divorce would serve the social good (May 23). The editor, Bruce Arnold, also wrote an especially complimentary piece about Garret FitzGerald on June 21, 8.

5. In addition to the de Valera family, the *Press* is now half-owned by an American-based trust. It has a circulation of 60,287 readers (*Ireland: A Directory*, 211).

6. Impressionistic evidence suggests, however, that in recent years there has been a noticeable increase in the amount of sensationalist stories featured in the *Irish Independent*.

7. Brady, 1985, 6. Conor Brady has held various editorial positions since 1969, most of them with the *Irish Times*.

8. John Whyte (1980, 269-70) reports that this observation was made by a number of prominent Catholics in 1951–1952.

9. Catherine Rose, 1975, 79-80.

10. Between April 23 and June 26 inclusive, the *Irish Times* had seventeen editorials and sixteen pieces by regular columnists on the amendment; the *Independent* had six editorials and two pieces each by two of its regular columnists in addition to an opinion piece by its political editor; the *Press* had five editorials on the amendment, including one in Irish on June 6, a column piece by its editor, and a piece in Irish by a regular columnist. I am happy to acknowledge my mother, Peg Dillon, for translating the editorial and other articles written in Irish in the *Press*.

11. *Irish Times*, June 9.

12. *Irish Press*, Apr. 24.

13. Ibid., June 25; Apr. 24. Risteard O'Glaisne, writing in Irish, also stressed the restrictiveness of the proposals in his column in the *Press* on June 20.

14. Tim Pat Coogan, June 21, 7. Coogan has been editor of the *Irish Press* since 1968. He is also the author of a number of books on issues of modern Irish history, including the IRA and the H-block prisoners' protests in Northern Ireland.

15. Apr. 24.

16. Apr. 24. See also Michael Finlan's column, *Irish Times*, Apr. 25, 10.

17. May 31; June 16. This line was also sounded by the *Sunday Tribune*. One of its editorials (Apr. 27) stated: "If the referendum is carried it will be the first clear signal that southern Irish society is not a mask for 'Rome Rule.' " On the Sunday preceding polling day, in an editorial titled "The Duty to Vote 'Yes,' " The *Tribune* (June 22) noted further that: "The hard fact is that the Protestant community in the North has believed—and not without some justification—that the Republic is a Catholic dominated State, which would not respect their religious liberties and cultural identity. The manner in which Catholic Church morality has been enshrined in the Constitution and laws of the Republic is testimony to the validity of part of that perception."

18. May 23.

19. June 25. A column piece in Irish by Risteard O'Glaisne, "Daoine a bhionn thios le scaradh" (*Irish Press*, June 20, 8), also commented on the relevance of passing the amendment in order to deprive Unionists in Northern Ireland from arguing that the Republic does not have the same civil freedoms as the North.

20. *Irish Times*, June 9.

21. *Irish Independent*, May 19.

22. *Irish Times*, June 26.

23. Ibid., Apr. 23; June 23; June 26.

24. *Irish Independent*, May 19.

25. Ibid. May 14; May 19.

26. Ibid., May 23.

27. *Irish Times*, June 12; June 16.

28. Nuala O'Faolain, ibid., May 16, 8.

29. Dick Walsh, ibid., May 15, 10.

30. Mary Holland, ibid. May 7, 10.

31. See for example, ibid., Apr. 23. This was not true of the *Sunday Tribune*, however, which was particularly critical of the Catholic hierarchy and the power the bishops wield on account of their "divine authority". The editorials in the *Tribune* (Apr. 17; May 18) emphasized that divorce was not a moral issue but one of sociological and political judgement, and thus moral guidance from the bishops was not required.

32. *Irish Times*, Apr. 24; May 14.

33. *Irish Press*, June 21.

34. *Irish Independent*, June 25.

35. Ibid. June 2, 8.

36. Ibid., June 23, 6.

37. Dick Walsh, *Irish Times*, May 1, 8.

38. June 9.

39. June 25.

40. June 21.
41. June 25.
42. *Irish Times* June 19.
43. Ibid.
44. June 25.
45. May 23.
46. May 21.
47. Dick Walsh, June 12, 10.
48. May 23.
49. June 19.
50. June 26.
51. John Healy, *Irish Times*, June 14, 20.
52. See the editorials in the *Cork Examiner*, Apr. 24; May 14; May 16; May 19; May 27; June 9; June 25. The *Cork Examiner* has a daily circulation of 58,149 readers (*Ireland: A Directory*, 211).
53. In Longford/Westmeath, for instance, the electoral constituency of Patrick Cooney, the dissenting cabinet member of FitzGerald's government, and of two prominent anti-divorce Fianna Fail shadow ministers, Mary O'Rourke and Albert Reynolds, and where 71 percent of the electorate voted against the amendment, neither the *Westmeath Examiner* or the *Longford Express* took an editorial stance on divorce.
54. In the absence of exit polls, these observations are based on the MRBI/ *Irish Times* poll conducted on June 19 and 20, five days prior to polling day. See table 1.
55. Here, when I refer to the media as a secular progressive voice I mean this relatively; compared to traditional sources of authority such as the Church, the mass media is a secular institution. This point, therefore, should not be taken to indicate my support for the perspective adopted by Lichter and Rothman (1981) that because those working in the media are an elite in terms of social background, education, attitudes, etc., consequently media content reflects these elitist liberal values. To the contrary, media content is largely a product of various organizational, economic, sociological, and sometimes legal, constraints (see Gans, 1979; and Tuchman, 1978, among others, for good examples of this type of analysis). This view was also maintained by Michael O'Toole of the *Evening Press* in his interview with me. He stated that the "deadlines and routines of news production as well as internal editorial controls militate against personal biases" being advocated by journalists.
56. Conor Cruise O'Brien is an internationally known writer and author. On Irish society, he is particularly critical of what he considers overly romantic nationalist sentiments regarding aspirations toward a united Ireland. As Labour minister for posts and telegraphs in the 1973–1977 Fine Gael/Labour coalition government, he was the minister responsible for amending the Broadcasting Act prohibiting interviews with or reports of interviews with members of the IRA. See section 31 of the Broadcasting Authority (Amendment) Act, 1976.

57. *Irish Independent,* May 24, 8.
58. Ibid.
59. Ibid., June 21, 8.
60. Ibid.

SEVEN   Television's Framing of the Debate

1. The Broadcasting Act in Ireland requires that: "in a matter of public controversy or a matter which is a source of current public debate, information, news or a feature presented about it, is presented by RTE (Radio Telefis Eireann) objectively, impartially and without any expression of the Authority's own views. . . . [and should be] fair to all interests concerned" (Broadcasting Authority Act, 1960, section 18; Broadcasting Authority (Amendment) Act, 1976, section 18). In the U.S. the Communications Act states that broadcasters must serve the "public interest, convenience and necessity" (United States Communications Act, 1934). More specifically, the Fairness Doctrine, which was repealed in August 1987, required broadcasters to cover controversial issues and to do so fairly. Broadcasters maintain that such rules have a "chilling effect." Afraid of offending certain sectors of the public by not presenting controversial issues in a fair manner, broadcasters tend to refrain from presenting them altogether or else do so in a superficial way. For a good overview of the American experience of broadcast regulation see Powe, 1987; and of the Irish experience, see Fisher, 1978; and Feeney, 1984.

2. The anchor/interviewers are: John Bowman, also a radio presenter and a historian who has written a book on Eamon de Valera and the Ulster question; Brian Farrell, associate professor of political science; Pat Kenny, also a radio presenter, with economic and managerial interests in the communication production industry; and Olivia O'Leary, a journalist who at the time of the divorce campaign was on leave with Channel Four in England.

3. Kelly, 1984, 89.

4. RTE, Annual Report, 1986, 7.

5. Irish Television Audience Measurement (TAM) ratings, various weeks, April, May, June, 1986.

6. TAM ratings indicate that this edition of "Today Tonight" was the second most watched program on RTE for the week ending June 22.

7. Further evidence of the combative style program introduction of "Today Tonight" was also evident, for example, in their second program. The lead-in here stated; "Tonight the opening shots in the debate. The arguments for and against" (Apr. 24).

8. May 22.

9. Apr. 23.

10. Apr. 24.

11. May 22; June 3.

12. June 24.

13. Apr. 23. This was suggested despite the fact that when the all-party parliamentary committee on marital breakdown issued their report in 1985, they

did not call for the introduction of divorce precisely because Fianna Fail members dissented from the rest of the committee on this recommendation.

14. May 22; June 3; June 10.

15. May 22.

16. A senior parliamentarian from Fianna Fail was featured on the panel in the two audience participation programs (June 3; June 10) as well as in a final campaign review program before polling day (June 19).

17. Reporter Una Claffey, "Today Tonight," June 19.

18. Apr. 23.

19. Ibid.

20. May 22; June 3; June 10.

21. Apr. 24. Similarly, at the DAG press conference, broadcast on Apr. 24, a "Today Tonight" reporter asked, "Could you withstand pressure from the Catholic Church?"

22. June 19.

23. See note 1 above.

24. Hallin (1983) uses this phrase in noting the difficulties broadcasters have to confront in imposing balance on what is after all an unbalanced reality. Although the broadcasting legislation does not specify the word "balance," and while all of the people whom I interviewed at RTE, both executives and those working on "Today Tonight," stressed that the statutory requirements do not specify or mean "balance," I believe that Hallin's phrase captures the complexity of the task involved in maintaining impartiality, objectivity, and fairness.

25. One piece that came closest to approximating this kind of reporting was one short segment featuring an interview with a community welfare officer from the Southern Health Board about the increase in the numbers of people applying for assistance in relation to problems of marital breakdown (Apr. 24). A separate "Today Tonight" program produced prior to the announcement of the referendum—"Marital breakdown: What happens when the dream of a lifetime breaks down"—presented, without commentary, detailed interviews with four people with broken marriages and was transmitted during the divorce campaign, but it was not integrated with the issues raised by the amendment. Apart from "Today Tonight," the ever-popular weekend live television light entertainment/chat show, "The Late Late Show" hosted by Gay Byrne, and which in over twenty-five years on the air has covered many controversial topics, often provoking heated public discussion and outrage, also departed from its customary format. Excluding its usual lively and engaged audience, the one show devoted to the divorce referendum followed a sterile courtroom format. Simply introduced by Gay Byrne, the "program" featured a presiding retired High Court judge, lawyers, and expert witnesses presenting the pro- and anti-divorce cases.

26. In my interview with a senior management executive at RTE, he pointed out that "you always have to include the politicians" in sensitive debates.

27. Apr. 23; May 22; June 17.

28. This point goes against Stuart Hall's argument, for instance, that despite the legal obligations faced by the British television authorities: "Formu-

lating the agenda for discussion, comment and debate, the right of selecting the speakers and of chairing the debate, have been . . . in the hands of the broadcaster" (Hall et al., 1981, 91).

29. The media's emphasis on dramatic conflict is well documented in studies of mass media. Esslin (1982, 6) emphasizes that "the language of television is none other than that of *drama;* that television . . . is, in its essence, a *dramatic medium*" [emphasis in original]. Gouldner (1976, 124) summarizes: "The press, in short, dramatizes violence and, more generally, features *conflict*" [emphasis in original]. Gitlin (1980, 27) also observes media frames of polarization and emphasis on internal dissension.

EIGHT   Values in Tension

1. On the negative effects of divorce Arendell, 1986, argues "One major effect of the continued high divorce rate has been the dramatic growth of families headed by mothers. . . . Directly related to the increase in female-headed households has been the impoverishment of women" (1).

2. See Mansbridge, 1986, particularly chapter 5, which she titles, "59 Cents."

3. Lakatos, 1970, argues that a scientific research "programme consists of methodological rules: some tell us what paths of research to avoid (*negative heuristic*), and others, what paths to pursue (positive heuristic). . . . All scientific research programmes may be characterized by their '*hard core*'. The negative heuristic of the programme forbids us to direct the *modus tollens* at this 'hard core'. Instead, we must use our ingenuity to articulate or even invent 'auxiliary hypotheses', [positive heuristic] which form a *protective belt* around this core, and we must redirect the *modus tollens* to *these*" [emphasis in original] (132-33).

4. Ludwig Wittgenstein, *Philosophical Investigations*, 232e.

5. The duality of opposing values is also clearly evident in other forms of public discourse in Irish society where appeal is made simultaneously to the values of tradition and to those of modernity. The discourse of corporate advertising is one arena that provides a good example. For instance, in adopting as its new logo a Celtic representation of Noah's ark and the dove, Allied Irish Bank (AIB), a major Irish-based, international bank explains: "The eighties were a decade of unprecedented change. Over the period AIB has taken the lead in change in the Financial Services Industry in Ireland and in the expansion of Irish banks abroad, becoming a truly international bank. . . . As we start in the 1990s, we are signaling our readiness for the future and we are expressing this readiness with a new identity. . . . It is a symbol that reflects security, recognises our past while heralding a future" (AIB, 1990, 24). Many readers may be familiar with the advertisements of the Irish Industrial Development Authority (IDA) in the United States, which feature historic images of Ireland juxtaposed with photographs of the well-educated Irish young Europeans. Commenting on this pattern, Luke Gibbons argues that "The most striking feature of IDA promotional material is that it does not simply acknowledge but actively

perpetuates the myth of romantic Ireland, incorporating both modernity and tradition within its frame of reference" (1988, 211).

6. Sica, 1988, 139.

7. Weber, "Science as a Vocation", 143, quoting Tolstoy. See also 138-56. Weber argues that none of the intellectual or scientific disciplines—natural science, modern medicine, aesthetics, jurisprudence, sociology or the historical and cultural sciences—can tell us what is worthwhile. They provide us with technical means but do not ask whether the pursuit is worth the effort.

8. Bellah et al., 1985, 79.

9. See Payne (1984) for a historical overview of the Church in Spain.

10. Mujal-Leon, 1982, 32.

11. Lovenduski, 1986, 54-55. See also Matsell, 1981, for a review of the status of women in Spain.

12. Lovenduski, 105-106.

13. See Wolchik's (1989) discussion of changes in Eastern Europe following World War II. Elsewhere, she notes (1981, 253) that "in accordance with Marxism-Leninism political elites in Eastern Europe have explicitly affirmed their commitment to women's equality in all areas of life".

14. Bogdan Szajkowski (1983) argues that "even for those who were by no means religious, the Church offered the only opportunity of openly expressing their disapproval of the government by attending Sunday mass" (3). At the same time as the Church and Catholicism constituted an oppositional culture for the Poles, the Church hierarchy let itself be used by the Communist party in order that Polish independence from Russia would be maintained. Szajkowski notes that "The Church agreed to restrain Solidarity from making overtly political demands which could undermine the regime and disquiet the Soviet Union. . . . The Catholic hierarchy saw a continuous threat to Polish independence and regarded its preservation as paramount" (102, 125).

15. Weber, 1981, 184.

16. See Beckwith, 1985 and 1987.

17. Wertman, 1982, 89-105.

18. Kuhn, 1962.

19. William Ogburn, [1957] 1964, 92-93, argues that societal upheaval brought about by revolution tends to cause cultural lags to crumble. Differentiating revolutions from rebellions, Skocpol (1979, 4) argues: "Social revolutions are rapid, basic transformations of a society's state and class structures; and they are accompanied and in part carried through by class based revolts from below. Social revolutions are set apart from other sorts of conflicts and transformative processes above all by the combination of two coincidences: the coincidence of societal structural change with class upheaval; and the coincidence of political with social transformation. In contrast, rebellions, even when successful, . . . do not eventuate in structural change."

20. Ogburn, [1957] 1964, 93-94, argues that war is another event that facilitates the dismantling of cultural lags.

21. Keogh, 1988, 98-196, discusses Ireland's neutrality and World War II.

22. See Carter, 1988, 10-24.

23. Brown, 1985, 180.
24. For a general overview of the status of women in Swiss society, see Baumann and Naf-Hoffman, 1978. The Cantons in which women were not allowed to vote were Appenzell Ausser Rhoden and Appenzell Inner Rhoden.
25. For a report on this, see the *New York Times*, Apr. 5, 1990, A14. The discussion here prompts me to speculate that the notion of a normative "culture clock" may be relevant to understanding societies in the same way as a "social clock" applies to individuals. When an opportunity in which to enact societal initiatives has gone by, for a variety of reasons, it becomes more difficult to embrace change at a later time. It may well have been easier for Ireland to introduce divorce in the 1970s when most other Western countries were liberalizing their divorce laws and when Irish society itself was undergoing economic and social change. Similarly, because Swiss women did not receive the right to vote when other European women did so, either in the first decades of the century (as did the Irish and the British), or following the end of World War II (when Italian and French women did so), their achievement of the franchise at a later time became more difficult.
26. For a discussion of the Church in America see Deedy, 1987; and O'Brien, 1989.
27. When asked about sources of personal influence on a range of issues, on divorce, 40 percent of the Irish people said the church, compared to 14 percent who stated the media. See MRBI, 1987a, table 1B (ii), 13.
28. Bendix, 1964, 6. See Bendix, 1964; Smelser, 1968, 126-27; and Smelser, 1976, 148-63, for a discussion of the process of economic development and modernization. Importantly, Bendix, 1967, 329, notes that "modernization in some sphere of life *may* occur without resulting in modernity" [emphasis in original].
29. Smelser, 1976, 148.
30. Eisenstadt (1973, 25) emphasizes the centrality of social change to modernization. He states: "Modernization implies . . . the development of a social, economic or political system which not only generates continuous change, but unlike many other types of social or political systems, is also capable of absorbing changes beyond its own institutional premises."
31. Gerschenkron, 1962, 353.
32. Clark Kerr et al., 1960, 284-85, 296.
33. See Smelser, 1968, especially 140-44; Smelser, 1976, 148-62; Bendix, 1964, 10; and Inkeles and Smith, 1974, 311, for remarks on the uneven nature of modernization.
34. See Ogburn's discussion, [1957] 1964, 86-95, of cultural lag. Citing the greater death and crime rates in urban as opposed to rural areas, Ogburn interprets this as indicative of a lag in adjustment to the modernized, urban environment.
35. Inkeles and Smith, 1974, 29, argue that: "The modern man . . . has a marked sense of personal efficacy; he is highly independent and autonomous in his relations to traditional sources of influence, especially when he is making basic decisions about how to conduct his personal affairs."

36. Bendix, 1967, 328.

37. Black, 1966, 27, argues that modernization "is a process that is simultaneously creative and destructive, providing new opportunities and prospects at a high price in human dislocation and suffering."

38. See Jackson Lears, 1981, for an interesting discussion of antimodernism in America between 1810 and 1920; and Hunter, 1983, for an analysis of evangelicalism as a response to modernity.

39. Bellah, 1970, 64.

40. Bellah et al. (1985) discuss various efforts by Americans to recreate community values and a sense of societal belongingness in their private "individualistic" lives.

Bibliography

Alexander, Jeffrey. 1983. *Theoretical Logic in Sociology. The Classical Attempt at Theoretical Synthesis: Max Weber.* Berkeley: Univ. of California Press.

Allied Irish Bank. 1990, Spring. *One-To-One.* Dublin: Mac.

Arendell, Terry. 1986. *Mothers and Divorce: Legal, Economic and Social Dilemmas.* Berkeley: Univ. of California Press.

Baumann, Margit, and Marlies Naf-Hoffman. 1978. "The Status of Women in Society and in Law." In *Modern Switzerland,* ed. J. Murray Luck. Palo Alto: The Society for the Promotion of Science and Scholarship.

Beale, Jenny. 1987. *Women in Ireland. Voices of Change.* Bloomington: Indiana Univ. Press.

Beckett, J.C. 1966. *The Making of Modern Ireland, 1603–1923.* London: Faber and Faber.

Beckwith, Karen. 1985. "Feminism and Leftist Politics in Italy: The case of UDI-PCI relations." In *Women and Politics in Western Europe,* ed. Sylvia Bashevkin. London: Frank Cass.

———. 1987. "Response to Feminism in the Italian Parliament: Divorce, Abortion, and Sexual Violence Legislation." In *The Women's Move ments of the United States and Western Europe,* ed. Mary Fainsod Katzenstein and Carol Mueller. Philadelphia: Temple Univ. Press.

Bellah, Robert N. 1970. *Beyond Belief: Essays on Religion in a Post-Traditional World.* New York: Harper and Row.

Bellah, Robert. N., Richard Madsen, William Sullivan, Ann Swidler, and Steven Tipton. 1985. *Habits of the Heart: Individualism and Commitment in American Life.* Berkeley: Univ. of California Press.

Bendix, Reinhard. 1964. *Nation-Building and Citizenship.* New York: Wiley.

———. 1967. "Tradition and Modernity Reconsidered." *Comparative Studies in Society and History* 9:292-346.

Binchy, William. 1984. *Is Divorce the Answer?* Dublin: Irish Academic.

Black, C.E. 1966. *The Dynamics of Modernization: A Study in Comparative History.* New York: Harper and Row.

Blackwell, John. 1989. *Women in the Labour Force*. Dublin: Employment Equality Agency.

Boylan, Tom, Chris Curtin, and Liam O'Dowd. 1988. "Politics and Society in Post-Independence Ireland." In *Irish Studies: A General Introduction*, ed. Thomas Bartlett, Chris Curtin, Riana O'Dwyer, and Gearoid O'Tuathaigh. Dublin: Gill and Macmillan.

Brady, Conor. 1985. "Ownership and Control of the National Newspapers in Ireland." In *Is the Irish Press Independent? Essays on Ownership and Control of the Provincial, National and International Press in Ireland*, ed. Desmond Bell. Dublin: Media Association of Ireland.

Breslin, Ann, and John Weafer. 1985. *Religious Beliefs, Practice and Moral Attitudes: A Comparison of Two Irish Surveys*. Maynooth: Council for Research and Development.

Brown, Terence. 1985. *Ireland: A Social and Cultural History, 1922–1985*. London: Fontana.

Bunreacht na hEireann: Constitution of Ireland. 1937. Dublin: Stationery Office.

Byrne, Gay. 1989. *The Time of My Life: An Autobiography*. [With Deirdre Purcell]. Dublin: Gill and Macmillan.

Carter, April. 1988. *The Politics of Women's Rights*. London: Longman.

Catholic Press and Information Office. 1986. *Nullity of Marriage in the Catholic Church*. Dublin: Veritas.

Central Statistics Office. 1989a. *Census '86: Summary Population Report*. Dublin: Stationery Office.

———. 1989b. *Ireland: Statistical Abstract, 1986*. Dublin: Stationery Office.

Chodorow, Nancy. 1978. *The Reproduction of Mothering: Psychoanalysis and the Sociology of Gender*. Berkeley: Univ. of California Press.

Clancy, Patrick, Sheelagh Drudy, Kathleen Lynch, and Liam O'Dowd, eds. 1986. *Ireland: A Sociological Profile*. Dublin: Institute of Public Administration.

Clarke, Desmond. 1985. *Church and State: Essays in Political Philosophy*. Cork: Cork Univ. Press.

Coakley, John. 1990. "Minor Parties in Irish Political Life." *Economic and Social Review* 21:269-97.

Cooney, John. 1986. *The Crozier and the Dail: Church and State, 1922–1986*. Cork: Mercier.

Corish, Patrick. 1985. *The Irish Catholic Experience: A Historical Survey*. Dublin: Gill and Macmillan.

Cremin, Joseph. 1986. "Divorce." *Irish Times*, June 25, 11.

Crotty, Raymond. 1966. *Irish Agricultural Production*. Cork: Mercier.

———. 1986. *Ireland in Crisis: A Study in Capitalist Colonial Underdevelopment*. Dingle: Brandon.

Cullen-Owens, Rosemary. 1984. *Smashing Times: A History of the Irish Women's Suffrage Movement, 1889–1922.* Dublin: Attic.

Daly, Cahal. 1982. "Ireland in the Eighties." *Social Studies* 7:5-12.

Daly, Gabriel. 1986. "Weighing the Arguments." In *Divorce. Facts, Catholic Viewpoints.* Dublin: Dominican.

Deedy, John. 1987. *American Catholicism: And Now Where?* New York: Plenum.

Dillon, Michele. 1990. "Perceptions of the Causes of the Troubles in Northern Ireland." *Economic and Social Review* 21:299-310.

Duncan, Greg, and Saul Hoffman. 1985. "A Reconsideration of the Economic Consequences of Marital Dissolution." *Demography* 22:485-497.

Eisenstadt, S.N. 1973. *Tradition, Change and Modernity.* Malabar, Fla.: Krieger.

Eisler, Riane. 1977. *Dissolution: No-Fault Divorce, Marriage, and the Future of Women.* New York: McGraw-Hill.

Esslin, Martin. 1982. *The Age of Television.* Stanford: Stanford Univ. Press.

Eurobarometer. Public Opinion in the European Community. Trends, 1974–1990. 1991. Brussels: Commission of the European Communities.

Family Solidarity. 1986. *Understanding the Divorce Amendment.* Dublin: Family Solidarity.

Fanning, Ronan. 1983. *Independent Ireland.* Dublin: Educational.

———. 1985. "Fianna Fail and the Bishops." *Irish Times,* Feb. 13 and 14.

Feeney, Peter. 1984. "Censorship and RTE." *Crane Bag* 8:61-64.

Fisher, Desmond. 1978. *Broadcasting in Ireland.* London: Routledge and Kegan Paul.

Fogarty, Michael, Liam Ryan, and Joseph Lee, eds. 1984. *Irish Values and Attitudes: The Irish Report of the European Value Systems Study.* Dublin: Dominican.

Freyne, Sean. 1986. "Marriage, Theology and the Real World." *Irish Times,* June 5, 13.

Gallagher, Raphael. 1981. "Morality in a Changing Irish Society." *Furrow* 32:713-724.

Gans, Herbert. 1979. *Deciding What's News.* New York: Pantheon.

Gardiner, Frances. 1988. "Euro-Elections: The Future for Women." *Annual Journal of the Women's Political Association* 24:12-14.

Gerschenkron, Alexander. 1962. *Economic Backwardness in Historical Perspective.* Cambridge, Mass.: Harvard Univ. Press.

Gibbons, Luke. 1988. "Coming out of Hibernation? The Myth of Modernity in Irish Culture." In *Across the Frontiers: Ireland in the 1990s,* ed. Richard Kearney. Dublin: Wolfhound.

Gilligan, Carol. 1982. *In a Different Voice: Psychological Theory and Women's Development.* Cambridge, Mass.: Harvard Univ. Press.

Ginsburg, Faye. 1989. *Contested Lives: The Abortion Debate in an American Community.* Berkeley: Univ. of California Press.

Gitlin, Todd. 1980. *The Whole World is Watching: Mass Media in the Making and Unmaking of the New-Left.* Berkeley: Univ. of California Press.

Glendon, Mary Ann. 1987. *Abortion and Divorce in Western Law: American Failures, European Challenges.* Cambridge, Mass.: Harvard Univ. Press.

Gouldner, Alvin. 1976. *The Dialectic of Ideology and Technology.* New York: Oxford Univ. Press.

Gramsci, Antonio. 1971. *Selections from the Prison Notebooks.* Trans. Quentin Hoare & Geoffrey Nowell Smith. New York: International Universities Press.

Grogan, Vincent. 1967. "Towards the New Constitution." In *The Years of the Great Test, 1926–39,* ed. Francis MacManus. Cork: Mercier.

Hall, Stuart, Ian Connell, and Lidia Curti. 1981. "The 'Unity' of Public Affairs Television." In *Popular Television and Film.* London: Open University.

Hallin, Daniel. 1983. "The Media Go to War—From Vietnam to Central America." NACLA *Report on the Americas* July/August.

Hannon, Patrick. 1976. "Catholics and Divorce." *Furrow* 27:470-73.

———. 1986. "Divorce." *Irish Times,* June 26, 11.

———. 1992. *Church, State, Morality and Law.* Dublin: Gill and Macmillan.

Hayes-McCoy, G.A. 1976. "Conciliation, Coercion and the Protestant Reformation, 1547–71" and "The Completion of the Tudor Conquest and the Advance of the Counter-Reformation, 1571–1603." In *A New History of Ireland. Early Modern Period, 1534–1691,* ed. T.W. Moody, F.X. Martin, and F.J. Byrne. Oxford: Clarendon.

Hechter, Michael. 1975. *Internal Colonialism: The Celtic Fringe in British National Development, 1536–1966.* Berkeley: Univ. of California Press.

Hoffman, Saul, and Greg Duncan. 1988. "What *are* the Economic Consequences of Divorce?" Demography 25:641-45.

Hout, Michael. 1989. *Following in Father's Footsteps.* Cambridge, Mass.: Harvard Univ. Press.

Hout, Michael, and Andrew Greeley. 1987. "The Center Doesn't Hold: Church Attendance in the United States, 1940–1984." *American Sociological Review* 52:325-45.

Hunter, James Davison. 1983. *American Evangelicalism: Conservative Religion and the Quandary of Modernity.* New Brunswick: Rutgers Univ. Press.

Inglis, Tom. 1982. "Legalism and Irish Catholicism." *Social Studies* 7:33-41.

———. 1987. *Moral Monopoly: The Catholic Church in Modern Irish Society.* Dublin: Gill and Macmillan.

Inkeles, Alex, and David Smith. 1974. *Becoming Modern: Individual Change in Six Developing Countries.* Cambridge, Mass.: Harvard Univ. Press.

Ireland: A Directory 1992. 1991. Dublin: Institute of Public Administration.

Irish Catholic Directory. Various years. Liverpool: Universe Publications.

Irish Episcopal Conference. 1971, 1973, 1978, 1982, 1983a, 1983b, 1983c, 1986a, 1986c. *Official Statements.* Dublin: Catholic Press and Information Office.

———. 1975. *Human Life Is Sacred.* Dublin: Veritas.

———. 1985. *Love Is for Life.* Dublin: Veritas.

———. 1986b. *Marriage, the Family and Divorce: A Statement of the Irish Bishops.* Dublin: Veritas.

Irish Episcopal Conference Delegation. 1984. *New Ireland Forum: Report of Proceedings, #12.* Dublin: Stationery Office.

———. 1986. *Questions Relating to Marital Breakdown in Ireland.* Dublin: Catholic Press and Information Office.

Jackson, Pauline. 1983. *The Deadly Solution to an Irish Problem—Backstreet Abortion.* Dublin: Open Line Counselling.

Kelly, Brian. 1976. "Catholics and Divorce." *Furrow* 27:562-64.

Kelly, Mary. 1984. "Twenty Years of Current Affairs on RTE." In *Television and Irish Society: 21 Years of Irish Television,* ed. Martin McLoone and John MacMahon. Dublin: Radio Telefis Eireann/Irish Film Institute.

Kennedy, Robert. 1973. *The Irish: Emigration, Marriage, and Fertility.* Berkeley: Univ. of California Press.

Keogh, Dermot. 1986. *The Vatican, the Bishops and Irish Politics, 1919–1939.* New York: Cambridge Univ. Press.

———. 1988. *Ireland and Europe, 1919–1948.* Dublin: Gill and Macmillan.

Kerr, Clark, John Dunlop, Frederick Harbison, and Charles Myers. 1960. *Industrialism and Industrial Man: The Problems of Labor and Management in Economic Growth.* Cambridge, Mass.: Harvard Univ. Press.

Klatch, Rebecca. 1987. *Women of the New Right.* Philadelphia: Temple Univ. Press.

Kuhn, Thomas. 1962. *The Structure of Scientific Revolutions.* Chicago: Univ. of Chicago Press.

Lakatos, Imre. 1970. "Falsification and the Methodology of Scientific Research Programmes." In *Criticism and the Growth of Knowledge,* ed. Imre Lakatos and Alan Musgrave. Cambridge: Cambridge Univ. Press.

Lasch, Christopher. 1979. *The Culture of Narcissism: American Life in an Age of Diminishing Expectations.* New York: Warner.

Lears, T.J. Jackson. 1981. *No Place of Grace: Antimodernism and the Transformation of American Culture, 1880–1920.* New York: Pantheon.

Lee, J.J. 1973. *The Modernisation of Irish Society, 1848–1918.* Dublin: Gill and Macmillan.

————. 1978. "Women and the Church Since the Famine." In *Women in Irish Society: The Historical Dimension,* ed. Margaret MacCurtain and Donncha O'Corrain. Westport, Conn.: Greenwood.

————. 1989. *Ireland 1912–1985: Politics and Society.* Cambridge: Cambridge Univ. Press.

Levine, June. 1982. *Sisters: The Personal Story of an Irish Feminist.* Dublin: Ward River.

Lichter, S. Robert, and Stanley Rothman. 1981. "Media and Business Elites." *Public Opinion* Oct./Nov.: 42–46, 59-60.

Litton, Frank, ed. 1982. *Unequal Achievement: The Irish Experience, 1957–1982.* Dublin: Institute of Public Administration.

Longford, The Earl of, and Thomas P. O'Neill. 1970. *Eamon de Valera.* London: Hutchinson.

Lovenduski, Joni. 1986. *Women and European Politics: Contemporary Feminism and Public Policy.* Amherst: Univ. of Massachusetts Press.

Luker, Kristin. 1984. *Abortion and the Politics of Motherhood.* Berkeley: Univ. of California Press.

Lynch, Kathleen. 1989. *The Hidden Curriculum.* London: Falmer.

Lyons, F.S.L. 1973. *Ireland Since the Famine.* London: Fontana.

MacEoin, Gary. 1966. *What Happened at Rome? The Council and Its Implications for the Modern World.* New York: Holt, Rinehart and Winston.

MacGreil, Micheal. 1977. *Prejudice and Tolerance in Ireland.* Dublin: College of Industrial Relations.

MacNamara, Vincent. 1986. "There Is a Moral Case for Divorce." *Irish Times,* Feb. 12, 13.

Manning, Maurice. 1978. "Women in Irish National and Local Politics 1922–77." In *Women in Irish Society: The Historical Dimension,* ed. Margaret MacCurtain and Donncha O'Corrain. Westport, Conn.: Greenwood.

Mansbridge, Jane. 1986. *Why We Lost the ERA.* Chicago: Univ. of Chicago Press.

Market Research Bureau of Ireland. 1983. *Irish Times/MRBI Poll: Voting Intentions in the Constitutional Referendum.* Dublin: MRBI.

————. 1985. *Irish Times/MRBI Poll: Public Reaction to the Government and Party Leaders, and to the Issue of Divorce.* Dublin: MRBI.

————. April 1986. *Irish Times/MRBI Poll: The Divorce Issue. The Government, Party Leaders, Current Party Support.* Dublin: MRBI.

————. June 1986. *Irish Times/*MRBI *Poll: The Constitutional Referendum Article 41.* Dublin: MRBI.

————. 1987a. *Eire Inniu: An* MRBI *Perspective on Irish Society Today.* Dublin: MRBI.

————. 1987b. *Irish Times/*MRBI *Poll: Current Party Support, the Extradition Act, and Other Issues.* Dublin: MRBI.

Matsell, Catherine. 1981. "Spain." In *The Politics of the Second Electorate: Women and Public Participation,* ed. Joni Lovenduski and Jill Hills. London: Routledge and Kegan Paul.

McBrien, Richard, P. 1990. "A Papal Attack on Vatican II." *New York Times,* Mar. 12, A17.

McCarroll, Joseph. 1985. *Marriage or Divorce—the Real Issue.* Dublin: Four Courts.

McMahon, Bryan. 1985. "A Sense of Identity in the Irish Legal System." In *Ireland: Towards a Sense of Place,* ed. J.J. Lee. Cork: Cork Univ. Press/ UCC-RTE Lectures.

McNamara, Kevin. 1985. *Pluralism: Unravelling a Riddle of Our Time.* Dublin: Veritas.

McSweeney, Bill. 1980. *Roman Catholicism: The Search for Relevance.* Oxford: Basil Blackwell.

Messenger, John. 1969. *Inis Beag: Isle of Ireland.* New York: Holt, Rinehart and Winston.

Mujal-Leon, Eusebio. 1982. "The Left and the Catholic Question in Spain." In *Religion in West European Politics,* ed. Suzanne Berger. London: Frank Cass.

New Ireland Forum. 1984. *Comparative Description of the Economic Structure, North and South.* Dublin: Stationery Office.

Nic Ghiolla Phadraig, Maire. 1977. "Moral Values of Catholics in the Irish Republic." *Doctrine and Life* 28:38-42.

————. 1986. "Religious Practice and Secularisation." In *Ireland: A Sociological Profile,* ed. Patrick Clancy et al. Dublin: Institute of Public Administration.

————. 1992. "Trends in Religious Practice in Ireland." *Doctrine and Life* 42: 3-11.

O'Brien, David. 1989. *Public Catholicism.* New York: Macmillan.

O'Callaghan, Denis. 1986. "Giving Adultery Respectability." *Irish Times,* Feb. 12, 13.

O'Carroll, J. Patrick. 1984, April. "Bishops, Knights; and Pawns? The Politics of the 1983 'Abortion Referendum Debate' in the Republic of Ireland." Paper presented at the meeting of the European Consortium of Political Science, Salzburg.

Ogburn, William, F. [1957] 1964. "Cultural Lag as Theory." In William Ogburn, *On Culture and Social Change.* Chicago: Univ. of Chicago Press.

O'Hearn, Denis. 1990. "Tales and Realities: Reply to Barrett and Gong." *American Sociological Review* 55:603-608.

O'Tuathaigh, Gearoid. 1988. "From United Kingdom to Divided Island: Aspects of the Irish Experience, 1850–1922." In *Irish Studies: A General Introduction,* ed. Thomas Bartlett, Chris Curtin, Riana O'Dwyer, and Gearoid O'Tuathaigh. Dublin: Gill and Macmillan.

Parliamentary Debates, Dail Eireann. 1986, May and June. Dublin: Stationery Office.

Parliamentary Debates, Seanad Eireann. 1986, May and June. Dublin: Stationery Office.

Payne, Stanley. 1984. *Spanish Catholicism: An Historical Overview.* Madison: Univ. of Wisconsin Press.

Peillon, Michel. 1982. *Contemporary Irish Society: An Introduction.* Dublin: Gill and Macmillan.

Phillips, Roderick. 1988. *Putting Asunder: A History of Divorce in Western Society.* New York: Cambridge Univ. Press.

Powe, Lucas. 1987. *American Broadcasting and the First Amendment.* Berkeley: Univ. of California Press.

Rabinow, Paul. 1977. *Reflections on Fieldwork in Morocco.* Berkeley: Univ. of California Press.

Radio Telefis Eireann. 1986. *Annual Report.* Dublin: RTE.

Report of the Joint Committee on Marriage Breakdown. 1985. Dublin: Stationery Office.

Riddick, Ruth. 1988. *Making Choices: The Abortion Experience of Irish Women.* Dublin: Open Line Counselling.

———. 1990. *The Right to Choose: Questions of Feminist Morality.* Dublin: Attic.

Robinson, Mary. 1978. "Women and the New Irish State." In *Women in Irish Society: The Historical Dimension,* ed. Margaret MacCurtain and Donncha O'Corrain. Westport, Conn.: Greenwood.

Rose, Catherine. 1975. *The Female Experience: The Story of the Woman Movement in Ireland.* Dublin: Arlen.

Rottman, David, and Philip O'Connell. 1982. "The Changing Social Structure of Ireland." In *Unequal Achievement: The Irish Experience, 1957–1982,* ed. Frank Litton. Dublin: IPA.

Ryan, Liam. 1979. "Church and Politics: The Last Twenty-five Years." *Furrow* 30:3-18.

Sayers, Peig. 1936. *Peig.* Dublin: Talbot.

———. 1974. *Peig: The Autobiography of Peig Sayers of the Great Blasket Island.* Trans. Bryan MacMahon. New York: Syracuse Univ. Press.

Schluchter, Wolfgang. 1979. "The Paradox of Rationalization." In G. Roth and W. Schluchter, *Max Weber's Vision of History: Ethics and Methods.* Berkeley: Univ. of California Press.

————. 1981. *The Rise of Western Rationalism: Max Weber's Developmental History*. Berkeley: Univ. of California Press.

Sennett, Richard. 1978. *The Fall of Public Man*. New York: Vintage.

Sexton, J.J., and Michele Dillon. 1984. "Recent Changes in Irish Fertility." *Quarterly Economic Commentary* May: 21-40.

Sica, Alan. 1988. *Weber, Irrationality, and Social Order*. Berkeley: Univ. of California Press.

Skocpol, Theda. 1979. *States and Social Revolutions: A Comparative Analysis of France, Russia, and China*. New York: Cambridge Univ. Press.

Smelser, Neil. 1968. *Essays in Sociological Explanation*. Englewood Cliffs: Prentice Hall.

————. 1976. *Sociological Aspects of Economic Development*. Englewood Cliffs: Prentice Hall.

Stone, Lawrence. 1989. "The Road to Polygamy." Review of *Putting Asunder: A History of Divorce in Western Society*, by Roderick Phillips. *New York Review of Books* 36:12-15.

————. 1990. *Road to Divorce: England, 1530–1987*. New York: Oxford Univ. Press.

Szajkowski, Bogdan. 1983. *Next to God . . . Poland: Politics and Religion in Contemporary Poland*. New York: St. Martin's.

TAM. 1986, April, May, and June. *Television Audience Measurement Ratings*. Dublin: TAM.

The Pope in Ireland. Addresses and Homilies. 1979. Dublin: Veritas.

The Sixteen Documents of Vatican II and the Instruction on the Liturgy. Boston: Daughters of St. Paul.

Tuchman, Gaye. 1978. *Making News: A Study in the Construction of Reality*. New York: Free.

Twomey, Vincent. 1986a. "When Theology Began to Lose Touch." *Irish Times*, June 19, 8.

————. 1986b. "Divorce." *Irish Times*, June 19, 11.

Twomey, Vincent, et al. 1986. "More Views on Divorce." *Irish Independent*, June 11, 8.

United States Bureau of the Census. 1990. *Statistical Abstract of the United States: 1990*. Washington, D.C.: GPO.

Wall, Maureen. 1961. *The Penal Laws, 1691–1760*. Dundalk: Dundalgan.

Ward, Peter. 1990. *Financial Consequences of Marital Breakdown*. Dublin: Combat Poverty Agency.

Weafer, John. 1986. "Change and Continuity in Irish Religion." *Doctrine and Life* 36:507-17.

Weber, Maria. 1981. "Italy." In *The Politics of the Second Electorate*, ed. Joni Lovenduski and Jill Hills. London: Routledge and Kegan Paul.

Weber, Max. [1904] 1949. " 'Objectivity' in Social Science and Social Policy." In *The Methodology of the Social Sciences*, trans. and ed. Edward Shils and Henry A. Finch. New York: Free.

————. [1919] 1946. "Science as a Vocation." In *From Max Weber: Essays in Sociology,* trans. and ed. H.H. Gerth and C.W. Mills. New York: Oxford Univ. Press.

————. 1968. *Economy and Society,* ed. Guenther Roth and Claus Wittich. Volume One. Berkeley: Univ. of California Press.

Weitzman, Lenore. 1985. *The Divorce Revolution.* Berkeley: Univ. of California Press.

Wertman, Douglas. 1982. "The Catholic Church and Italian Politics: The Impact of Secularisation." In *Religion in West European Politics,* ed. Suzanne Berger. London: Frank Cass.

Whyte, John H. 1966. *The Tenant League and Irish Politics in the Eighteen-fifties.* Dundalk: Dundalgan.

————. 1980. *Church and State in Modern Ireland.* Dublin: Gill and Macmillan.

Wittgenstein, Ludwig. 1974. *Philosophical Investigations.* Oxford: Basil Blackwell.

Wolchik, Sharon. 1981. "Eastern Europe." In *The Politics of the Second Electorate,* ed. Joni Lovenduski and Jill Hills. London: Routledge and Kegan Paul.

————. 1989. "Women and the State in Eastern Europe and the Soviet Union." In *Women, the State and Development,* ed. Sue Ellen Charlton, Jana Everett, and Kathleen Staudt. Albany, N.Y.: SUNY Press.

Index